Gestures of Love

Also in the series

William Rothman, editor, *Cavell on Film*

J. David Slocum, editor, *Rebel Without a Cause*

Joe McElhaney, *The Death of Classical Cinema*

Kirsten Moana Thompson, *Apocalyptic Dread*

Frances Gateward, editor, *Seoul Searching*

Michael Atkinson, editor, *Exile Cinema*

Paul S. Moore, *Now Playing*

Robin L. Murray and Joseph K. Heumann, *Ecology and Popular Film*

William Rothman, editor, *Three Documentary Filmmakers*

Sean Griffin, editor, *Hetero*

Jean-Michel Frodon, editor, *Cinema and the Shoah*

Carolyn Jess-Cooke and Constantine Verevis, editors, *Second Takes*

Matthew Solomon, editor, *Fantastic Voyages of the Cinematic Imagination*

R. Barton Palmer and David Boyd, editors, *Hitchcock at the Source*

William Rothman, *Hitchcock: The Murderous Gaze, Second Edition*

Joanna Hearne, *Native Recognition*

Marc Raymond, *Hollywood's New Yorker*

Steven Rybin and Will Scheibel, editors, *Lonely Places, Dangerous Ground*

Claire Perkins and Constantine Verevis, editors, *B Is for Bad Cinema*

Dominic Lennard, *Bad Seeds and Holy Terrors*

Rosie Thomas, *Bombay before Bollywood*

Scott M. MacDonald, *Binghamton Babylon*

Sudhir Mahadevan, *A Very Old Machine*

David Greven, *Ghost Faces*

James S. Williams, *Encounters with Godard*

William H. Epstein and R. Barton Palmer, editors, *Invented Lives, Imagined Communities*

Lee Carruthers, *Doing Time*

Rebecca Meyers, William Rothman, and Charles Warren, editors, *Looking with Robert Gardner*

Belinda Smaill, *Regarding Life*

Douglas McFarland and Wesley King, editors, *John Huston as Adaptor*

R. Barton Palmer, Homer B. Pettey, and Steven M. Sanders, editors, *Hitchcock's Moral Gaze*

Will Scheibel, *American Stranger*

Nenad Jovanovic, *Brechtian Cinemas*

Gestures of Love

Romancing Performance in Classical Hollywood Cinema

Steven Rybin

Cover (clockwise from top left): Cary Grant and Katharine Hepburn in *Holiday* (Columbia, 1938), Lauren Bacall and Humphrey Bogart in *To Have and Have Not* (Warner Bros., 1944), and Rock Hudson and Dorothy Malone in *Written on the Wind* (Universal, 1956).

Published by State University of New York Press, Albany

© 2017 State University of New York

All rights reserved

Printed in the United States of America

No part of this book may be used or reproduced in any manner whatsoever without written permission. No part of this book may be stored in a retrieval system or transmitted in any form or by any means including electronic, electrostatic, magnetic tape, mechanical, photocopying, recording, or otherwise without the prior permission in writing of the publisher.

For information, contact State University of New York Press, Albany, NY
www.sunypress.edu

Production, Eileen Nizer
Marketing, Fran Keneston

Library of Congress Cataloging-in-Publication Data

Names: Rybin, Steven, 1979– author.
Title: Gestures of love : romancing performance in classical Hollywood cinema / by Steven Rybin.
Description: Albany : State University of New York Press, [2017] | Series: SUNY series, horizons of cinema | Includes bibliographical references and index.
Identifiers: LCCN 2016031471 (print) | LCCN 2016047977 (ebook) | ISBN 9781438465517 (hardcover : alk. paper) | ISBN 978143846552-4 (pbk. : alk. paper) | ISBN 9781438465531 (ebook)
Subjects: LCSH: Love in motion pictures. | Motion pictures—United States—History—20th century. | Motion pictures—Production and direction—United States—History—20th century. | Motion pictures—California—Los Angeles—History—20th century. | Motion picture acting.
Classification: LCC PN1995.9.L6 R93 2017 (print) | LCC PN1995.9.L6 (ebook) | DDC 791.43/6543—dc23
LC record available at https://lccn.loc.gov/2016031471

10 9 8 7 6 5 4 3 2 1

Contents

List of Illustrations   vii

Acknowledgments   xiii

Prelude: Little Bursting Bubbles   xv

Introduction: The Actor's Heartbeat   1

Part I: Screwball Love

1. Love's Final Irony: John Barrymore and Carole Lombard in *Twentieth Century*   33

2. Wicked Jaws, Lanky Brunettes: Myrna Loy and William Powell in *The Thin Man* and *Libeled Lady*   57

3. "You Look So Silly": Katharine Hepburn and Cary Grant in *Sylvia Scarlett*, *Holiday*, *Bringing Up Baby*, and *The Philadelphia Story*   83

Part II: Noir Amour

4. Love's Possession: Dana Andrews and Gene Tierney in *Laura*   119

5. Wooing Bogie, Courting Bacall: Humphrey Bogart and Lauren Bacall in *To Have and Have Not*, *The Big Sleep*, *Dark Passage*, and *Key Largo*   147

Part III: Love and Melodrama

6. Lipstick on a Teacup: Performance in Vincente Minnelli's *The Cobweb* and *Tea and Sympathy* — 185

7. Hudson, Bacall, Stack, Malone: Love and Gesture in Douglas Sirk's *Written on the Wind* — 209

Coda: Modern Love — 239

Works Cited — 249

Index — 257

Illustrations

Figure P.1.	Myrna Loy dreams in *Consolation Marriage* (RKO Radio Pictures, 1931).	xvi
Figure I.1.	Pierre Brasseur as Frédérick Lemaître in *Children of Paradise* (Pathé Consortium Cinéma, 1945).	2
Figures I.2 and I.3.	Miriam Hopkins and Herbert Marshall in *Trouble in Paradise* (Paramount, 1932).	13
Figures I.4 and I.5.	Miriam Hopkins and Herbert Marshall—as they disappear—in *Trouble in Paradise* (Paramount, 1932).	14
Figure I.6.	Kay Francis and Herbert Marshall, in *Trouble in Paradise* (Paramount, 1932).	17
Figures I.7, I.8, and I.9.	Miriam Hopkins sketches Gary Cooper and Fredric March in *Design for Living* (Paramount, 1933).	21
Figure 1.1.	John Barrymore, Carole Lombard, and performance pedagogy: *Twentieth Century* (Columbia, 1934).	34
Figure 1.2.	John Barrymore, Carole Lombard, and the raising of tears above reality: *Twentieth Century* (Columbia, 1934)	35
Figures 1.3 and 1.4.	Carole Lombard floats and bobs with William Powell in *My Man Godfrey* (Universal, 1936).	38
Figure 1.5.	John Barrymore, in a moment of multiplied self-admiration, in *Twentieth Century* (Columbia, 1934).	44
Figure 1.6.	John Barrymore, commanding our attention, in *Twentieth Century* (Columbia, 1934).	47

Figures 1.7 and 1.8.	Carole Lombard's impending response, and her little little kicks, in *Twentieth Century* (Columbia, 1934).	54
Figure 2.1.	Myrna Loy and William Powell being nutty. Production photo for *The Thin Man* (MGM, 1934) Author's collection.	58
Figure 2.2.	Myrna Loy falls into William Powell's lap in *Manhattan Melodrama* (MGM, 1934).	60
Figure 2.3.	William Powell and Kay Francis, bejeweled and besotted, in *Jewel Robbery* (Warner Bros., 1932).	66
Figure 2.4.	Myrna Loy in *The Barbarian* (MGM, 1933).	68
Figure 2.5.	William Powell and Myrna Loy are the life of the party in *The Thin Man* (MGM, 1934).	70
Figure 2.6.	Myrna Loy, playfully disregarding plot, in *Libeled Lady* (MGM, 1936).	77
Figure 2.7.	William Powell burning away the narrative in *Libeled Lady* (MGM, 1936).	78
Figure 3.1.	Cary Grant and Katharine Hepburn, looking so silly in *Bringing Up Baby* (RKO Radio Pictures, 1938).	84
Figures 3.2 and 3.3.	Wind me up again: Cary Grant and Katharine Hepburn in *Bringing Up Baby* (RKO Radio Pictures, 1938).	85
Figures 3.4 and 3.5.	Katharine Hepburn, taking pleasure in her performance, in *Sylvia Scarlett* (RKO Radio Pictures, 1935).	89
Figure 3.6.	Cary Grant, with Katharine Hepburn's treasured childhood toy, in *Holiday* (Columbia, 1938).	94
Figure 3.7.	Cary Grant, and the knowledge the hard floor provides, in *Bringing Up Baby* (RKO Radio Pictures, 1938); Katharine Hepburn looks on.	101
Figure 3.8.	Katharine Hepburn, gazing radiantly at Cary Grant, in *Bringing Up Baby* (RKO Radio Pictures, 1938).	103
Figure 3.9.	Katharine Hepburn, writing with movement, in *The Philadelphia Story* (MGM, 1940).	108

Figure 3.10.	Katharine Hepburn, in the center so as to be admired, in *The Philadelphia Story* (MGM, 1940).	109
Figures 3.11 and 3.12.	Hearth fires: Katharine Hepburn and Jimmy Stewart in *The Philadelphia Story* (MGM, 1940).	111
Figure 4.1.	Falling in love with a painting: Gene Tierney and Dana Andrews in *Laura* (Twentieth Century-Fox, 1944).	120
Figure 4.2.	Gene Tierney, in stillness, in *Leave Her to Heaven* (Twentieth Century-Fox, 1945).	129
Figures 4.3, 4.4, 4.5, and 4.6.	Herbert Marshall and Gene Tierney, never making a gesture without imparting beauty to it, in *The Razor's Edge* (Twentieth Century-Fox, 1946).	131
Figures 4.7 and 4.8.	Dana Andrews falls in love with a painting in *Laura* (Twentieth Century-Fox, 1944).	138
Figures 4.9, 4.10, and 4.11.	Dana Andrews interrogates Gene Tierney in *Laura* (Twentieth Century-Fox, 1944).	142
Figure 4.12.	Dana Andrews and Gene Tierney—it might be the beginning of a kiss—in *Laura* (Twentieth Century-Fox, 1944).	143
Figure 4.13.	Dana Andrews, Gene Tierney, and a kiss across a door in *Laura* (Twentieth Century-Fox, 1944).	146
Figure 5.1.	Humphrey Bogart and Lauren Bacall, keeping an eye out, in *To Have and Have Not* (Warner Bros., 1944).	148
Figure 5.2.	Lauren Bacall scoping out Humphrey Bogart in *To Have and Have Not* (Warner Bros., 1944).	153
Figures 5.3 and 5.4.	Lauren Bacall, dancing with a match, in *To Have and Have Not* (Warner Bros., 1944).	154
Figures 5.5 and 5.6.	A shared world of performance in *To Have and Have Not* (Warner Bros., 1944).	157
Figure 5.7.	Prelude to a kiss: Humphrey Bogart and Lauren Bacall in *To Have and Have Not* (Warner Bros., 1944).	162

Figure 5.8.	Lauren Bacall, with some help from Humphrey Bogart, in *To Have and Have Not* (Warner Bros., 1944).	164
Figure 5.9.	Humphrey Bogart, Lauren Bacall, and the dance between gesture and glance in *The Big Sleep* (Warner Bros., 1946).	171
Figure 5.10 and 5.11.	Lauren Bacall and a slow burn in *Dark Passage* (Warner Bros., 1947).	177
Figure 5.12.	Bogart's gift of a metaphorical ring to Bacall in *Key Largo* (Warner Bros., 1948).	180
Figures 5.13 and 5.14.	Bogart, Bacall, and an open future in *Dark Passage* (Warner Bros., 1947).	182
Figure 6.1.	John Kerr and Lauren Bacall in *The Cobweb* (MGM, 1955).	186
Figures 6.2 and 6.3.	Stevie's paintings, freezing moments of Richard Widmark's performance in still tableaux, in *The Cobweb* (MGM, 1955).	188
Figures 6.4 and 6.5.	Charles Boyer and Lillian Gish, refigured in Stevie's paintings in *The Cobweb* (MGM, 1955).	189
Figures 6.6, 6.7, and 6.8.	Sue (Susan Strasberg) painted in red in *The Cobweb* (MGM, 1955).	190
Figure 6.9.	John Kerr, the troubadour, in *Tea and Sympathy* (MGM, 1956).	200
Figure 6.10.	Deborah Kerr and John Kerr, in the moment he will kindly talk about years from now, in *Tea and Sympathy* (MGM, 1956).	207
Figure 7.1.	Douglas Sirk, directing Rock Hudson, Lauren Bacall, and Robert Stack on the set of *Written on the Wind* (Universal, 1956).	210
Figure 7.2.	Robert Stack, pursued by invisible demons, in *Written on the Wind* (Universal, 1956).	211
Figure 7.3.	Lauren Bacall, and overcast light cutting across a purple floor, in *Written on the Wind* (Universal, 1956).	218

Figure 7.4.	Robert Stack, in a quietly magical moment, in *Written on the Wind* (Universal, 1956).	221
Figure 7.5.	Robert Stack and Lauren Bacall in *The Gift of Love* (Twentieth Century-Fox, 1958).	228
Figures 7.6, 7.7, and 7.8.	Lauren Bacall, pouring her face and eyes sorrowfully into her hands, in *Written on the Wind* (Universal, 1956).	230
Figures 7.9 and 7.10.	Dorothy Malone, courting a dream in *Written on the Wind* (Universal, 1956).	235
Figure C.1.	Griffin Dunne in *After Hours* (Geffen Company, 1985).	240
Figure C.2.	Scorsese's camera encounters potential lovers in *After Hours* (Geffen Company, 1985).	242

Acknowledgments

I send the deepest gratitude to the brilliant and tireless editor of the Horizons of Cinema series at SUNY Press, Murray Pomerance, and I thank him for his mentorship throughout the process of writing and revising this book. I suspect this project would never have gotten off the ground without his support, or perhaps I would not have had the confidence to write it.

I had the opportunity to present an early version of part of the chapter on Katharine Hepburn and Cary Grant at the 2014 Society for Cinema and Media Studies conference in Seattle. That panel stimulated thought that went into the revising and writing of the manuscript. I would like to thank Murray Pomerance, William Rothman, and Linda Ruth Williams, my fellow panelists at that conference, all of whom stimulated challenging discussion and thought directly related to this book's major concerns with the love of performance. I would also like to thank the especially thoughtful audience in attendance at the panel that day, in particular Christian Keathley, whose thoughtful feedback deepened my use of the concept of *découpage*, and who directed me to Timothy Barnard's invaluable book on the subject. I also want to extend my profound gratitude to Will Scheibel for his professional support, friendship, and for his very useful comments on an earlier draft of this book's first chapters.

Early research that informed this book was conducted at the New York Public Library and in the Special Collections department at the Margaret Herrick Library in Beverly Hills. I want to thank all of the librarians and staff at both libraries for their patience and attention to detail as they helped me locate, acquire, and, where necessary and possible, make photocopies of important research materials.

At SUNY Press I want to thank James Peltz and Rafael Chaiken for their very professional work and communication as this book was put into production. I also want to thank the two peer reviewers of the manuscript, whose insightful comments and suggestions for revision significantly improved the book, particularly its introduction. Finally, thanks also to Eileen Nizer and Fran Keneston at SUNY for their work on the production and marketing of this book.

I would also like to thank my many other friends, colleagues, and family, whose various forms of precious support help make a project like this feasible in the first place. The most special thanks of all must go to Jessica Belser, for the friendship and love she gives me every day: the most cherished gestures of all.

June 2016
Atlanta

Prelude

Little Bursting Bubbles

A moment from a film . . .

In a scene early in the melodrama *Consolation Marriage* (1931), the main character, an earnest reporter named Steve (Pat O'Brien), strides with confidence to see the woman he loves. He persists in the belief that she will still be interested in leaving with him on a vacation, despite a letter he has received earlier in the week revealing that she is abandoning him for another man. "She" is Elaine, played by Myrna Loy. Steve arrives at her house, eager. On a small table in his paramour's living room, he spies two books, for one of which he heads directly, as if intuiting that this volume preoccupied his lover in sleepless reading the night before. He gathers it up. In close-up: *Romeo and Juliet*. He opens to a page, glances without much thought. A maid appears, and anxiously tells him that the household has not been informed that Elaine is supposed to go on any kind of vacation. "Just tell her Romeo is here," says Steve, handing the book to her as he caresses a piece of fabric left behind in its pages—fabric, no doubt, that has touched Elaine's skin, fabric left in the book the previous evening, before she ambled upstairs to sleep and dream about the poetry she had read.

The maid dutifully bounds up the stairs to report "Romeo's" presence. Miss Elaine, however, is sleeping. In a high-angle medium shot (figure P.1), we are shown Myrna Loy in repose. Her right arm, bent at the elbow, rests on the pillow next to her head. As she wakes, her dreamy gaze immediately removes us from the rather prosaic narrative reality the film *Consolation Marriage* has presented up to this point. What vivid dream can have been interrupted here? Was it a dream sparked by the pages of *Romeo and Juliet* that her eyes caressed the night before?

Figure P-1. Myrna Loy dreams in *Consolation Marriage* (RKO Radio Pictures, 1931).

"Ro-me-oh?" she asks confusedly, in Loy's inimitable and charming lilt of voice. Were Romeo and Juliet on the page—did she read them, or did she dream them in sleep? She holds the book in her hands for a moment, and thinks about it. Yes, perhaps she only read about Romeo the evening before; but perhaps, too, the dream Romeo had reality. And perhaps real-world men, existing outside of the enchantment of dream, would like to assume themselves Romeos in the face of her erotic power.

She goes downstairs to discover this "Romeo" truly *is*.

The astonishing thing about what immediately follows, and about Loy's performance in that moment, is Elaine/Loy's earnest effort to convey to the sturdy, secure, and mundane Steve/O'Brien the content of this vivifying dream as she felt it, even with the demands of social reality, and the words it insists she must use, compelling her to describe the event in ways that may not be commensurable to the textures of dreams. Loy walks down the steps, the camera following in a low-angle tracking shot. Steve and Elaine meet on the staircase, internally framed by pillars. "I've been trying to tell you—I'm married," Elaine says; "it's true, Stevie." She spills out the narrative information necessary to the machinations of *Consolation Marriage*'s plot: that she is committed to some other man; that she cannot go on the vacation Steve has planned. In poetic counterpoint to this tedious information, delivered by the actress and her character according to the demands of the film's script, is, once again, Myrna Loy's lilting voice—and also her hair (that overtly dyed hair, reminding us that the figure in front of us may be a conjuring somewhat different from the characters Loy plays in other films), and also the satin fabric of her nightgown, a sign not of the erotic pleasure viewers might take in gazing upon her but rather and more powerfully a lingering reminder of the pleasure her dream held for her. After Loy/Elaine has delivered all the necessary plot information, her vocal lilt glides ahead to something altogether more enchanting, something altogether about enchantment, a description of how she came to be besotted by her new husband:

> ELAINE: Oh, I know dear. Please don't look like that. I don't understand it myself. The minute I saw him everything else evaporated like little bursting bubbles . . . I can't explain it, dear. Please, Stevie . . .

The plot of this film would have us assume that the lover of whom she speaks is the man she has mentioned in the dialogue just previously, the man she married and who now prevents her from leaving with Pat O'Brien. But as to this man: we never see him in the film at any point. The narrative is palpably uninterested in him. The next time Elaine appears in the film, it will be after a one-year stint of marriage, when she is divorced, and ready to return to Steve. At this moment on the staircase, we may well wish to hear the name of this mysterious other man, the character she has married, the man who is preventing O'Brien's character from going off with her rather than suffering a disappointment that sends him into a cause-and-effect narrative chain where he must succumb to the consolation marriage of the title (with Irene Dunne). Yet the husband's name is treated as only perfunctory, a placeholder for the more deeply romantic "Romeo" she dreamed about, whom she dreams about still while awake in Steve's more practical presence.

Elaine doesn't know how it happened that she came to love this unseen man; it could be because he doesn't actually exist—that he's nothing but fantasy, an imagined variation upon the Romeo in the great play. She claims only to be able to describe the experience of her encounter with this dream of a man, who has been enough to distract her from reliable Pat O'Brien, as if her dream were a cascade of "little bursting bubbles"—*little bursting bubbles* that take rhythmic shape across the waves of Myrna Loy's sing-song lilt. Even as she strives to share these "bubbles" with Steve, they are uniquely and irrevocably hers, can be spoken of by no one with quite her vocal inflection. Yet that uniqueness is not their ultimate value. Rather than keeping her dream to herself, she desires to share the mystery of this moment, here, with Steve. She is stunned, enchanted, and wants him to know. And he seems to have stunned her as much as Myrna Loy is stunning me as I strive to convey the shape and tremor and floating of the little bubbles I encounter in this particular filmic moment that more than eighty years ago she worked to create, fragile and evanescent bubbles that can float in the air without popping for only so long, and then only if they are delicately and carefully held.

Little bubbles of affection will course throughout this book. I share Elaine's deeply registered feeling that when we fall in love, in this case with figures in cinema, who come to us as if in a dream, we do not know how or exactly why, or what we are to do with this feeling. We could explain the how and the why, of course, through various forms of semiological or social response—dutifully reminding ourselves that film is a capitalistic industry built on the exploitation of viewer emotion; that various psychoanalytical frameworks exist to suggest the love we feel is not really ours, but that it belongs to some other authoritative voice who will explain to us the idea of an id-ego-superego structure, a structure that, again, is not really the property of any one of us, but which rather determines us; that stars are always already defined in their meanings for us, as if the industry wanted to rob us of our experience of performance before we have had the chance to have it, through publicity campaigns and marketing materials; and finally reminding ourselves that we always risk possible social embarrassment if we share our love for an actor in a way that eschews the aforementioned methods and proceeds forward in full acknowledgment of that figure's power over us. But I persist in the belief that, like Elaine, those who love cinema and the figures who live within it may be better off in never fully awakening from that dream— neither ignoring reality nor "escaping" from it but rather investing it with more humanity. Does Elaine share with Delmore Schwartz the notion that, in dreams, begin responsibilities? Like her, I write this book in the belief that, if we do our very best to describe the particular shape or music our love for performance in cinema takes, others can perhaps find such descriptions useful—and in ways that cannot be presumed or predicated before the interrelated acts of viewing and reading. As if it could distend those few seconds into three-hundred pages, this whole book is written in the space between Elaine waking up and her walking down the stairs to describe that love as *little bursting bubbles*, three little words that describe how, now awake in the reality in which she must live, she was wooed away in her dream.

I am carried along by the lilt of her voice, so that perhaps I might find my own.

Introduction

The Actor's Heartbeat

LACENAIRE: You practice a peculiar craft.

LEMAÎTRE: The best.

LACENAIRE: No doubt. But you make hearts beat every night at the same hour.

LEMAÎTRE: You don't understand. That's the beauty of it! The wonder! To feel and hear your own heart and the heart of the audience beat at the same time.

LACENAIRE: How promiscuous!

—Marcel Carné's *Les Enfants du Paradis* (1945)

THIS BOOK TELLS A STORY ABOUT the performance of courtship and love across three genres of Classical Hollywood cinema: the screwball comedies of the thirties, forties noir, and the family melodramas of the fifties. It is also about how love for performance is shaped and shared by writing, endeavoring as writing can to linger upon those truly stunning moments when an actor, herself playing a character whose heart beats and mind races at the sight of another, besots, causing hearts to beat and minds to race in turn.

There are many fine books on performance in cinema studies, but there are precious few which query how one writes about films, or indeed watches films, as an enchanted viewer, a viewer enthralled—wooed—by a particular actor or actors moving and gesturing in a given cinematic moment. Some scholars studying the subject of love and performance

Figure I.1. Pierre Brasseur as Frédérick Lemaître in *Children of Paradise* (Pathé Consortium Cinéma, 1945).

have nevertheless pushed in this direction, selecting certain performers for close study, and noting how attachment to a beloved star can refigure a film's shape and meaning. Martha P. Nochimson, for example, selects for analysis those stars who form dynamic, engaging, heterosexual couples in Hollywood movies. She locates the value of these tandems in the way they subvert the ideological norms most films reinforce: "When an onscreen couple generates powerful energy and boosts the image to prominence as a structural element in the film," she writes, the performance of romance tends "to disrupt the formulas in interesting ways so as to create highly distinctive perspectives on the social practices embedded in the usual narrative pattern" (8–9). Other scholars, too, grapple with the challenge of analyzing certain remarkable actors, noting how writing itself is a vehicle for contemplation of the viewer's experience of performance. Virginia Wright Wexman, in her study of romance in classical cinema, reminds her reader that the kinetic experience of film performance poses challenges for analysis, for although "performance is continuous . . . its analysis must approach this phenomenon in terms of discrete (or *digital*) units" (21). This challenge comes paired with the fact that enchanting onscreen couples in cinema are more often than not played by actors whose success, Wexman writes, "is often explained by referring to the 'magic' of their personalities rather than to their skills as actors" (22). Perhaps the greatest difference between this book and these earlier volumes on the performance of coupledom, however, is that I strive to take the magic out of quotation marks—I am earnestly interested in the magic of film performance, not the "magic." I want to know more about how the viewer is or might be wooed. A study of the performance of love, I argue, must thus also meditate upon the love of performance, as experienced and then shared in the act of writing: that tantalizing encounter between the devoted lover of film and the film player, an experience which, in discussions of cinephilia and film pleasure, is often not acknowledged. Murray Pomerance wisely notes the intellectual stakes at work in the contemplation of a pleasing moment of film performance: "How is the special mode of relationship established that permits intimacy without commitment, revelation without implication? What surrender of the viewer's self is implicit in every acceptance of acted reality?" (128).

This book aims to sharpen our sense and understanding of that surrender, particularly as it pertains to Classical Hollywood. I offer an understanding of the place and participation of the film lover at the scene of performance, and in particular the performance of love, in different varieties of this classical cinema. While studies of film stars frequently explore the role of the audience in the making of stars and their meaning (see, especially, Dyer 1998 and 2003, Gledhill 1991, and Morin 2005), scholarship on film performance—that is, work focused on the moment-by-moment unfolding of gesture, movement, and expression rather than extra-textual matters of persona or celebrity—tends not to comment on how the viewer's attachment to actors might shape an understanding of the unfolding of performance and its meaning. A rare exception is Ana Salzberg's admirable study of female stardom in studio-era Hollywood, in which she declares an interest in "the more sensual engagement between star and viewer," one in which the viewer responds "to the star's onscreen affect"—and where "the spectator 'wraps' the performer up in a visceral embrace that is unique in its sensation—not abstract, but utterly intimate" (15). Yet by and large, most writers on film acting keep the performer at a distance. A typical star study, for example, taking an individual actor as its subject, might suggest that a film character is understood in large part by the viewer's consumption of other media material, such as interviews or publicity appearances; or, if it is a performance study or actor biography, how a player's evolution of acting style inform the creation of a character. A study of genre might slot the actor within a set of well-worn conventions, constructing the viewer as one who expects the actor to give the typical performance one expects from a given formula. What I am after, by contrast, following Pomerance and Salzberg above, is a kind of "cinephilia of the actor," a love of film that takes the performer as its beloved—or, more accurately, a love of film that acknowledges besotment by a figure on the screen. (The viewer, after all, does not "take" the performer; the viewer is taken.) Yet cinephilic writing on film, while typically writing from the energy produced by what Barthes (25–26, 1981) called the *punctum*, or piercing feeling, that a uniquely noticed inscription on a strip of film provokes in the viewer, often loses sight of the actor: where cinephiles often direct their attention to the visual marginalia or obscure details of a film in order to win perceptual and social distinction and status, the actor, by contrast, is not a marginal figure. Often they are at the center of the frame, and everyone, cinephile or not, has been moved by a performer at one time or another. What I want to know more deeply is what place the lover of film has in our understanding of the performed moment of love, and what place the love of the actor has in our understanding of love as depicted subject in cinema. Further, what does this viewer become when he sets out to write about such moments? What story does the writer tell of gestures and movements experienced and remembered—not the story of the film, but the story of film's experience, freshly told? A viewer's affection for certain actors, if we take it seriously rather than dismissing it as the product of celebrity culture, or as somehow not "cinephilic" enough (everyone loves actors); if we resist giggling with embarrassment or social anxiety when moved by a figure on the screen—becomes a very crucial part of film experience; it can come to refigure the content of the films as described in writing. As our eyes follow, moment-by-moment, gesture-by-gesture, beat-by-beat, she or he who has enchanted us for a time, the lover with this eye, if she takes to writing, is thus inscribing, in the mind's eye and then later on paper, how this time spent watching the actor's movements, gestures, and expressions felt, and what this feeling is taken to mean.

Through this book's discussion of Classical Hollywood's variation on what Pomerance calls this "special mode of relationship" connecting the actor to the viewer, I aim to explore a question that cuts to the quick of a very special kind of experience that happens at the movies: the engagement between the figure who sits in the theater (the committed lover of film) and that special figure on the screen who inspires, through her gestures, movements, and expressions, a deeper contemplation of what is of value in watching cinema. In this study, I acknowledge the narratives films ostensibly tell without remaining beholden to them; my larger interest is to discover how beloved onscreen couples dart off on a new narrative—one that is not exactly articulated within the films as scripted but which comes to a kind of completion only when a smitten cinephile is carried along on a journey across the stars. This is not a book, then, about the "star images" formed by legendary movie couples, already set in historical stone. It is a book about the experience of watching, again and again, how individual, fascinating performers create figures who court one another, and find alongside the viewer (or, especially in some of the noir and melodramas I will study, fail to find) a common philosophy of life, a shared passion in their pitching of woo. Thus, the narrative fact of the screen "couple" is less interesting, I think, than the play and performance of desire that uses narrative as a pretext to make desire palpable in a larger and shared context. In charting these gestures, movements, and expressions, the analyst of film is doing more, or something other than, charting biography and articulating already-established star personae. Pomerance, for example, in the passage quoted earlier, is of course discussing a biographically and historically situated actor (Janet Leigh in Alfred Hitchcock's *Psycho* [1960]); but what he is ultimately more interested in are those particular actors from the past who are still alive in the present-day watching of movies—performers who ongoingly intervene in film experience, and who possess memorable ways of gesturing, moving, laughing, crying, quivering, and so on, as well as looking at and loving others with whom they share the screen. Commentators often discuss how the camera changes or inflects a viewer's perception of a figure, but the actor, as a special component of film experience, and as a special component of moments in movies memorable to us, might even throw into relief, through her special distinction, the cinematic armature surrounding her, a structure that, in the presence of another actor, might have come across as conventional or dull (see, for a discussion of just this sort of comparative test, Thompson, "Commutation Test"). In other words, the film actor is not only in the space—she might change the space of a given film moment, as much or perhaps more than it has changed her.

In this study of love's performance in classical cinema I aim to describe and analyze particular qualities each of my selected actors offer, through a close look at interconnected moments from their various films in three different classical genres. It is difficult to know, of course, how a performer might impact a viewer in film experience; there is no universal position or spectatorship that can presume, for sure, how a gesture will touch the eyes and heart at this moment, or how it will find its way into writing subsequently. This ongoing vitality of both the classical cinema and its greatest performances insures that our understanding of these films can never settle into ossified response: the contingent encounter with performative gesture—the viewer's participation in the social event of love onscreen—demands a new account, in writing, a new circulation of performance's impact in and across cinephile culture. In writing of performance within and for an intersubjective community of film lovers, I aim to suggest how each vision of woo created in these performances intervenes into our understanding of love as a social form: as a primarily heterosexual form in thirties screwball and forties noir, and a more complicated grouping of performers coming to form threesomes and quartets in a handful of family melodramas of the fifties. Hollywood, of course, has a prevailing tendency to imagine courtship in an exclusive and normative context: white, ostensibly heterosexual couples whose union more often reinforces, rather than challenges, the dominant ideology. Yet our pleasure in performance, I argue, exceeds social determination in its contingent unpredictability and the varieties of emotional response the experience of Classical Hollywood cinema elicits. Although the subject of my work is the performance of particular social rituals—flirting and courtship—in cinema, I am most attracted to performative moments not because they illustrate social conventions of romance during the 1930s, 1940s, and 1950s, but rather because they intervene in those conventions, offering inventive examples of the tendency, in the frame of cinema, to imagine and hope that love might provide a better future and a different kind of narrative, through the creation of characters who strike out against or apart from convention or typicality. As these moments are linked together in this book, and put into dialogue with thought on acting, historical reflection on the moment of production, and more general reflections on screen performance, they will constitute a story of performed love in Classical Hollywood cinema, a way to ongoingly experience and rewrite the excitement of that cinema and some of its greatest characterizations.

Of course, I have not so much selected actors to write about but rather, they have selected me; I have not simply plucked them from a batch of existing films as possible "case studies" but have rather focused on Myrna Loy and William Powell rather than, say, Claudette Colbert and Clark Gable, because one pair has utterly and thoroughly and repeatedly besotted me while the other—while brilliant, beautiful, important, and thoroughly entertaining—has not. (Where my own choice of performers might differ from the reader's, I humbly encourage that reader to engage with this book in a kind of counterpoint, refracting my thoughts on those who have wooed me through your own thoughts, however they might be shaped by this book, by those who have wooed you.) In the context of my reception of the Classical Hollywood cinema, these actors have changed the way my heart beats during performance. For me, they generate, as Nochimson might say, a powerful energy; because, as Wexman might put it, I find that the particularity of this energy poses an intriguing challenge to my writing on film; and because, following Pomerance, I have found that in watching these figures I have not simply been witness to an actor imitating a pre-written character but have rather surrendered a very important part of my identity and desire to their existence in cinema during, and indeed sometimes after, the duration of their movies. Nochimson is certainly right that the writer concerned with analysis must take care to pick the most interesting and energetic actors, and Wexman is justified to remind us of the distance that marks performance's experience from performance's analysis. But as I have suggested, it is also true that the actor may not so much be selected by the viewer as intervene powerfully in the film lover's experience of cinema and in efforts to transcribe this experience in writing. Christian Keathley writes more generally of what he calls the "cinephiliac moment"—that privileged moment in film experience that stands salient in our memory, rift from its original context of narrative—in which a film might "step into our lives" in unpredictable and perpetually powerful ways (152). An actor might, too.

The Beating Heart of *Mise-en-Scène*

All of the actors and couples I especially like in the Classical Hollywood cinema tend to converge, more or less, around three particular genres: the screwball comedy of the thirties, the film noir of the forties, and the family melodrama of the fifties. Each of these genres offers distinct and varying contexts for the performance of love. Because performance in Classical Hollywood is often understood as a salient component of *mise-en-scène* presented to the audience through the pre-planned organization of framing, camera movement, and analytical editing (a blend of technique that French cinephiles call *découpage*), this study of love's performance in Classical Hollywood cinema is in part a story about love's changing rhythms and inflections in the context of various evolutions of classical style across three distinct genres. In the 1930s screwball films I discuss, for example, the smooth, seamless continuity of image works in tandem with the playfully physical grace and dexterity of individual performers: Katharine Hepburn, in *Bringing Up Baby* (1938) bounding across golf course, night club, and countryside in her madcap pursuit of Cary Grant; Myrna Loy and William Powell, in *The Thin Man* (1934) delectably serving and consuming martinis while entertaining a room of guests and solving mysteries; Carole Lombard, in *My Man Godfrey* (1936) zanily bouncing out of a shower, fully dressed, somehow convinced of William Powell's love. Indeed, the grace of these performers serves to hold together the seamlessness of classical continuity during Hollywood's golden age of the 1930s, while nevertheless imbuing that continuity with a screwy energy few other players or films from that decade can match. While the classical continuity of Hollywood remains firmly in place in 1940s noir (see Bordwell, Staiger, and Thompson 74–77), love's movement through classical noir is no longer as smooth, or as self-assuredly inventive, as in screwball, and at times the seamlessness of the system begins to break down, and performance bears the weight of anxiety and deceit. Watch, as Gene Tierney tries to wriggle free of a web of male possession in *Laura* (1944); and as Humphrey Bogart and Lauren Bacall, in a matching of wary wits, learn to trust one another in *To Have and Have Not* (1944) and *The Big Sleep* (1946). Finally, in the 1950s family melodrama, couples, although living in an ostensibly prosperous post-noir world, find the old continuities of classical cinema crumbling all around them, a stylistic parallel to fractured hearth and home. Here, the couple's very form as a traditionally heterosexual twosome is called into question. In Vincente Minnelli's *Tea for Sympathy* (1956), for example, John Kerr grapples with homosexual desire, and the possibility of various unconsummated couplings, in a society not shaped to accommodate his love. In Douglas Sirk's *Written on the Wind* (1956), meanwhile, the nascent modernism of the film itself gestures toward the modern love of the decades to come.

What each of these classical genres might be said to offer is a different proscenium for the performed moment of love. Of course, as the arrangement of the chapters implies, there is plenty of variation within each genre, to the extent that every individual film constructs its own unique proscenium for its actors. As Stanley Cavell points out, genres are themselves quite like mediums, wherein members of a group that take up the medium "inevitably seem at first not to fit with the features of the others, hence that each is in argument over what defines the genre" (*Cities of Words* 150). That is, when Carole Lombard, Myrna Loy, and Katharine Hepburn, and John Barrymore, William Powell, and Cary Grant perform in what have historically been called screwball comedies, they make various kinds of performative claims about how behavior might take shape under a certain kind of known proscenium, claims that are themselves open to variation within the evolution of each actor's specific career. This idea compels us to ask how performance in genre, if genre is to be taken as a kind of medium, impacts the viewer with its own palpable variations.

All of the films discussed in this book, of course, are part of a larger mode of production: the Classical Hollywood cinema, a cinema built upon cause-and-effect, narratively motivated images, and continuous editing. However, highly variable, genre-specific performances have the power to inflect the flow of this continuity editing, or what some writers call *découpage*, with a certain quality of feeling, a certain texture of encounter, that perhaps cannot finally be rationalized or predicated in advance. Richard deCordova claims that the typical Hollywood movie "renders performance according to genre-specific rules" (116); but there may be a more supple way to regard performance in Classical Hollywood movies (an articulation which might place the rendering in the hands of the actors, in relation to the frameworks provided by their directors, and not the genre itself). To divine this, it is worth contemplating further the precise quality of the word *découpage*, this chimerical French term that, as Timothy Barnard reminds us, refers to "scene conception" (12), or "something created by the camera and their sequencing as envisioned at an earlier stage of the film's creation" (6). As Dudley Andrew has pointed out, it was Roger Leenhardt, in the pages of *Esprit*, who located great value in *découpage*, and used the word to simultaneously refer to both the structure created through planning in pre-production and the structure realized through the shooting of the film itself. Importantly, this broader definition implicitly incorporates all of the various cinematographic properties contributing to the rhythm of a film, including framing and its duration, camera movement, and staging. Leenhardt, in Andrew's words, praised "filmmakers who probe the temporality within their material as it runs up against a developing whole to which it contributes" (34). As Andrew goes on to suggest, working from Leenhardt, "'In English . . . *Découpage*, is called *continuity*,' and continuity is experienced as rhythm, 'the control exercised by the mind over the material which has been filmed or is to be filmed.' This aesthetic notion . . . links matter to memory, letting the mind parse the world so as to bring out its significance" (34). Later, the French critics writing in *Cahiers du Cinéma* used this concept of *découpage* in its two conventional senses: as a means to understand the breakdown of a film's treatment before shooting, and as a word used to refer to the assemblage of the filmed pieces in the editing stage. But they also employed the concept in order to describe the cinephile's experiential investment in a given film's inflection of temporality, continuity, and genre.

While the *Cahiers* critics privileged auteurs, their ideas about the experiential qualities of *mise-en-scène* offer a suggestive prompt for how we might write about the performance of love as a part of what creates, rather than something that is merely contained within, film style. Jean-Luc Godard, for example, articulates the logic behind classical film style directly in relation to the movement of love's performance:

> If direction is a look, montage is a heart-beat. To foresee is the characteristic of both: but what one seeks to foresee in space, the other seeks in time. Suppose you notice a young girl in the street who attracts you. You hesitate to follow her. A quarter of a second. How to convey this hesitation? *Mise en scène* will answer the question, 'How shall I approach her?' But in order to render explicit the other question, 'Am I going to love her?,' you are forced to bestow importance on the quarter of a second during which the two questions are born . . . This example shows that talking of *mise en scène* automatically implies montage. When montage effects surpass those of *mise en scène* in efficacity, the beauty of the latter is doubled, the unforeseen unveiling secrets by its charm in an operation analogous to using unknown qualities in mathematics (*Godard on Godard* 39).

Timothy Barnard (52–53) argues that Godard is speaking more of "cutting" in this passage rather than *découpage*—that is, that Godard is interested in how the film is created in the editing room through juxtaposed shots rather than how the film's total rhythm is created out a conception which overlaps the various processes and procedures of pre-production, production, and editing. However, I concur with Adrian Martin that this passage is nevertheless a sign of Godard's interest in how the orchestration of all the various elements of film technique are related, an interest in "the overlap of the phases of on-set direction and editing" (Martin 55)—that is, the close relationship between the gestures and rhythms of what we perceive as *mise-en-scène* and the gestures and rhythms of cutting. In turn, what I am most interested in is the performer's share in this cinematic creation of space and time in the Classical Hollywood romance. The hypothetical "narrative event" Godard discusses in this passage—the beginnings of a love affair—is, of course, familiar from scores of Hollywood films. However, by describing how *mise-en-scène* and montage might complement and intensify one another, Godard's insight shows how such techniques, handled in a particular way, can invest formulaic situations with present-tense, embodied aliveness ("direction is a look, montage is a heart-beat").

Of course, Godard's theoretical example is a nearly complete abstraction: two imaginary figures, boy and girl, bereft of gestural specificity, exist on the page of his criticism, a realm where no performance happens: they must wait for an actor to come along and make them live. Crucially, as Godard points out, they also need a viewer to love them: throughout the passage, he addresses a hypothetical "you," a viewer whose moment-by-moment attention to the movements and gestures of performance (performance as manifest within the overall temporality of a filmmaker's framing and cutting) surrenders the viewing self to the actor and the character she creates. Here Godard may be somewhat close to Ana Salzberg's suggestion that viewers can themselves create kinds of close-ups through their affection for particular figures in the frame, regardless of the specific kind of shot distance the director has chosen to frame the actor at any particular moment. In writing of her admiration of Katharine Hepburn's unique way of moving onscreen, for example, Salzberg conceives of a kind of close-up framed not by the filmmaker but by the viewer's loving eye, a pleasurable and intense mode of visuality generated by both the actor *and* by the love of the viewer: "One could arguably build on the notion of close-up vision to consider the intimacy between viewer and star. More precisely, one could suggest that Hepburn invites a close-up *on* vision itself—a heightened awareness of the visual pleasure inspired by the actress's onscreen form" (40). Such a conception not only goes some way to suggesting the important role actors play in the realization of *découpage*; it also suggests—in its provocative idea that the viewer's intimate gaze, when touched by the figural power of a performer, creates a close-up in the act of viewing (regardless of the choice in shot distance by the director)—that the act of scene construction and conception in fact extends to the act of viewing itself, where our meditation upon the meaning of space and our reflection upon qualities of time are stimulated not only by choices made by the filmmaker and the actor but also by our own eyes, driven by a heart that beats on the screen.

Of course, Godard, in the aforementioned passage, only describes in a very cerebral way the moment in which his two lovers come together—he ignores, in his description of this imagined example, all of those little nuances, rituals, and flirtations that defer the moment of coupling even as they gesture toward it. Yet Godard's larger insight is that the heartbeat of the actor, inflected by the eye of the adoring viewer, can imbue the mechanical engineering of each classical film's deployment of continuity with human, present-tense aliveness. For Godard, the *découpage* and editing of a given film do not merely "contain" or predetermine, in the planning of directorial treatment, film performances; nor does the editor "save" the performances in the cutting room. Instead, actors and the cinephiles enchanted by them become the key elements in the construction of the scene, part of a larger *découpage* that is perpetually reconstructed and reconceived every time a Classical Hollywood film is felt deeply by its viewer and then perhaps written about. In fact, Godard's observations compel us to wonder if actors themselves can even be quite considered fully a part of the "staging" that is one of the components of *découpage* by those who conceive of it mostly as "pre-planned treatment." One cannot stage or entirely pre-plan a gesture, in all of its embodied contingency. A gesture may be a part of *découpage* (or, in terms of narrative, the social form of courtship and love), but ultimately gesture works to intervene in such a framework and in such pre-planned forms. Certainly the viewer's own share in this scene conception cannot quite be pre-planned or fully anticipated by the filmmaker.

The viewer's perception of performance, then—the beating heart of *mise-en-scène*, montage, and other stylistic techniques Godard is concerned with—becomes a lived experience of love's performance in film. Following Godard, this cinephile finds that the structure of *mise-en-scène* created in the watching of a given film does not merely "contain" the performances (just as the "social form" of love, either as expressed in the diegesis or in the cultural moment during which the film was made, does not fully contain them, either) but is in fact the very structure generated through the encounter of one lover with another, and through the encounter between the figure on the screen and the lover of film. In cinema, love is not depicted, it creates; *découpage* does not exist, in Godard's sense, until these lovers approach, and because lovers always meet in an irreducibly particular way, performers and their viewers ultimately achieve singular inflection of the classical style Godard discusses, and different idealizations of how love takes on social form. By striking at the erotics of encounter that lie at the heart of classical cinema's editing practice, Godard finds in love not simply the *content* of the Hollywood movie; it is the very heart that makes continuity style live and breathe.

A Matter of Time

And yet the actor's heartbeat extends beyond the moment of first encounter. In most of the films discussed in these pages, the initial encounter between lovers happens quickly, and often with no clap of thunder. What matters, finally, is how this encounter is extended beyond the first moment, to the ones to follow subsequently: in other words, what matters is how each couple's life, lived through love, is marked by a distinctive quality of time. An Ernst Lubitsch film that prefigures the screwball comedies I write about in the first part of the book offers suggestive opportunity for thinking further about how to live and breathe alongside the actor, and how to trace love in cinema from the moment of initial encounter to a life that might be ongoingly—and playfully—shared.

Lubitsch's *Trouble in Paradise* (1932) is exquisitely sensitive to the varying qualities of time different actors give us. Early in the film, Lily (Miriam Hopkins) meets Gaston (Herbert Marshall) in a posh Venice hotel under the pretense that Hopkins is a Countess and Marshall is a Baron. Anticipating the playful disposition of later screwball characters such as Susan Vance (*Bringing Up Baby*) and Irene Bullock (*My Man Godfrey*), Lily plays a game of tease. Her playmate is the dignified Herbert Marshall, who, poised as this fraudulent Baron, looks believably American but behaves, convincingly, like a sophisticated European. Their wooing takes the shape of thieving. He reveals he has stolen a pin (and intimates, as he gives it back to her, that its central jewel may still be missing); after restoring the pin to her dress, Lily asks for the time. But time is in Lily's hands; like all great movie characters, Lily has stolen time away from us, just as the Baron realizes, in a beat, that she has stolen his watch. And what is time for, these actors seem to be asking us, if not to flirt? This is the question Lubitsch seems to want us to ask as he shows us the Baron revealing the last great purloined object in this wooing sequence: Lily's garter (figures I.2 and I.3; how in the world, and where and at what point in this hotel room did the Baron manage to lift it off her leg, without her noticing?). No mere look of pleasure now, for Hopkins: she shrieks a "*darling!*" and throws herself at the Baron, who will reveal himself, to a look of deep satisfaction from Lily, as the famed thief Gaston Monescu.

They kiss. A dissolve. Stretched out, now, the lovers on a couch: it is fair to ask how much time has passed (is this still the first copulation, or the lull between the second and the first?). And the viewer knows there is something more happening with this dissolve than the typical passage of time; there is the insinuation of the viewer's response into the space of the scene, which colors our interpretation of the gestures to follow. Marshall sits by Hopkins's waist; she is lying down, and he is leaning toward her in a kiss, before pulling back to appreciate once again her

Figures I.2 and I.3. Miriam Hopkins and Herbert Marshall in *Trouble in Paradise* (Paramount, 1932).

powers of thievery (the display of which has generated this attraction). As always in Lubitsch's cinema, how one responds to insinuation—the preceding dissolve—will color how these gestures and positioning are read. If we believe they have already had sex, then thievery itself, rather than physical copulation, will serve as the object and aim of the convoluted courtship to follow. But if we believe the moment of physical coupling has yet to take place, then the veritable striptease which has occurred with the shedding of lifted items in the preceding scene will flirtily extend itself across the entire film (and here Lubitsch will stay away from the normativity of a legal union, delaying the copulation of his characters through more crime). Regardless of our quality of response, the important thing is that the response has occurred, that it is keyed to the gestures of desire expressed by Hopkins and Marshall which extend across the entire film (with Kay Francis soon to be introduced as the third instrument in this erotic trio). We are, in other words, complicit with the play of Lubitsch and his actors: that intimate involvement with performance, rather than the "representation" of such-and-such a class subverting such-and-such another, is the social reality Lubitsch's cinema is most interested in, which extends beyond the diegesis into the space of the theater and implicates the audience in the circulation of desire on film.

The texture of this playful engagement with the actors, regardless of the exact quality of our response, is framed as a dream a moment later by Lubitsch, when, timed to a kiss, he dissolves his lovers out of the image, and leaving us, for five languorous seconds, with the sight of the abandoned sofa upon which these figures of cinema were a moment ago perched as lovebirds, and upon which we might now project an entirely fresh range of fulsome, naughty thoughts.

Figures I.4 and I.5. Miriam Hopkins and Herbert Marshall—as they disappear—in *Trouble in Paradise* (Paramount, 1932).

Critics have responded to this second, equally ambiguous and much more magical dissolve in divergent ways. For William Paul, in *Ernst Lubitsch's American Comedy*, it is part and parcel with the "brilliant romantic tenor" of the first long sequence in Venice in the film, prior to the introduction of a more blatant satire in the arrival of Madame Colet in the first Paris sequence (44). Sabine Hake listens closely to this romantic tenor and finds in the dissolve of the lovers into the ether of celluloid halide "the image of an empty sofa cast in twilight, an image that, once again, bears witness to the gains and losses involved in all relationships" (179). Lubitsch's biographer, Scott Eyman, sees it is as part of a "dazzling Möbius strip of erotic allusion, genial irony, and dégagé visual lyricism and elegance" (193). James Harvey writes that the film bears a double consciousness, glimpsed in moments such as the above dissolve, in which "Lubitsch, it seems, wants us to have the dream with a full and continuing ironic consciousness that it *is* a dream" (53). My own response is to suggest that what the dissolve confirms, with its introduction of the passage of time into what was a beat earlier the representation of a languid kiss in the *mise-en-scène*, is that what these two thieving lovers put onto a pedestal is not each other—unlike in the later screwball comedies, which, as Stanley Cavell points out, involve the instruction of the characters in the avoidance of idealizing the everyday lover (see *Pursuits of Happiness* 121). Instead, what Lily and Gaston are idealizing, what they put on a pedestal, is the moment itself, in their attempt to hold onto it against the passage of time signaled by the dissolve. As our eyes sinuously wind through cinema in pursuit of those moments that will occupy us, perhaps for a lifetime, Lily/Hopkins and Gaston/Marshall themselves, too, want to fill that moment with a gesture of love full enough with desire so that it may last in idealized memory for as long as they live. This dissolve not only ironically suggests the impermanence of the moment and thus the folly of their intentions to idealize time; it is also Lubitsch's own elegant, melancholic counterpoint to the intense intentions of this onscreen love. Here, the response Andrew Sarris has to moments such as this dissolve is closest to my own: "A poignant sadness infiltrates the director's gayest moments, and it is this counterpoint between sadness and gaiety that represents the Lubitsch touch, and not the leering humor of closed doors" (643). The director appreciates the ideal yearned for by the characters but reminds the viewer that efforts to hold onto time will never quite be fulfilled; in its place is found a rueful melancholy.

But Lubitsch is alive to the varieties of ways his performers and characters have of trying to hold onto time—or, more precisely, of generating those languid moments of love that they, in turn, try to hold onto. And so as the plot of *Trouble in Paradise* continues lightly on its way, Lily and Gaston realize they will need to commit more thievery to bankroll a lifestyle allowing for such fleeting moments of plenitude. They will thus devise to rob perfume industrialist Madame Colet (Kay Francis) of her money. But as one watches Marshall flirt with Francis in subsequent scenes, with the same quality of duplicitous performance that sparked his discovery of love for Lily (this time, as Monsieur Laval, a former man of means who has lost most of his fortune), one realizes that it is not expensive objects Gaston/Laval is in search of (these objects are merely the means to what he really wants), but rather more moments, more slices of time that he might share with another woman of distinction, all in the ongoing attempt to put the experience of time itself, as love, on a pedestal. It is not, then, that he is cheating on Lily, exactly, or at least not yet; he is putting two different qualities of time into counterpoint, to see which is best suited to his performance. And he certainly finds these moments rival what Marshall created earlier with Hopkins. As William Paul notes of a scene in which Madame Colet contemplates the purchase of an expensive trinket from a jeweler, Kay Francis exudes a kind of languid sensuality that throws into contrast the quicker, tighter, more narrowly directed gestures and movements of Miriam Hopkins: "When she says 'But it's beautiful,' her brisk line-reading suddenly slows down and lingers on 'beautiful,' almost as if she could taste the word as she speaks it . . . The real currency this character deals in is sensuality" (56). Unlike Hopkins, who characterizes Lily as a woman "constantly on the move about [Gaston's] room, both as if to explore it and to establish her own space," Francis "repeatedly lapses into frozen positions" as she creates her Collet (64). (Lily, by contrast, only freezes when Gaston kisses her—and even then, another movement is nigh.) Paul summarily describes this difference in performance style between the two female leads as a dialectic between "Hopkins' bouncy allegro playing in counter-rhythm to Francis' sensuous adagio" (65). The musical metaphors aptly describe the different qualities of time each woman spends with Gaston. With Lily, it is forward movement, the enjoyment of duration foreshortened by the need to acquire the economic means to support the next one. With Colet, the sensuality of time quivers on the surface of Kay Francis's body as she attempts to hold a still pose while alternately anticipating Gaston, greeting Gaston, or waiting for his next arrival.

Later in the film, after Gaston reveals his identity to Madame Colet, Gaston follows Lily out the door, leaving Kay Francis alone. She hears footsteps down the stairs, suggesting Gaston's reunion with Lily and departure from her life. Placing her hands at her sides, eyes cast downward, Francis moves slowly over to a sofa, freezing herself in another tableaux. She is suspended here above two possibilities: Gaston is either gone forever; or perhaps he will come back. He comes back—Lubitsch returns the sounds of the footsteps to the soundtrack, walking up this time—and, as Gaston stands over her, Colet strikes a tentative smile up his way. As she raises to her feet, however, Gaston tells her, with great politesse, that their love is impossible, and that if he were to stay, surely a policeman would be knocking on their door to arrest him for his crimes the next morning. Francis casts her eyes away from him, offscreen right—as if glimpsing the invisible, magical dream space into which Lily and Gaston earlier dissolved, and into which she will now not have access (figure I.6). "But that terrible policeman," Francis says. Lubitsch, finally, calls upon us to watch performance through a filter of sophisticated irony; we must not miss the very question the characters themselves yearn to ask, *was this time well spent?*

These moments from *Trouble in Paradise* remind us of the relationship between our love of performance and our experience of duration, as

Figure I.6. Kay Francis and Herbert Marshall, in *Trouble in Paradise* (Paramount, 1932).

viewers measure the value of time spent with onscreen lovers engaged in both public and private pitching of woo. Time, of course, and the evaluation of time, is essential to courtship as both public and private ritual, and flirtation as lived event. To flirt is to take Godard's twinned questions in his theorem of lovestruck *découpage*—"How shall I approach her? and "Am I going to love her?"—and stretch them as far as they might go in time, all in an effort to defer the moment of commitment and institutionalization. If, as Godard reminds us, "in order to render explicit the . . . question, 'Am I going to love her?,' you are forced to bestow importance on the quarter of a second during which the two questions are born" (*Godard on Godard* 39), in flirtation one takes that quarter of a second and stretches it out to many seconds, many minutes, hours, perhaps years. Psychoanalyst Adam Phillips conceives flirting as the continued deferment of duty and goals in favor of the ongoingly pleasurable play with time:

> If our descriptions of sexuality are tyrannized by various stories of committed purpose—sex as reproduction, sex as intimacy—flirtation puts in disarray our sense of an ending. In flirtation you never know whether the beginning of the story—the story of a relationship—will be the end; flirtation, that is to say, exploits the idea of surprise . . . space is being created in which aims or ends can be worked out; the assured wish for the more or less obvious sexual combinations, or commitments, may be a way of pre-empting the elaboration of, making time for, less familiar possibilities. Flirtation, if it can be sustained, is a way of cultivating wishes, of playing for time. Deferral can make room. (xix)

Diegetic deferral, as these few moments of flirty encounter in *Trouble in Paradise* suggest, makes temporal room for the film lover, too, giving her space and time for her own heart to beat as she watches gesture, movement, and expression unfold in the performances of two or more figures on the screen. The sort of deferral Phillips discusses in his theory of flirtation might also have something very much to do with the cinephile's desire to return, beyond narrative consumption or clarification of character psychology or motivation, to moments of performance created by beloved actors, again and again: to revisit the work of a beloved actor is to make time for possibilities, to find new surprises, to flirt with new meanings and feelings in one's reencounter with a performance one knows well, or thinks one knows well.

Sketching Love

Trouble in Paradise, then, through its drawing of our attention to the flirtation with another in and across time, suggests the shape of the method I use to tell the story of courtship's performance in classical cinema. But given the force of the idea of performance's description in Marshall's implicit comparison of the time he spends with Hopkins and Francis—that is, the idea that Marshall implicitly describes to himself, or weighs, the contrasting qualities of time Francis and Hopkins mean to offer him, the possible transformation of social form that might occur should he take his intimacy with one or another of these women further—the role of description in my method is worth one additional preliminary consideration (with, again, some help from Lubitsch).

Description, as a method to extend the time of viewing into the time of writing and close analysis, has played an important role throughout the history of film performance studies. Charles Affron, for example, in his 1978 masterpiece *Star Acting: Gish, Garbo, Davis*, sees a parallel in the pleasures of giving a performance and the pleasures of attending to one as a viewer:

> Effective screen acting exploits this perceptual dynamics—it not only invites and withstands the activity of our scrutiny, it mirrors the activity. It sets a standard for variation, for composition and recomposition . . . As our ear is trained to distinguish musical themes, their variations, and permutations in the constantly shifting framework of a sonata or a symphony, as our eye is challenged by the tension of masses in sculptured marble or chiaroscuro on canvas, so the screen actor, by the richness of his being and manner, by his comfort in photographic contexts, sets us a challenge . . . screen acting plays elaborate games with our perception, forcing it to behold complexities of space and attitude that take on resonance through recurrence. (*Star Acting* 7)

Of contemporary scholars, Andrew Klevan has especially risen to Affron's challenge of perceiving and describing the richness of being and manner in a variety of performers most directly. Klevan, dialoguing with Affron and the work of Lesley Stern and George Kouvaros (in their collection *Falling for You: Essays on Cinema and Performance*), persuades us to consider the act of writing on performance as a "process of evocation," in which privileged moments from cinematic works "disclose themselves with equal vivacity;" and, crucially, Klevan explores the role of duration at play in this act of appreciation and description, writing further that "our effort to appreciate will forever be in process, in pursuit, there will always be more of their achievement to emerge" (16–17). By placing emphasis on the act of description which follows and answers the challenge of perceiving performance, these writers place criticism on film acting squarely in the history of *ekphrasis*, which in the traditional arts is a word that refers to the description, in writing, of a scene painted in a picture (see Krieger, *Ekphrasis*, especially 3–21). For Stern, likewise, such questions of *ekphrasis* are intimately linked to the writer's desire to evoke the presence of a lost object (no matter how repeatable on home video, at the moment of the act of writing this sentence full attention to the actor is irrevocably absent) and the concomitant result that a certain degree of fictionalization (of the creation of a new narrative as the writer strings a series of privileged moments together) will always be involved in the serious cinephile's effort to evoke the experience of performance in all of its complexity (Stern 17). In all of these senses, criticism of film performance is also simultaneously a means of describing and measuring the value of time spent. Whenever actors are attended to and described in prose, the writer is tacitly responding to the implicit question *Trouble in Paradise* asks as performance is viewed: How closely did you watch the actors as they created their characters alongside you—and was it worth it?

Thus, the interactions between characters who come to love one another in films themselves have much to teach us about how to pay attention to and describe the fluctuations of actors in movies. As I have already suggested, in *Trouble in Paradise*, Lubitsch draws our attention to the different qualities of lived time Herbert Marshall spends with, first, Miriam Hopkins and, then, Kay Francis. This line of thought may be concluded by returning, one final time, to Lubitsch, to glimpse one more example of how the writer on performance might contemplate cinema as itself a source of inspiration for describing performance. In *Design for Living* (1933), the film Lubitsch made one year after *Trouble in Paradise*, Miriam Hopkins plays Gilda, the illustrator for an American ad agency with offices in Paris. On a train, she meets two other American artists, Tom Chambers (Fredric March), a playwright who writes, in his words, "unproduced plays"; and George Curtis (Gary Cooper), a painter. She happens upon the two of them in a train compartment, where they lay asleep. After busily putting away luggage and taking off gloves, she takes enough of a moment to glimpse March and Coop snoozing. But she does not fall in love with them, not right away—*Design for Living* is not that kind of Hollywood romance. She first wants to draw them.

And so she does—in the same notebook which contains her sketches for an underwear ad featuring Napoleon in his skivvies, she captures the slightly disturbed, open-mouthed snoring of March and the left-to-right head-nodding sleep of Coop in a sketch that successfully (the two men will glimpse it in a moment) captures a fleeting moment of the performance Hopkins/Gilda has witnessed. It is not easy, of course. She needs to get up from her chair, and move close to March, to capture the detail in his dimple; March proves himself to be a willing subject, for almost as if on cue, as Hopkins moves closer to him, March turns his head leftward, as if to give her a better angle for his chin. The camera moves in closer, in rhythm with Gilda's own studious, aesthetic attention, progressively in close-ups and then extreme-close-ups on March's head and the movement of his tongue and mouth as he sleeps. Drawing March was a matter of details, but Coop, by contrast, is more demanding of Gilda's illustrative powers. His expressions keep changing. He is frowning in his sleep one moment. Smiling the next. And in the next, the head droops a little lower. She needs to erase, and re-draw, in response to his changed position in the moment. Satisfied, eventually, with her rendering (although Lubitsch delays showing the illustration to the audience), Gilda puts her sketchbook away. Then she falls asleep herself (figures I.7, I.8, and I.9).

Figures I.7, I.8, and I.9. Miriam Hopkins sketches Gary Cooper and Fredric March in *Design for Living* (Paramount, 1933).

When this drawing is revealed, later in the sequence, after the two men are awake, Gilda's illustration unveils itself as a marvelous likeness of March snoring and Coop sleeping. She has captured the handsome length of Coop's face, and the curl of his bangs; she has found the right strokes for the dimple in March's chin, and the boyish gape of his yawn. She has somehow achieved that most difficult of goals for the analyst of film actors: to describe them, moment-by-moment, within the aesthetic interpretation of their quivering and snoring that is her drawing. Andrew Klevan, in writing of the beautiful difficulties of living with film performances as they unfold, says something that is equally true of the writer on film acting as it is of Gilda herself. He means to celebrate "the achievement of fluency by a selection of film performers and [to indicate] the way in which, as each action flows fluidly into the next or as one move integrates with another, they make it difficult for us to isolate or crystallize meaning" ("Living Meaning" 35). Has not Gilda appreciated the gentle fluency of movement comprising the sleep of these two men—and have we not, in turn, appreciated the gentle fluency of Hopkins herself as she performs the character whose appreciation of March and Coop is recorded in her drawing? Interpreters of film are often quick to analyze scenes on trains as emblematic of the modernity theories of Wolfgang Schivelbusch, whose work inspires thinkers on cinema to draw parallels between the panoramic perception of traveling on trains and the aesthetic attentiveness viewers are compelled to perform while watching cinema (see Keathley 42–44; and Doane 44). And this is fine, but what Hopkins and Lubitsch are contemplating in this scene happens a beat after the event of cinematic perception: the description of Coop and March (through ink and paper); the interpretation of what they are doing (for Hopkins/Gilda has her own, ever-so-slightly caricatured way, of appreciating what they are doing); and the love of these two sleepy men, signaled in *Design for Living* in the fact that Hopkins will soon feel more than cursory aesthetic interest for the two figures who have, in the first few minutes of the film, occupied her time.

It is not insignificant to either the plot of *Design for Living* or to the tenor and concerns of my own study that Gilda falls in love with both Chambers and Curtis as the film progresses; the entire narrative circles around her desire to maintain the *ménage-à-trois* and refuse finally to choose between them, a thematic strand that is often cited as emblematic of the film's special place in the saucy Pre-Code era of Hollywood cinema. And yet the scene teaches still more: in falling for film actors, the viewer need not be monogamous (notice how, even in star studies which pivot around the analysis of a single performer, our attention is often drawn to the figures who function as the chosen star's co-stars); that, in being so promiscuous, we may distinguish between the different qualities of time we might spend with different actors (justifying this book's approach on three interconnected yet distinct kinds of genres, as well as a variety of onscreen couplings); and that, in gazing upon these moments of performance that occupy us as they occupy Gilda, we are doing something, as Klevan also reminds us, which is in fact quite difficult, and worthy of contemplation and consideration as we ask ourselves how best to perform our descriptive and critical acts. Of course, Lubitsch, in this scene, makes clear that a kind of blush might pass across the face of the viewer as she sets about crafting her performative descriptions, a potential social embarrassment which descriptions and evaluations of our most beloved actors always seems to risk, for Gilda's lovely sketch of March and Coop is preceded by several rather awkward drawings, in her sketchbook, of Napoleon stripping down to his underwear—suggesting again her interest in drawing these two men may be equally comic, aesthetic, and erotic: a blend difficult to convey in normative, "useful" language.

The writer on performance, though, will ultimately do well to shed whatever social inhibitions prevent her from conveying affection for the actor, and for actors. Instead, follow Gilda's example. In the subsequent chapters, of course, my own "fictionalization" of treasured moments of performance pays some attention to the surrounding cinematic structures through which auteurs frame the achievements of their actors; but I remain always open to the possibility that the actors themselves may in turn inflect their auteur's ways of seeing them through gesture and movement (in effect, performing their own fictionalization, their own search, in tandem with their diegetic lovers, for a different time, another kind of story).

Unqualified Surrenders, Mirroring Replies

These Lubitsch films offer preliminary examples of lived-in variations of Godard's moment of loving encounter, extending the initial lovestruck moment across stretches of time. But they do not fully account for the fact of having been struck by an actor in a film at all, and of wanting to write about her. Perhaps the most initially magical aspect of engaging deeply with the fact of having your attention fully immersed in a projected human being while watching a film for a given set of minutes is that who precisely does this to and for us cannot usually be anticipated. When an actor does make herself felt in cinephilic life, most writers have resolved the problem—that is, failed to really address the experience—by either ignoring or repressing the affection, whether out of social embarrassment or commitment to some other form of analysis (as in most of what goes under the label of "narrative analysis," which often says a lot about characters but very little about actors and what they do to create those characters moment-by-moment). When writers do address the intervention of an actor into film experience, it usually takes the form of fetishizing some detail of her appearance (as is so often done in star publicity and marketing campaigns). That is, she is extricated from her participation in the surrounding *mise-en-scène*, and the existential, thematic, temporal, and cinematic complexity of her performance is thereby reduced. Most often, this sort of writing fixates on some purely physical aspect of the actor, finding ecstatic fulfillment not in the location of the actor within form or medium but in the delirious (and potentially masochistic) encounter between willingly submissive cinephile and a star god or goddess. The most dangerous threat to a seriously loving attention toward the actor in film is precisely this temptation to place the actor on a pedestal, for it removes the progressive possibilities of love's performance out of intersubjectivity and complexity, and into an asocial, fetishistic, worshipful sphere. In other words, it removes the performance from the rhythms of time.

The most deliriously infatuated of such paeans once flowed from the pen of French Surrealist Jacques Rigaut, writing on silent-film star Mae Murray: "Her little laugh you'll never control, her latest lies, her next lies, her gowns, her exasperating childishness, her ultimata about a glove or stroll, things you're unaware of, the terror and desire of an inevitable parting, her tenderness when you'd given up hoping for it, her incorrigible gaiety, and the recollection of this long, too agile body, of an extravagant reward, of vice, I'm in love with Mae Murray" (205). Rigaut's stream-of-fetish sentence is, implicitly, itself a writerly riposte to the place of the actor in Lev Kuleshov's theory of film editing, wherein the juxtaposition of an image of an actor's face with an image of some corresponding object produces performative, emotional content regardless of the quality of the actor's expression (see *Kuleshov on Film: Writings* 200). In lieu of merely reporting the successful transmission of an idea that has come to the viewer through the relationship between actor and image, Rigaut records his own successive, breathless inventory of the actress's body and soul, all finally culminating, at his breathless sentence's end, with a declaration of a rather helpless cinephilic love. A more reserved version of this tradition persists in the writing of Kenneth Tynan on Greta Garbo, who condenses his own affection for the star into a more modestly swooning appreciation of the various inflections this actress could achieve with mere tilt of head: "Garbo's most radiant grins were belied always by the anxiety in the antennae-like eyebrows; and by the angle of her head she could effect a transition, not alone of mood, but of age. When it was tilted back, with the mouth sagging open, she was a child joyously anticipating a sweet; when it was tipped forward, the mouth still agape, she became a parent wide-eyed at her child's newest exploit" (349–50). None of this, it should be noted, has anything to do with Garbo's specific films: she never played a child, having come to cinema in adulthood, and on the very rare occasions when she played a mother (in Edmund Goulding's *Love* [1927], for instance), she could not be properly described as "wide-eyed." Rather than commit himself to a proper description of what Garbo actually does, Tynan removes Garbo from the surrounding *mise-en-scène* and from the temporal rhythms of her films in order to enjoy her more fully and freely for himself. Substantiating Barthes's similar claim that "Garbo still belongs to that moment in cinema when capturing the human face still plunged audiences into the deepest ecstasy" (*Mythologies* 56–57), Tynan nevertheless lifts her not only from that moment but from all successive moments, onto the pages of a film criticism that does with her what it pleases.

There is something fundamentally possessive about this kind of prose, which freezes the actor in a kind of atemporal space; even as Rigaut admits in the first clause of his ode to Mae Murray that his cinematic beloved will never be finally subject to the control of his prose (he even laments the fact that his would-be object of desire is "too agile"), his writing moves ceaselessly onward with the goal of possessing her. Yet this tendency to lift the actor from the surrounding temporal and spatial context of film experience has life in more outwardly sober film writing, in which the face, abstracted from surrounding space, affects ecstatically. The most renowned theorist in this tradition is Béla Balázs. Although his conception of film was inherently musical, like Tynan, Balázs nevertheless extracts the film actor away from cinema's rhythms. While only "the leading melody meets the eye" in everyday life, the close-up in cinema has the power to reveal "the most hidden parts in our polyphonous life," teaching us "to see the intricate visual details of life as one reads an orchestral score" (130). Of these details in close-up, the most dizzyingly polyphonous was the human face, which Balázs is compelled to lift free of all other spatial and social contingency: "The facial expression on a face is complete and comprehensible in itself and therefore we need not think of it as existing in space and time. Even if we had just seen the same face in the middle of a crowd and the close-up merely separated it from the others, we would still feel that we have suddenly been left alone with this one face to the exclusion of the rest of the world" ("The Close-Up" 131). Balázs rhapsodizes physiognomy as another dimension of emotion, a dimension populated by figures such as Asta Nielsen and Lillian Gish: in Nielsen, in a narrative about seduction, he finds a face which deviously "registers a sham, a pretense of love" as Nielsen's character sets her sights on the rich young man she is aiming to trick; in Gish he finds, from out of the narrative of *Broken Blossoms* (1919), something more pure, "a warm emotion" that turns the face into a luminous, honest expression of "intangible nuance" (133). However, it is telling that in order to read the play of features in the faces of these actresses, Balázs still needs recourse to the temporal and spatial contexts he elsewhere denies—the faces which take presence in his writing require a narrative, and the corresponding perspective of a lover or suitor (in Nielsen, the hapless rich man, and with Gish, the Chinese merchant played by Richard Barthelmess) in order to perform their transcendence.

In the writing of Charles Affron, the location of fulfillment in the polyphonic close-up is more fully and consciously contextualized than it is in Rigaut, Tynan, and Balázs. Rather than lifting the face out of its filmic, temporal contexts, Affron delights in relating its various vibrations and tremors to the filmic world surrounding the performer. Affron, in *Star Acting: Gish, Garbo, Davis*, situates the actors in various aesthetic contexts crafted for them by their directors (4). This move allows Affron to situate his rapturous engagement with the face in a fluctuation of sensitive engagement with the performance of the actor, and the form of the entire film. Affron, no less than Balázs, finds fulfillment in the faces of the actors he loves as they shed the social masks of their characters in moments of close-up. But his writing on the performative face carries more power because it is produced from out of a total engagement with the surrounding structures of the films which contain the lively musicality of the faces he adores. On Garbo: "She was . . . an actress of reflection, of long durations, and one whose talent enabled her to sustain a legato line with a fineness and clarity that belied its length" (104). Notice how Affron's temporal focus on reflection, duration, sustenance, and rhythm avoids Tynan's pitfall of fixing certain Garbo gestures into either that of a child or a mother. On Bette Davis: "When Davis's face almost fills the frame during Herbert Marshall's death scene in *The Little Foxes* (1941), dramatic art is not mimicking life. It is forming patterns that invite our perceptions to play with its articulatable and verifiable processes" (6). Note how the face forms patterns here, and invites perception and involvement with the rhythms of cinema in which the performance is found: rather than fixing Davis onto the atemporal realm of the page, Affron emphasizes how her performances engage our perceptual and critical faculties across time. Of Gish's most memorable gesture in *Broken Blossoms*—her use of her fingers to mold her mouth into a fake smile—Affron writes: "The restrictions of chronology control a degree of stylization appropriate to this extraordinary mixture of face and mask. The pained eyes burn through the pitiful, forced smile; the actress unites expression and emblem. She forces our attention to that line where art is hinged on its artificial conventions and its verisimilitude" (18). In this passage on Gish, note how the actor is given agency to force viewer attention; she has a say in how perception is shaped and to what it is directed. This does not deny Affron's occasional delight in finding ecstatic fulfillment in the figure of a face enveloping the entire frame, as his separate paeans to Garbo, Davis, and Gish make abundantly clear. But even those delights place their emphasis on rhythm, movement, duration, perception—on the lived life of both performer onscreen and viewer perceiving this performed life. Affron's desire is to locate those moments of performative transcendence, but he always returns—eventually, inevitably, in descent from a moment of ecstasy—to consideration of surrounding narrative and directorial form, which attends responsibly to the context which enables the face's enchantment, and the context that this enchanting face might in turn change.

Affron's occasional attention to his leading ladies' various co-stars (Barthelmess with Gish and Marshall with Davis) echoes my own study's concern with various movie couples. But his division of chapters according to single actors—and his tendency to adore only female figures—belies a privileged interest in learning how to inhabit the affective spaces created by his chosen leads. Taking a cue from Affron's later book, *Cinema and Sentiment* (1982), which goes beyond the single-actor focus of his initial study, George Toles (in a piece tantalizingly subtitled "The Film Critic as Actor") acknowledges the powerful lure an engagement with one actor can compel us to have and encourages us to locate this involvement by reference not only to surrounding filmic structure but also to our separate and no less intense attachments to their co-stars. In his discussion of *A Place in the Sun* (1951), for example, Toles describes the starry presence of both Elizabeth Taylor and Montgomery Clift, and finds in their romantic close-up a startling intensity:

> What is most enlightening about this stretch of the film is the split between Taylor's announcement that she is being looked at (and her turn to the camera's forcefully intrusive presence for confirmation) and her immediate location of what she takes to be a secure refuge from prying eyes. She assumes, perhaps rightly, that after catching the camera observer in avid voyeuristic proximity, she can leave the 'otherness' of the camera eye behind, appropriating its capacity for engulfing enlargement and subjective intensification for purely private ends. Her look to the camera, and to us, would at first suggest that we have been spotted—and thus apprehended—as unwarranted trespassers into her rapt communion with Clift. Once

she has become self-conscious about the camera's inescapable nearness, how can she, and by extension we, get away from our unwelcome selves? The answer seems to be that she must simply return to her beloved's gaze, making an unqualified surrender of her attention to him and winning a reciprocally comprehensive regard from Clift in mirroring reply. The camera is more *on top* of the lovers than it was before, and if ever the word 'crowding' could be employed to signify camera pressure on the face, it would seem to be here. But strangely, and I would argue, mystically, the camera no longer feels as though it is outside the lovers, scrutinising them from the perspective of a troubling other, as it has just finished doing. It is now inside them. We are beholding their faces as they prepare to kiss from behind the space where their mutually enfolding gaze originates. We are within the charged field of their locked gaze, from which all competing stimuli and stirrings of memory have been (as by a feat of mesmerism) excluded. We too expand within the radiance of their seeing and almost experience, in our tremulous isolation, the transient, totalising connection of their kiss. (98–99)

Here Toles, remarkably, weaves in his prose an inhabitation of two performances at once. What an astonishing thing to have achieved and found in writing on cinema, something which amounts to a transcendence of the physical laws of time and space—yet a transcendence that emerges from and eventually descends back to the time and space from which the moment takes flight, finally giving it meaning. Both Taylor and Clift are here separately understood, of course (even as her "unqualified surrender" of attention bears witness to his rhyming and "mirroring reply"). Toles, too, wraps his prose around the camera's initially autonomous presence, describing the intense, even suffocating means by which it overtakes the faces of the actors. And then, strikingly, at this heightened, unequivocal moment of melodramatic fulfillment, the camera (and the writer) disappear in one rapturous moment in which a mesmerizing engagement with two separate actors becomes even more impossibly enthralling through our complete cinematic involvement with both of them, together. However, unlike Balázs, Tynan, and Rigaut (but quite like Affron), Toles descends from this moment with his chosen couple, as they themselves descend into a "soon-to-be experienced falling away from this momentous, momentary world of answers" back into "the realm of mortal limitations and aggravated separateness"—and back into rhythms of the film's larger context (99). Importantly, Toles does not simply select such moments for critical attention but rather locates them in the total work of a given film as he creatively thinks his way through and alongside it, and finds in this case two separate performances becoming momentarily conjoined before they fall back into a world of separateness and doubt. Toles usefully urges us to be "equally mindful of edges separating one *kind* of performance from others in film" (95)—a mindfulness added to the equally important task of recognizing those moments when two or more performances blur those edges. This is a challenge for writers meditating upon film acting: it requires not only appreciating the to-and-fro created in the undulating rhythms of two performers, but also appreciating what happens to the totality of a film's space, and the trajectory of its story, when two separate affective and expressive ways of inhabiting the world are intimately aligned.

Not every performance and film in this book, of course, is orchestrated quite like *A Place in the Sun*, and part of the work of the subsequent chapters is to discover the precise qualities of to-and-fro that exist between two (or three, or four) actors, and between these tandems and the total film. The slow crescendo into fulfillment and accompanying descent into the larger context of film space Toles finds in *A Place in the Sun* seems most characteristic of the family melodrama as a genre; in my final two chapters on fifties melodrama later in this book, when I turn to films by Vincente Minnelli and Douglas Sirk, there appear moments of intense fulfillment in which two or more actors consummate, temporarily, our attentions and in doing so transcend the strictures of both camera and debilitating social context. (In Minnelli and Sirk, alas, these transcendences are short-lived.) But in screwball comedies, such as *Twentieth Century* (1934) and *Bringing Up Baby*, extrication from social context is never really an issue: the *mise-en-scène* is often a playground enabling the discovery of expressive sympathies between two stars, and if these two stars manage to transform our vision of the possibilities of their worlds' social settings, this will occur without any overt melodramatic intervention. In the noir films, meanwhile, close-up moments of emotional intensity seem to signal precisely the reverse of what Toles finds in *A Place in the Sun*: rather than emotional fulfillment and ecstatic privacy, close-ups of Bogart in *The Big Sleep* seem to confirm an alienated spirit that only discovers the possibility of a more utopic social world once Lauren Bacall leads him from out of shadow. (At the end of *Key Largo* [1948], Bacall literally opens a pair of windows to let light stream in, in preparation for Bogart's return from vanquishing Edward G. Robinson.) Nevertheless, regardless of the genre or the star, Toles and Affron persuade us to locate our intense moments of performative inhabitation in a larger context.

Loving actors is important because through it the viewer claims a meaningful share of the emotional rhythms of a film. These rhythms, in turn, set our thoughtfully creative imaginations into motion, and as a result, in response to gesture or expression, the writer on film might see more or something other than perhaps even what the character herself felt. Of course, many philosophers of love have explored the idea that the lover sees in the beloved something that may not actually be there; this is usually reduced to the idea of "sentimentality," which adorns the beloved figure with qualities she may not actually possess (Jollimore 48–73). However, film characters can also see things we can't see; gestures slip away from viewers just as they do from onscreen partners, and film characters color their beloveds with their own particular form of sentiment. And once the lover thinks she knows her partner well, another gesture or movement gives birth to a new thought or desire—and the relationship continues to evolve.

All of this means that there will be an intimacy between viewer and actor that only partially overlaps the affection held between two characters onscreen. One of the reasons I respond to *The Thin Man*, of course, is because I delight in seeing William Powell and Myrna Loy performatively respond to one another. But there can be no clap of thunder between two actors if the distinctive pleasures of each performer's abilities are not felt, to some degree, in separation. That something in each partner escapes the vision of the other in classical cinema is precisely what makes the eventual coupling so delightful. And because certain details of the lover escape the other lover's purview, this suggests there is room for ongoing discovery of deepened qualities of time in love, a perpetual flirtation even after certain kinds of commitments are made. As Roland Barthes puts it in *A Lover's Discourse*, the future of love rests on the idea that it might last "*a little longer*" (22–23). The lover of actors, in glimpsing something beyond or above what one or more members of a screen romance might feel in a moment, suggests not a lack but a future promise, a space of value the lovers in the film may yet discover—if only that they might last together, *a little longer*. Engaging with performance always implicitly believes in the future promises of love—its ongoing ability to transcend, its promise to inflect, challenge, or change limits of social possibility, to find a home.

This book offers, then, one way to dwell within, to think about both the homes our lovers search for, and the beloved actors who have worked so beautifully to create them.

Part I

Screwball Love

1

Love's Final Irony

John Barrymore and Carole Lombard in *Twentieth Century*

> But there is one side of acting that has always stirred me . . . This is the superiority of the actor over reality . . . Of the few actors that I have known who had the genius, I admired most Jack Barrymore . . . he was the greatest actor of my time.
>
> —Ben Hecht (*A Child of the Century* 431)

❦

ASPIRING ACTRESS MILDRED PLOTKA—Carole Lombard—is crying. Theatrical impresario Oscar Jaffe—John Barrymore—has broken her down. Poor Mildred is to play Mary Jo Calhoun in Jaffe's latest production, *Hearts of Kentucky*. In this play, she is to assume the stage moniker "Lily Garland," the dreamt-up name of the star Jaffe would like Miss Plotka to become. But she can't get the cry right. Blocking and directing her movements on the stage with zig-zagging chalk, Jaffe has made sure Mildred knows where to stand. But she doesn't yet know how to project her voice and body theatrically. When her character's character is to react to her father's death, Lombard raises her hands to her throat and gazes up at the heavens with a subtlety only a film camera could register. And Howard Hawks's camera does register Lombard's

Figure 1.1. John Barrymore, Carole Lombard, and performance pedagogy: *Twentieth Century* (Columbia, 1934).

perfectly expressed manifestation of what is, in the context of Jaffe's theater, Mildred's performative failure. But, of course, in the world of *Twentieth Century* (1934), Mildred is not rehearsing for a movie. Mildred must project loudly enough to be heard in the back row. So Barrymore expresses Jaffe's exasperation with her by providing a model of the performance Mildred herself cannot at this point achieve. As Lombard raises her hands to her throat, Barrymore stretches his outward, in exaggerated counterpoint to her bound gesture and in the direction of the not-yet-present audience toward which Lombard's character will need to project on opening night. Slamming his script to the floor—in frustration, yes, but also to create an example of the kind of aural effect, heard throughout the theater, Mildred cannot yet successfully produce—Jaffe finally drives her to tears, tears more genuine than anything so far expressed in the rehearsal. And with this, Jaffe discovers, Mildred might yet become an actress. The discovery here, however, is not the tears themselves; Jaffe is uninterested in naturalism. What he wants is to bring those tears to surface, and to amplify surface loudly and beautifully enough so as to reach every row of his audience. He does not mine Mildred for tears because he wants reality; Jaffe wants to raise Mildred's tears above reality. When she successfully transcends the prosaic, Jaffe will know he has found his actress. And she is close to that transcendence here—Jaffe knows now he has something to work with. So he offers a touching appreciation: Barrymore cradles Lombard's tear-stained face in his hands, guides his finger along Lombard's left cheek, the cheek bearing an ever so slightly perceptible scar, and lightly pinches it (figure 1.2).

This little, intimate gesture is touching, and in its own quiet way, is also above the ostensible "reality" of the scene. For all of Barrymore's broad gesticulating and dramatic shouting in the preceding moments—for all of Jaffe's demands that Mildred project herself to the back row—this little caress of the scar on Lombard's cheek could only be detectable to a closely positioned camera. This gesture reminds us that while Jaffe and Lily are creatures of theater, Barrymore and Lombard are finally creatures of cinema, who touch us and make us laugh because the camera, piercing through their characters' theatrical pretensions (without invalidating them), guides us to the authentic, human hearts beating through their self-conscious commitment to a performative life. Because tricks of

Figure 1.2. John Barrymore, Carole Lombard, and the raising of tears above reality: *Twentieth Century* (Columbia, 1934).

photography and positioning often make the scar on Lombard's left cheek less than salient in her movies, it only becomes a part of her character when our attention is directed there (and when we are prepared to notice it). In this shot, Barrymore draws our eye there, guiding his fingers across Lombard's cheek with a quiet tenderness. Yet the scar serves no role in *Twentieth Century*'s narrative; unlike most facial expressions, which work to convey psychological content, Carole Lombard's scar does not serve as a sign of character interiority. (Is it even really Mildred's scar? If so, how did she get it? The film doesn't tell us. Perhaps actors can possess features that their characters do not.) That Barrymore's gestures should direct us, cinematically, to the surface of Lombard's skin, then, rather than the inner life of the character she is playing, is key to the meaning of *Twentieth Century* as experienced.

William Rothman writes, in his characteristically brilliant book *Must We Kill the Thing We Love?*, that something troubles him about this frequently missing interiority in Lombard's screwball performances. He asserts that Lombard's characters lack the rational, inner life of, for example, Katharine Hepburn's Susan Vance in *Bringing Up Baby*. For Rothman, *Bringing Up Baby*'s "close-ups of Susan (that is, of Hepburn) reveal that she is not really, or simply, the screwball she appears to be. Playing a screwball is internal to Susan's perfectly rational plan to keep David close by her side until he realizes he has fallen in love with her" (67). Of Lombard's screwball roles, only in *Twentieth Century* does Rothman find a brief moment of inner rationality guiding her "screwiness," pointing to a moment late in the film in which Lombard's Lily responds to Barrymore's gesticulating with a thoughtful, self-aware close-up. If, for Rothman, close-ups in screwball are opportunities for the performer, elsewhere entertaining us in long-shot with irrational behavior, to convey a thoughtful inner life, he argues that in Lombard's other screwball classics, Gregory La Cava's *My Man Godfrey* (1936) and William A. Wellman's *Nothing Sacred* (1937), there is no sign of this guiding intelligence. "When Carole Lombard plays screwballs," Rothman writes, "these characters really are 'screwy'" (67).

In Rothman's sensitively philosophical hands, he uses this notion to give us revelatory readings of other films and screen heroines. But Lombard's special kind of "screwiness" is finally readable as psychological failure only if rationality and thoughtfulness are *all* we expect to find in close-up, and if giddy, goofy pleasure is severed from the interior meaning it might potentially project. Lombard's rationality, in other words, takes on a delightfully screwy form, one perhaps easy to mistake as entirely unhinged. An early scene with William Powell in *My Man Godfrey* suggests this idea. Lombard's Irene Bullock encounters Powell's Godfrey at a city dump. He is a "forgotten man"—one of the Great

Depression's unemployed. Irene is at the dump to claim him as a prize—as part of her high society's absurd "scavenger hunt," she is to find a homeless man to win the trophy. This scene contrasts Lombard's character with her sister, Cornelia (Gail Patrick). Cornelia speaks to Powell's Godfrey in a condescending inflection of voice, treating him as an object when she offers him five dollars to return to the hotel lobby as proof she has found the "forgotten man" necessary to win the scavenger hunt. Lombard's Irene is there, at least initially, for the same purpose as her sister. Details of performance and costume, however, align our sympathies with Irene. For one, while Cornelia is wearing a dull black dress that absorbs the surrounding light rather than reflecting it, Lombard's shimmering silver gown (like her scar, another of the details that draw our attention to the surface of her performing body) both accepts and reflects light, and is reflective of her more generous and humane attitude toward Godfrey (even as it continues to align her with the largesse of a more privileged social class). Powell's movements toward Lombard parallel his earlier approach toward Gail Patrick, as he corners her to the edge of the frame just as he had cornered Cornelia into an ash pile. Here, the contrast between Powell's face (cloaked in low-key shadow as he confronts Irene) and Lombard's dress, sparkling and shimmering in the moonlight as she backs up to the right side of the frame, is vivid. As the scene goes on, Powell's Godfrey, at first impatient with her to leave, changes his mind, and tells her to sit down. When Powell asks her if she is a member of the "hunting party," Lombard says, quickly: "I was, but I'm not now." Before she can give any reason justifying this sudden abandonment of the scavenger hunt, Irene moves swiftly onto her next observation, at her amusement of Godfrey's cornering of Cornelia into the ash pile: "I couldn't help but laugh. I've wanted to do that since I was six years old." Recollecting the moment which has just passed, she bursts out laughing; but what makes the moment funny is not Irene's recollection itself (Godfrey's pushing of Cornelia into the ash pile was actually not that funny, to us), but the physical manifestation Irene's giddiness, as incarnated by Lombard, takes: the staccato, high-pitched laugh; the convulsions of her head as she snickers, accompanied by the playful bob of her curly bangs, which float above her forehead (figure 1.3); and the covering of her face with her gloved right hand, as if to suggest that any facial expressions which Lombard/Irene might be revealing here (and which are temporarily masked by the hand) are less important than the sheer physical convulsion of a woman delighting in her own capacity to regard events in her world with good humor (figure 1.4). And despite the fact that Powell's pushing of Gail Patrick into the ash pile is not particularly funny, Lombard's delightful physical orchestration of her character's own giddiness is. The performance guides

Figures 1.3 and 1.4. Carole Lombard floats and bobs with William Powell in *My Man Godfrey* (Universal, 1936).

us to the realization that what is delightful here is not what Lombard is laughing at but how Lombard is incarnating laughter, how her physical orchestration of laughter makes her viewer giddy in turn.

Powell's steady gaze and disapproving frown convey his character's impatience with all this. Powell's performance, in fact, confirms the use of the close-up as traditional revelation of psychological rationality and thoughtfulness, and stands in contrast to Lombard's. Where Powell's Godfrey wants to slow down and have, as he puts it, "an intelligent conversation," Lombard giddily jumps into the next moment, the next observation, the next source of laughter and joy. Lombard's character does not lack for inner life or thoughtfulness. Rather, she almost has too much inside her to express; she jumps breathlessly from one observation to the next, and through the art of this performance Lombard's own ability to translate a bubbly, vibrant interiority immediately into external behavior, onto the surface of her skin, is conveyed with brilliance.

For those who would need proof of rather more traditional thought in Irene, however, that is present in the scene, too. At the very beginning of the scene, having witnessed Cornelia's abhorrent behavior toward this homeless man, she has already made the decision to abandon the scavenger hunt. Later, she will confirm in dialogue that she is no longer willing to engage in such unethical behavior:

> IRENE: I've decided I don't want to play any more games with human beings as objects. It's kind of sordid when you think of it, when you think it over.
>
> GODFREY: Yeah, well, I don't know, I haven't thought it over.

Here Irene realizes Cornelia's treatment of Godfrey is unethical. Throughout the film, as if to demonstrate the content of this revelation, Lombard will work to convey her character's authentic love for Godfrey. But this burning inner desire and thoughtfulness is, in the context of *My Man Godfrey*, less important than the way Lombard takes her character's inner revelation and translates it into the medium of screwball—a medium she helped invent. For Lombard's characters, inner life matters, but what matters more is the way interiority manifests itself into external behavior, as if performance itself were a lesson in how to chiefly inhabit a way of life physically, not in place of thinking but in light of one's thoughts.

What Lombard creates, then—and what she works to achieve alongside John Barrymore in *Twentieth Century*—is a demonstration that there is no necessary division between performer and form: where in most conventional films the close-up serves to enable the performer's conveyance of inner life, in screwball—and in Lombard's screwball films especially—the swiftly moving expressive surface of the actor (her gestures, her movements, her expressions) returns us repeatedly to the *mise-en-scène* around her, as if the very surface of her body were an inimitably creative intervention into the world as such, rather than merely an illustration of a scripted psychology. Lombard's characters have ideas, but rather than taking ownership of them (say, through a close-up, in which the furrowing of eyebrows or the lowering of lips might convey an emotional state and thus a clear possession of an emotion or idea by the character), she throws them immediately out into the social world, through the medium of her body, to see if they stick or to witness what delightful and productive trouble they might cause. Joe McElhaney has noted that, in Classical Hollywood cinema, actors were often the "driving force" of films ("Howard Hawks: American Gesture" 32), and this is certainly true of Lombard in her screwiest moments. As one Lombard biographer writes, "If a movie is an orchestration of component parts, then Carole Lombard is the glamorous conductor of the screwball concerto . . . She defined the screwball comedy's style and progression, and its character mirrored her own" (Swindell 304). In reading her performances for character, however, we fall into a potential trap; rather than guiding us inward toward the psychological traits it is in her (or her character's) unique possession to grasp, Lombard throws us giddily back onto the surface of her films, and of herself, insisting that her goofy and charmingly screwy gestures, movements, and expressions be experienced as part of the film's dynamic force, and of its force on us.

This idea returns us to Lombard's scar, and Barrymore's gentle caressing pinch of it: Barrymore's gesture guides us to the "surprise enchantment" of the scar itself, and the star herself, who, when we open ourselves to her giddy movements across the surface of the screen, directs us to what it means to fully live like a screwball in light of one's thoughts. This is not meant to devalue the thoughtful role dialogue and interiority elsewhere play in the genre, and the role thoughtfulness in screwball has played in Rothman's (and Stanley Cavell's) peerless interpretations of screwball form as philosophically significant. It is meant simply to remind us of the equally important point that those thoughts won't matter much unless we first know how to inhabit them, that is, unless we know how to live like a screwball. Just as Barrymore/Jaffe teaches Lombard/Lily/Mildred how to position herself for the stage, Lombard tutors us not so much about what her films mean as how they feel, how the screwiest emotions first take shape and form on the surface of things before we can quite work through what they might mean for our inner lives or our social bearings.

There were few men in screwball comedy who could quite match Lombard in marrying the giddy surface of her gesturing and vibrations to the screwy surfaces of the films themselves. In *My Man Godfrey* William Powell's character is never quite as delectably goofy as Lombard (and this is an odd aspect of Powell's characterization in the film; his characters in *The Thin Man* films and *Libeled Lady* [1936], as the next chapter shows, can be thoroughly and giddily goofy). *Nothing Sacred* is another Lombard delight, too, but like Powell in *Godfrey*, Fredric March's character in that film is not intended to inspire the same delights of viewing that Lombard does herself.

Indeed, the only time in Lombard's career she would find a male match for her own delightfully comic performative style was with John Barrymore in *Twentieth Century*. This is because, unlike Powell in *Godfrey*, Barrymore responds to her movements with his own glorious, theatrical physicality, a physicality that renders immediately the thoughts and emotions of his character into joyous, bodily transcendence of whatever those around him, at any given moment, are prosaic and dull enough to understand or organize as "reality." And his caress of the scar, in the aforementioned moment, is his tacit approval of Lombard as a worthy onscreen match. The scar bears the mark of the sheer contingency of their coming-together in this film, the lucky chance by which this filmed moment in *Twentieth Century* even came to exist; for the scar on Lombard's left cheek reminds us of biographical events that might have precluded her from ever discovering, opposite Barrymore or anyone else, what giddiness her body discovers on the screen. Lombard suffered the injury leading to this scar in a car accident in 1926, shortly after she had won a leading role opposite Barrymore—who had approved her casting—in a screen production of *The Tempest* (1928). In words written by Gladys Hall, but revised by Lombard herself before being approved for publication, we are told in some detail about

> that Sunday afternoon when the young Carole went riding in a foreign-made car with Harry Cooper, son of a prominent Hollywood banker. They were driving through Beverly Hills. The car struck a bump. The catch of the removable seat unhinged. Carole was catapulted, face forward, into the windshield. The windshield shattered. And the beauty which was Carole's became a long, bone-deep, blood-masked gash from her upper lip to the middle of her left cheek. No anesthetic could be administered when the mangled face was sewn together. The surgeon at the Hollywood community Hospital—an emergency job was done on Carole, not the plastic surgery which has been reported—did not want the facial muscles to relax while he sewed up the wounds. Only a slight scar now remains of what was once wrecked beauty. But evidently there must be an inner scar, not so light, the result of those months when Carole moped about the house, sick at heart, believing that she must go through all her youth, all her life, unsightly in the eyes of men, her career ended before it had fairly begun. (Gladys Hall correspondence 7–8)

This is a scene from a horror story, actually lived, and pitched at a melodramatic level suitable for publicity. Yet this horror, which prevented Lombard from trying her chops at Shakespeare opposite Barrymore in the late twenties (she was quickly replaced in *The Tempest*), led to something else. Lombard lost her contract to Fox shortly after the accident; a subsequent string of performances in Mack Sennett pictures ended in a contract with Paramount in the late twenties, and a new direction in her career. When Barrymore lets his hand glide gently across Lombard's scar in the film they would eventually make eight years later, then, it is not only a gesture caressing this shared history (and of Lombard's own professional resilience, after her accident, which parallels Mildred's own in dealing with Jaffe). The gesture also reminds us of the temporary power the elder actor held in choosing his screen partner—for if the scar reminds us of Lombard's missed opportunity in *The Tempest*, it also reminds us that it was Barrymore himself who approved her as his co-star in the Shakespeare, just as he chose her to perform opposite him in *Twentieth Century*. If Barrymore is privileged to choose the one worthy of the opportunity to share in his filmic transcendence of prosaic reality, it is Lombard herself who at the very least equals, through her own performative prowess in *Twentieth Century*, the theatrical authority signified by Barrymore's knowing caress of her cheek.

❦

If the caress of Lombard's scar also reminds us of the benevolent power Barrymore held, in both 1926 and 1934, to select she who might match him, the way the caress is framed, composed, shot—the fact that it is framed, composed, and shot in a particular way—calls to our attention that it is Howard Hawks who crafts the proscenium upon which Barrymore and Lombard perform together. When Manny Farber describes Hawks's *His Girl Friday* (1941) as "a gymnasium of outrageous motion" (*Negative Space* 29) he is speaking of the rhythmic thrust of the film as a whole, and of how this vehicle is driven by the actors and engineered by Hawks the director (see also McElhaney, "Howard Hawks" 32). Hawks is, likewise, the engineer behind the "outrageous motion" of *Twentieth Century*—he deserves credit for what Farber calls the "gymnasium," a film designed for actors. A biographer goes so far as to credit Hawks in this film with the introduction of "the screwball comedy, in which attractive players, one of them a major star, horsed around and bounced off one another in a manner normally expected only of comedians or supporting types" (McCarthy 197). One thread in this myth goes beyond creation of genre to suggest that Hawks, as a Svengali, created Lombard the comic actress; that she was one of the tough and tomboyish "Hawksian women" (Wise 111-19), like Lauren Bacall and Jean Arthur, who Hawks essentially "re-made" through his intervention. There is a little truth to this, of course. Lombard is funny only in moments in her earlier pictures (often in delightfully goofy gestures that have little to do with the often non-comedic plots, such as her sudden *plonking* of a box of delivered flowers onto the floor once Clark Gable enters the room in the otherwise mostly serious *No Man of Her Own* [1932]). By contrast, she is funny throughout *Twentieth Century*. What Hawks gives Lombard with this film is a cinematic vehicle wholly comprised of a chain of scenes that enable giddy moments—a gift not unrelated to the one Barrymore gave her through his selection of her as an screen partner, and very much like the one Oscar Jaffe gifts to Mildred Plotka, who directs Mildred into becoming "Lily Garland," a persona that is soon fully under the actress's control once she becomes Lily, once she inhabits Lily expressively and, indeed, socially, as the star Jaffe so much wants her to become. And since this performance takes place in what may be Hawks's fastest film, it is not unimportant that the bulk of her performance in *Twentieth Century* takes place on a train, a vehicle which is not unlike the experience of the medium of cinema itself in the rapid alternation and succession of quickly changing exterior views (see Schivelbusch, *The Railway Journey*)—a vehicle that plunges us along a track that is already set in its place, but which nevertheless, as we experience the ride it offers, opens us up to the unpredictability of the contingent, perhaps even the possibility of a chance encounter between two lovers meeting one another, after some years, again.

But before they can reunite on the train, they first must split up: and to even form a couple in the first place, Jaffe must teach Mildred how to inhabit their coupledom theatrically. To return to the opening scene, prior to the moment of the caress of the cheek: we join the rehearsed scene-within-the-scene in the middle of one of Mildred's lines. Lombard, initially, is facing away from the camera, in a long establishing shot, with Jaffe's entire troupe. Her movements and positioning are, to use the terminology Cynthia Baron and Sharon Marie Carnicke (192–93) encourage us to use in performance analysis, a combination of a bound and free-flowing gestures: although fixed in one position on the stage, Lombard nods her head and swings her hands behind her back freely, as if waiting to unleash the manic energy that will flow from her body in the film's second and third acts. This rehearsal is a hilariously disorganized shambles; much of the first ten minutes of the film will focus on Jaffe's efforts to shape this chaos into a production worthy of his name, and to turn Mildred into a star. But it is clear from Lombard's performance that her character is already quite ready to act (if quite unconscious, as of yet, of her ability to do so): Mildred is the only one to notice that the stage director miscounts the number of gunshots heard off-stage (two, rather than one), and, upon completion of the line, she notices that one of her supporting players, the actor who is to play Mary Jo Calhoun's brother, has failed to take up his correct position in the scene. A beat later, as the stage director informs the cast to rehearse lines until Jaffe appears, Lombard, otherwise fixed in a bound position, tugs repeatedly at the left side of her skirt, as if to express the nervous energy that her character is as yet unable to translate into a good performance in this badly managed rehearsal. Lombard's movements throughout the scene give us an initial sense of Mildred as a character who has yet to find the right supporting player, or the right of idea of a theatrical life, toward which her energy might be directed. She must find this before she can take to the train.

Cue Barrymore: Jaffe, alone, in his magisterial office, with only his secretary as company; the environment is decorated with medieval armor and painted mirrors. These rarified aesthetic objects complement the aristocratic gestures and poses Barrymore uses to introduce Jaffe: as he speaks with an assistant about his inability to locate Lily Garland in the rehearsal, Barrymore leisurely leans, on the floor, against a pillow, signing some papers, casually adorning his left hand with a cigarette in between the fore- and index-fingers, a prop that suggests simultaneous care and indifference for the objects he holds closest to him. After the phone call, Jaffe prepares for his entrance to the rehearsal, and Barrymore conveys the care taken and self-admiration enjoyed by his character in his assured fling of a scarf around his neck while standing in front of a three-way mirror that affords Barrymore's character multiple gazes onto his aquiline, statuesque profile (figure 1.5). "The Great Profile" was, of course, Barrymore's moniker (so famous, indeed, was this profile, that rather than imprinting his hands into cement in front of the Chinese theater, he impressed his nose); and no doubt we are meant to read into this profile in *Twentieth Century* a further sign of Jaffe's achievement of aristocracy through success on the legitimate stage. But another key aspect of the Barrymore persona, subtending our understanding of Jaffe as a character, is a voluptuous weakness for women; and so it is

Figure 1.5. John Barrymore, in a moment of multiplied self-admiration, in *Twentieth Century* (Columbia, 1934).

important that, when Jaffe turns away from his own reflection in the mirror he should see before him, entirely by accident, the derriere of his bespectacled secretary, bent over in retrieval of documents Jaffe has left strewn all over the floor.

This book will, later, describe a moment in which Humphrey Bogart flirts with a similarly bespectacled young woman played by Dorothy Malone, in another Hawks film, *The Big Sleep*. Barrymore and the woman playing his secretary, an uncredited character actor named Gigi Parrish, generate no similar heat. This may have more to do with Jaffe than anything else; the potential of actual, prosaic sex, with an actual woman, in lieu of his preferred taste for the performance of love on a stage, wilts rather than intensifies Jaffe. After spying her bending over, Barrymore's voice lowers an octave and cracks in its delivery as Jaffe thanks the secretary for handing him his cane. Jaffe can walk just fine—Barrymore has his character bound out of the office with confidence—so the prop is here one more theatrical, aristocratic affectation that declares his desire for a life of pretend. And the cane also reminds us that, in the presence of a woman who is a part of a rather more boring normative world (with its shuffling of papers and other administrative duties), Jaffe will prefer the fiction of performance, and the performance of fiction. He will need the stage to realize his desire. "Lily Garland," who does not even yet know who she is, and who Jaffe has not yet even seen, is his fantasy, his dream; and he will only be able to fulfill this desire for an ongoing theatrical life—which requires for its transcendence of reality certain fixtures of that reality, including the secretary and also the presence of paying audiences willing to give Jaffe the benefit of their applause and approval—by creating her.

But is the desire only for her, for this eventual creation—or is it for theatricality itself, as a way of life, always in need of perpetual rediscovery? Jaffe, the film implies, has already been through a lot of actresses—professionally, certainly, perhaps also personally. The idea of the next actress is well in his head before he even begins working with Mildred Plotka; "Lily Garland" is a figure of his imagination not so much because she is the "perfect woman" (Jaffe does not suffer from placing women on pedestals, as Jimmy Stewart will, later, in *The Philadelphia Story* [1940]) but because she is a figure who will enable him to live his life theatrically, as a well-prepared show responding to the contingencies of whatever script is presented with dexterous gesture and vivid vocal elocution. And so it matters that, outside of the rehearsal space which opens the film, Carole Lombard is never actually seen performing Lily Garland performing Mary Jo Calhoun, the performance that, in the film's social world, makes Garland a star. Instead, the film only depicts the outcome of this stardom: the struggle of Jaffe and Lily to retain the theatrical, entirely artificial but still palpably present energy that brought them together; and the performances of Barrymore and Lombard as keyed to their character's struggle to find new ways, always with the desire to avoid a simply normative life, to theatrically be. This elision ensures that performance, in this film, is kept off the stage, in a private world (or, at least, a social form that the two leads keep greedily locked away all for themselves, their only public viewers the assistants, maids, co-actors, and train riders privileged enough to glimpse something of their gestures).

This becomes clear in the apartment scene, which takes place some three years after Mildred has become Lily and after Lily has become a star. At the beginning of the scene, Lily is getting dressed for a party at a club, dedicated to her honor—"Lily Garland night." A doorbell disturbs her. She grandly swings the doors to her bedroom as if making her entrance onto a theatrical stage, her eyes wide open, and holds the position in a tableaux for a few seconds, as if standing in ready for the arrival of a new audience into her home. Her dressing gown hangs open (in a way frank enough to have been impossible, merely two months after the release of this film in May 1934, under the new enforcement of the Production Code), a sign perhaps of Lombard's own lack of inhibition in front of the camera but also of Lily's own willingness to turn over whatever private aspect of her life still exists to whatever adoring public might want to look at her. But Lily abdicates this theatrical posture almost as quickly as she has assumed it, bounding in an instant, past her maid, to the front door, to verbally chastise whomever beyond the door is interrupting her. The sudden, seemingly improvisatory quality of the movement toward the door is the result of Lombard's ability to characterize Lily as a woman who, at any moment, might be given to do just about anything. But always with a theatrical flair, for the gesture of the closing of the gown is itself quite theatrical, a declarative statement that this woman owns the means of her self-presentation and self-performance. This sudden change in character—one cannot imagine Mildred Plotka having done any of this in the first scene—is a sign not only of how successful an actress Lily has become, but already, in her indignation over this interruption of her preparation to spend the evening out, in her assumption of her own theatrical autonomy in her private life. Once she opens the door, and sees that it is not Jaffe, but rather his publicist, Owen (Roscoe Karns) who lies beyond the door, one realizes the extent to which Lily no longer quite needs Jaffe to pull off a scene. She can now inhabit a stage, indeed determine where and what that stage might be, all by herself.

The scene thus poses a question that will hover around the rest of the film. If Jaffe, and now Lily, are able to command theatrical authority and generate viewer pleasure as individuals (Lily, from her various diegetic audiences within the film, and Jaffe, from his theatrical troupe of sycophants, and his eager actors; and Barrymore and Lombard, both separately and together, from us), why, after their impending rift, should they need to reconcile their coupledom? Since either one alone can inhabit the frame with a command of theatricality, what can they achieve together that they cannot achieve alone, as singular stars? Lily's very stardom, which continues after she leaves Jaffe, is itself a confirmation of the fact that she is interesting as a solo performer. A contrast in both character and performative style is, of course, evident from the opening of this film, where, as we have seen, Barrymore/Jaffe assumes a theatrical authority that Mildred (if not Lombard herself) is not quite ready to attain. But in the apartment scene there is an evolution in this contrast, whereby Lombard herself—and perhaps also Lily, to the extent that she is able to realize this achievement—begins to break away from the binary form of theatricality in which Jaffe instructs Lily in the opening scene. Jaffe, in those opening rehearsal scenes, assumes a division between audience and actor: The audience is something the actor must

Figure 1.6. John Barrymore, commanding our attention, in *Twentieth Century* (Columbia, 1934).

reach (through projection of voice and ostentation of gesture), but the boundary between them is never to become blurred. (It is his assistant, Oliver, played by Walter Connolly, whom Jaffe sends to the back row to act as an audience for Mildred's rehearsal; one can never imagine Jaffe, always close to the stage himself during rehearsals, deigning to remove himself from the lights.) To some extent Barrymore himself embodies Jaffe's own philosophy; as a traditional actor of the finest genealogical theater stock, and the grandest of cinematic presences, one can never quite conceptualize Barrymore gazing up to look at anyone else, so fully is he (certainly by 1934) unto himself. Jaffe, in a sense, reconfirms this when he does finally appear in the apartment scene a couple of minutes later, suddenly, in black hat and jacket, descending onto the scene like a villain in a silent melodrama and commanding the quiet attention of Lily without saying a word (figure 1.6). And he continues to carry on in the scene in this manner; as Lily begins to declare her dissatisfaction with his tyrannical monopolization of her life, Barrymore has Jaffe, silently, walk over to the window, open it, and gaze outside it, as if in contemplation of possibly jumping out of it.

James Harvey notes how Lombard, first in this scene but then throughout the remainder of the film, finds a way to subvert the presence of an actor and a character who demands a strict separation between actor and audience. As Harvey writes, "where Barrymore's hysteria is daunting, deranged, and wildly inventive, it's always a spectacle. Lombard's is an experience, something we don't just watch but get involved in too" (*Romantic Comedy in Hollywood* 120). I would question any intransigence in this binary—watching Barrymore play a theatrical ham turning himself into a spectacle is, of course, its own kind of experience. But what Harvey notices here, and what Lombard\Lily achieves in this scene in which she begins to carve out a space of performative autonomy from Barrymore\Jaffe, is that her audience is her lifeblood. Her devoted viewer, a devoted viewer of the cinema actor and not of the stage, delights in her slightest quivers (perhaps this is why Lily, after the rift with Jaffe, makes the decision to go into movies, after all); and her sudden movements, her most inspired subtleties of comic invention, will confirm that the cinema gives her the audience that she needs, that indeed would seem to need the most from her. Lombard's (and Lily's) audience, is, in other words, a modern audience, one that does not measure its favorite stars in terms of the heavenly distance that separates us from them (as Edgar Morin, for one, conceptualizes the relationship between viewer and a silent screen star; see *The Stars*, especially 1–26). Instead, this audience is itself involved with the everyday performance of life and wants to see from its favorite stars not mere filmic repetition of the quotidian which they already perform but rather subtleties of expression and nuance adding a touch of difference and spice to the everyday. (Louise Brooks, in her writing on the cinema, divined something very much like this, acutely suggesting that for the successful actor "it is necessary to add eccentricities and mystery to naturalness, so that the audience can admire or puzzle over something different than itself"; see 64–65.) John Barrymore, a creature originally of both theater and silent cinema, of course, transcends the everyday in equal measure; but he doesn't quite need devotion, or even cinephilia; his is a stardom predicated on, indeed, a great deal of distance, a distinction that separates. (That Barrymore would spend a good part of his late career poking fun at this "hammy persona," in films like *The Great Profile* [1940] and *Playmates* [1941] does not lessen the distance between him and the viewer; if anything, the ironic posture makes the distance even more acute, more knowing.) This is not to say that Barrymore is not a grandly cinematic creature, but only that his cinematic qualities are perceived to a certain degree as a cinematic adaptation of an essentially theatrical actor to the photoplay. Lombard, by contrast, is, moment-by-moment, creating, inhabiting a new, modern woman within the bounds of cinema, and a new, modern brand of performance (screwball, still being initiated into the public consciousness after *It Happened One Night* [1934] a couple of months earlier in 1934). To some extent, though, she has no place in Stanley Cavell's discussion of "the new woman" in *Pursuits of Happiness*, precisely because of how quickly Lombard/Lily moves beyond the instruction and education provided by Barrymore/Jaffe in the film's opening scenes (in Cavell's conception, the education of the women by the man takes place over the course of the entire narrative). To understand this performance, we must inhabit it ourselves, experience it, feel Lombard's radiant goofiness in our bones—have her teach us, as she has perhaps been taught by Barrymore—thus dissolving the distinction, at least while the movie is playing, between our viewing and her being.

Jaffe's trick, as Barrymore expresses it, is to turn the very contradiction of the stardom he has created for Lily—that she should no longer need him as a performative mate once she has achieved her own distinction and skill—into the very problematic of the scene and the ensuing rest of the movie. We last left Jaffe near the window, contemplating suicide. Barrymore walks over to the window, placing his hat and cape on a chair; he faces away from Lombard and from the camera. Facing away from the audience is a familiar acting move, after the late nineteenth century, to suggest psychological and interior depth (see William Archer, *Masks or Faces?*; and Naremore, *Acting in the Cinema* 52). But what happens when the desire for rhetorical flourish *is* the content of psychology—when the very desire for theatricality, the desire for surface rather than interiority, is precisely what the heart wants? Here, Jaffe's trick is to make the very distinction between Barrymore/Jaffe and Lombard/Lily as performers—his theatrical distance, Lily's improvisatory vitality—not a problem to keep them apart, but a dramatic conflict to be acted, to be taken as the departure for the very heartbeat of the performed life they might ongoingly share. After a beat, he returns to the window, now opening it, as if to signify less the sincerity of his possible suicide than a melodramatic transition in the scene. "What are you going to do?" Lily asks; having here become his audience of one, her question is less concerned with the actual possibility of his suicide than with her anticipation of the next narrative beat his performance is going to hit. "Nothing . . . while you're here," Jaffe says. The last line, and the gravitas with which Barrymore delivers it, punctuates Jaffe's point in the sequence. As long as they are together, the very contradiction ripping them apart (their performative distinction, and ostensible lack of use for one another once success has been achieved) might become the very subject whose dramatic content could keep them animated, in essence a subject that gives these two actors themselves as characters to play. And this is precisely what Lily, eventually, comes to admire: Jaffe's theatrical dexterity, nimbly jumping from one expressive mode (over-the-top comedy, in the film's opening scenes) to another (put-on melodrama with a touch of ham, in this one). So whether or not she "buys" what he is "selling" is not the point: it is not that Jaffe must convince Lily that he is really torn over her desire to leave him alone for the night, but rather that he can put on a good show for her, that he can be as good an actor for her as she has been for him. This is how he woos.

    As Barrymore, in a one-quarter profile medium-shot, stands at the window, feigning contemplation of defenestration, he waxes nostalgic, pining for the experience of being so warmly welcomed in the city's theatrical community during his youth. Cut to Lily, who tries to sneak away. But Jaffe catches her tiptoeing, demanding she stay—not to "save his life," but because he has yet to finish his makeshift scene, and he needs his audience! Speeding things up, he foregoes the rest of his speech and pulls his jacket halfway down, as if he were about to finally kill himself. Lily stops him, and Jaffe pulls back, not convinced "to live" but rather waiting, for a beat, for her to join him on his "stage." And she does (lifting her fur coat above her shoulders as if preparing for a grand entrance on a stage), but only to change the trajectory of the scene. Calling Jaffe a "horrible fake," she amplifies a laugh and turns around to walk away from Jaffe just as quickly as she approached him. The camera now follows, effectively breaking the fourth wall of Jaffe's makeshift proscenium and matching Lombard's fluid movements with its own tracking. "You cheap ham!" Lily admonishes. Where Jaffe ostentatiously changed the flow of the scene earlier, appropriating Lily's window as his theater and facing away from the camera in his declaration of performative autonomy, he now subtly answers her cue to answer the speed of cinema. Just as the camera tracks with Lily, Jaffe follows its approach to her, admonishing her, in a medium-shot, for her promiscuous dalliances with other men while pulling her fur coat off her shoulders to reveal the bare back that will be for all of these men to see. What Jaffe seems to be tacitly admitting here is that he is willing to follow Lily out of the theater, into the flux and flow of everyday life, as performed; he is willing to try and become the down-to-earth star that Lily became in movies. But if they are to proceed to this everyday life, they must still add some special distinction of theatricality, a little of that mystery and eccentricity to quotidian naturalness that makes stars interesting. Thus the very drama they create together, out of the clash of their personalities and the distinction between their performative styles, will be the subject of their ongoing performance. This is a dramatic conflict that will always ensure that these two will continue to grasp life as an opportunity for creativity and the full living through of a moment, unlike the rest of the world around them, which performs everyday life merely to go about business.

After their temporary reconciliation in the apartment, Jaffe has a private eye follow Lily to make sure she is not cavorting with other men; after Lily discovers this ploy, she punches the investigator in the eye, and makes her way for Hollywood on the Twentieth Century, Limited, the train that will take her to her success in movies. (All of this happens offscreen.) Some months pass—Jaffe finds another actress, but either she is not as good, or his direction of actors has lost its spark, its responsive mate. So Jaffe boards a train to New York in a desperate attempt to avoid his creditors in Chicago, the city where his latest play, a hopeless *Joan of Arc*, has failed. Lily is on this train too, heading back to Broadway to secure a contract with a rival producer; after winning over Hollywood, she wishes now to prove she can succeed on the New York stage without Jaffe, perhaps to further declare her performative autonomy and authority. Jaffe, however, seeks to restore their coupledom with a new theatrical contract. Upon entering her compartment, Jaffe finds only Lily's personal assistant, Sadie (Dale Fuller), who informs him she is taking a nap. But she's not. After a beat, Barrymore gazes away from Fuller, and into the washroom of the compartment (offscreen to us, visible to Jaffe). He spies Lily there, and decides to perform for her. Taking command of the center of the frame, in a pose that recalls the tableaux of many of his silent films, Barrymore lifts his finger in instruction to Sadie. But Sadie is not really his viewer.

Pleading that Sadie take care of Lily in his absence, Jaffe raises his voice in order to better direct his words to Lily, the offscreen presence toward which they are directed: "She's very delicate!" Such words, of course, do not rhyme with the star seen earlier in the movie, nor the star persona of the actress playing her—Lombard, who had a tomboy's childhood and a sailor's mouth, was hardly delicate. Barrymore, though, through his gesture offscreen, understands the irony of his words, challenging his co-star to emerge from the wings, and express her comic strength. Now, through just a sliver of mirror fixed on the washroom door, Lombard is visible, watching the performance that Barrymore/Jaffe directs toward her assistant, but which is really intended for her.

He is, of course, also bidding to direct her again, trying to guide the trajectory of her movements and gestures to match his own. Barrymore, too, issues his authority over the performative content of the scene, taking charge of the frame in a comic variation on his melodramatic poses from twenties silent films. Of course, once again Barrymore's command of the film frame reminds us that there is here a certain figural fullness to the actor at this stage of his career. For reasons owing to his legacy, he requires no co-star to give himself theatrical life and energy. Yet the very point of his performance in *Twentieth Century* is to play with this fullness: to use it as a gesture to invite another to achieve her own similar sort of stature, and to circle around the idea that a movie couple might find some sort of modern happiness through the sublime interconnection of their otherwise self-sufficient performative presences. At the very same moment in which he strikes this pose, then, he also makes the explicit admission that he is performing not for the purpose of establishing his own authority (which already exists), but to open a space, on the left side of the screen, for the imminent arrival of his co-star (and his most important viewer), and for the words, movements, and poses she herself brings. He feigns to sit down to wait for Lily to wake up; but when Lombard enters a beat later, he rises again. For the balance of the scene, Barrymore will now find himself in an equally responsive position, charged with creating expressivity that conveys the inherent theatricality of the romantic relationship he means to rekindle. She approaches: "What do you want . . . *scorpion?*" Barrymore (and Jaffe) hilariously anticipates Lily's insult; right after she delivers the line, his eyebrows jut up with jagged alarm. Lombard conveys, with equal preparedness and timing, the way in which Lily is fully and equally prepared for the *bon mot* Jaffe is about to throw her way. "If it makes you any happier to *call me names,*" Barrymore intones, "*go ahead . . .*" Even before Barrymore can finish his sentence, Lombard is lifting her hands in comically feigned exasperation. "Oscar, you're complete! The most horrible excuse for a human being that ever walked on two legs!" she says, as she plops down on the chair in front of Jaffe.

Of course he is—complete, that is. His (and also Barrymore's) "horrible excuse" is that, as an impresario, he has traded in, has risen above, his normative humanity, in exchange for a more heightened, theatrical brand of living, one he needs not in order to establish "relationships"— he's full enough of himself—but rather one he uses to find those like-minded persons fully attuned to the playful possibilities of this alternative mode of life. The most important of these people is the woman he helped turn into a star who now reclines on the chair before him. Jaffe gets right to the point: he objected to the suitor she brought on the train, the yawn-inducing George Smith (Ralph Forbes), not because he was innately jealous of another lover possessing her charms, but because Smith (if not necessarily Forbes) is a dull actor. The great lover of Lily—the woman, after all, whom Jaffe has named—must also be a great performer.

I will explore again, in the next chapter, this desire on the part of a woman in a couple for the man to earn her woo by performing: in *The Thin Man* series, Myrna Loy makes demands on William Powell that he perform, for her pleasure (since they no longer need the money), as a private investigator; while, later on in this book, in *Holiday* (1938), Katharine Hepburn will welcome Cary Grant into her upstairs playhouse in order to perform circus feats and tricks that prove they should be together. And so Jaffe's convincing of Lily that he is the right performer for her, a performer who, indeed, can adapt, despite his theatrical pedigree, to the rhythmic cinematic context provided by the speeding train on which they are acting in the final two-thirds of the movie, is part of the explanation for their reconciliation as a theatrical couple in the final act. But something else also happens near film's end, a touch in Lombard's performance that suggests this coupling is, ultimately, meant to give *her* flight—beyond Barrymore, and into future delightful movies. Jaffe, in the train car, still trying to win Lily back over to his brand of theatricality, expresses his regret for never before fully appreciating Lily's innate talent during their productions together. Lily does not quite see through this; instead, she recognizes there is nothing through which to see. In a medium-shot, she approaches the sitting Jaffe, and cradles his head in her hands: "We're not people, we're lithographs. We're only real between curtains." The entire point of the movie, of course, has been to prove that at least half of this statement is not quite true—their performativity owes nothing to curtains, adaptable as it is to experience beyond the traditional theater. Jaffe, taking this cue, gets up, and admonishes Lily for acting in movies. Lily sits in exasperation while Barrymore has Jaffe begin to act out the theatrical production he imagines they might realize next: the Passion Play, with Lily as the Magdalene. Kneeling before Lily, Jaffe conjures his delectably ridiculous vision with his fingers, and then grasps Lily by the shoulders. For a moment, Lily buys in. She sits up and looks away from Jaffe, off-camera, as if envisioning her own role in the imaginary *mise-en-scène* Jaffe conjures. But just as Lily begins to stake out her own authorship in Jaffe's imagined production, Barrymore takes over the scene again, acting out the part of various extras and animals he envisions in the play. During this charade, Hawks cuts to a shot of Lily, gazing at Jaffe with sudden realization, raising her eyebrows—those inimitable eyebrows raised, here as in so many of Lombard's films, to suggest not only a knowingness, but also an impending physical and emotional response (figure 1.7). So when Jaffe ends his narrative of this possible play with a description of the character Lily is to play as a "pathetic little figure"—somewhat distant from the empowered woman Lily was earlier describing—Lily convulses in laughter. Standing up, for a moment, to face Jaffe, Lily admonishes him for taking advantage of her marquee name in his imagined Passion Play, and refuses to sign the contract, while Jaffe reminds her of her past as a common shop girl. Now falling back on the chair, with Jaffe continuing to loom over her, Lombard wards off Barrymore's approach with a series of little kicks (figure 1.8), sudden cycling movements of legs and feet that, for a moment, do not so much "drive the film" but keep it running beautifully in place. For a brief pause, as we experience these little kicks, we forget we are on a train; and we might even forget, at least for a moment, about Barrymore. Lombard now commands full attention.

These little kicks come late in the movie, but they were filmed relatively early in the production. One biographer confirms that this scene was key to Lombard's self-discovery of herself as a comic actress

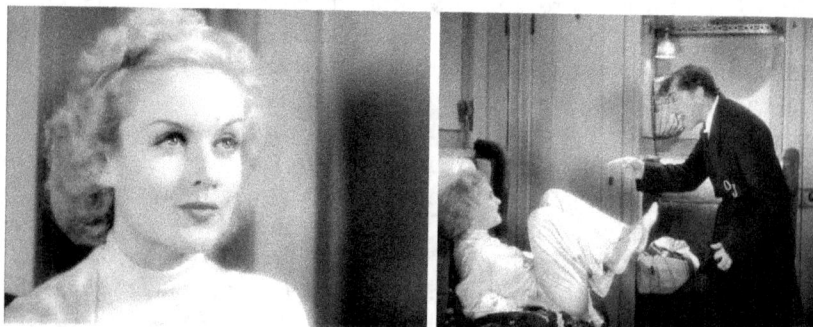

Figures 1.7 and 1.8. Carole Lombard's impending response, and her little kicks, in *Twentieth Century* (Columbia, 1934).

(see McCarthy 202). Legend tells us these kicks were prompted by a question Hawks had asked Lombard, regarding what she would do if someone like Jaffe had spoken to her like he does to Lily in real life. "I'd kick him the balls," she told Hawks (Gehring 119–120). And, so, in this scene, she kicks—but whatever authorship or inspiration Hawks (or Barrymore, or indeed Jaffe) might claim over the moment or the entire film or Lombard's stardom is relinquished in the moment of the kicks themselves, belonging as they irreducibly do to Lombard's particular talent for comically amplified flutter. What Lombard wins in this scene is something Lily, of course, continues to struggle for, given that dramatic conflict is the very heartbeat of the love she shares with Jaffe; at the end of the film, she is still quarrelling with her lover. But Lombard would continue kicking, delightfully, in three more comic gems in the years to follow: *My Man Godfrey*, *Nothing Sacred*, and *To Be or Not to Be* (1942).

Twentieth Century, then, leaves us an interesting question for the story this book tells of love's performance. Within the narrative of the film, Lily and Jaffe solve their problems by imbuing everyday life with qualities of theatricality, and by making the very contrast between their performance styles the substance of a dramatic conflict that makes coupledom ongoingly exciting. Their bickering in the final shot of the film, on the rehearsal stage, confirms this. Yet Carole Lombard—apart from encouraging her studio to cast the actor in a minor role three years later in *True Confession* (1937)—would make no more movies with John Barrymore. Lombard would indeed eclipse Barrymore as a movie star in the second half of the thirties, kicking herself into other memorable movies without him. We are thus left with a question explored further in pages to follow: if one is performatively possessed all by oneself, why does one need another?

2

Wicked Jaws, Lanky Brunettes

Myrna Loy and William Powell in *The Thin Man* and *Libeled Lady*

We found a table. Nora said: "She's pretty."

"If you like them like that."

She grinned at me. "You got types?"

"Only you, darling—lanky brunettes with wicked jaws."

"And how about that red-head you wandered off with at the Quinns' last night?"

"That's silly," I said. "She just wanted to show me some French etchings."

—Dialogue between Nick and Nora Charles, from Dashiell Hammett's *The Thin Man* (2-3)

❦

SOMETIMES, CLASSICAL HOLLYWOOD comedies end ambiguously. As Stanley Cavell writes, "the principal pair, in reentering that state of matrimony, are crossing some border that leaves us out, behind, and with no visible secure embrace of their own, nothing to insure the risk

Figure 2.1. Myrna Loy and William Powell being nutty. Production photo for *The Thin Man* (MGM, 1934). Author's collection.

that they will find, or rather re-find, their happiness" (*Cities of Words* 159). This quote applies vividly to a film I will explore in the next chapter, *The Philadelphia Story*, in which the future narrative of Katharine Hepburn's reunion with Cary Grant lies beyond the frame of both George Cukor's film and the stealth journalist in the story who seeks to snap a picture of the two lovers for the society pages. By contrast, comedies pairing Myrna Loy with William Powell exude an unwavering confidence in both the present and the future of its central couple. The harmony Powell and Loy create together, particularly in their characterizations of Nick and Nora Charles in the six films in *The Thin Man* series (1934–1947), is perhaps unparalleled in Classical Hollywood. This does not mean the Loy-Powell onscreen romance is bereft of flirtation or play. Jeanine Basinger calls them "Fred and Ginger *off* the dance floor" (109), so successfully do Loy and Powell retain their individuality as performers even as they perfectly complement one another. If Lombard and Barrymore end with the question of why a distinctive, performatively self-sufficient star even needs another, Loy and Powell's performances create characters unyielding in their coupled commitment. Whatever Loy and Powell need to learn in order to live in harmony together in *The Thin Man*, they have already learned before the film begins. On film together, they are perfectly in tune; and whenever they are seen apart, rhymes and parallels in their individual performances continue to remind us of the essential rightness of their eventual reunion. Part of the pleasure of watching them perform together is becoming privy to this secret interplay, a model of ongoing happiness within marriage that other thirties comedies, such as those Cavell studies, displace into future unscreened uncertainty. Powell and Loy convey this secret through their nuance, nobility, and subtlety, eschewing, as Maria DiBattista (139) points out, the usual histrionics of the "battle of the sexes" paradigm so often framing the performance of love. The performative harmony they create together is the apex of untroubled coupledom in Classical Hollywood cinema.

The first to recognize the unique bond between these two performers was director W. S. Van Dyke, who brought Loy and Powell together on *Manhattan Melodrama* (1934). The director already had worked with Myrna Loy on *Penthouse* (1933) and *The Prizefighter and the Lady* (1933), two films in which Van Dyke, as Elizabeth Kendall puts it, "coaxed out more of Loy's laconic, prairie-style wit, which combined so interestingly with the seductive, too-available woman MGM still insisted Loy was" (55). In *Manhattan Melodrama*, Loy plays Eleanor, the girlfriend of gangster Blackie (Clark Gable) who is sending her to occupy politician friend Jim Wade (Powell) for a few hours before Blackie arrives. Her first moment with Powell onstreen begins, after Eleanor jumps into the cab, with a fall onto Powell's lap—a fall that comes off as slightly artificial, as it does not quite match to the velocity of her motion in the match-on-action cut linking this shot to the previous one. At the beginning of the shot, Loy is almost frozen in space, in a pose that precedes her performance of the fall (figure 2.2). The momentarily fixed quality of the shot implies Van Dyke took as his priority in the direction of this scene not the shot-by-shot accuracy of gesture and movement but rather the special sort of kinetic relationship at play within the shot, between Loy and Powell in a moment of shared performance. Where shot-reaction shot, in Godard's conception of *découpage*, brings most couples together, Loy and Powell already seem perfectly right for one another from the very moment they begin to share the frame. They are ready to inhabit the same emotional and philosophical universe in an instant, with their ensuing performance of courtship only a playful confirmation of the fact. Where Lombard and Barrymore's independent self-sufficiency leads us to question, ultimately, the need of one for the other, Loy and Powell's is an unquestionably committed union, with each always expressive of the

Figure 2.2. Myrna Loy falls into William Powell's lap in *Manhattan Melodrama* (MGM, 1934).

need of the other, above and beyond whatever question of commitment might be happening in the plot.

This quality of committed but still playfully alive interaction would carry over into the depiction of marriage in *The Thin Man* films. In that series, Loy and Powell delight in one another through their respective mastery of two specific performative instruments: Powell's humorous wielding of drink and Loy's charming vocal lilt. Powell's way of reaching for, imbibing from, holding, walking with, and placing down various cocktail glasses throughout *The Thin Man* series is an example of the use of what James Naremore calls "expressive objects" in cinema, objects which, when used in a certain way, express how "feelings or psychological states are communicated by the way that one handles things" (*Acting in the Cinema* 84). What makes Powell's handling of the cocktail glasses in *The Thin Man* films unique, however, is the salient restraint of expressivity in his gestures, as if the consumption of drink and ensuing intoxication were in support of a self-possessed willingness to let others serve as potential objects of expressive interest and attention. For the archetypal Powell character, the cocktail is less a sign of a psychology requiring expression than a sign of his general amiability and sociability, his own gentlemanly openness to the needs and interests of others. When Loy is in the room, of course, Powell's amiability toward society in general shifts into a more specifically focused ardor; as James Harvey has written, in these films Powell "is everybody's servant in a way—and totally beyond their reach. All this changes when he turns to *her*. [Loy] has the real attention, unmixed and delighted" (178). If Powell's mixing of martini makes him a good-natured social player—likable enough not only to have attracted Nora in the first place but also socially attuned enough to solve crime after crime in the series—it is Loy's equally intoxicating presence that fills Powell's Nick with meaningful, directed expressivity, the kind a dry martini can complement but never match. Powell's drinking in *The Thin Man*, then, is throughout a sign of his individuality and sociability, but also of his commitment and courtesy; he is never so drunk that he cannot acknowledge the woman he loves. Even more delightfully, his expressive drinking indicates his ability to sway between these two positions, bouncing back and forth between self-indulgence and social politesse with the manner of a lover who knows how intimacy might be performed in public.

For Loy, meanwhile, it is her voice—mischievously cutting through the placid surfaces of the domesticity surrounding her heiress characters in these films—which drives attention simultaneously first to her own unique subjectivity (her way of speaking) and then to the specific quality of the performer from which the voice emerges. Loy's enchanting lilt is at least a partial justification of Michel Chion's otherwise essentialist idea that "the voice of the woman seems to possess an ubiquity by nature" (119). Indeed, there is a certain intangible quality of *phonogeny* that lets Loy's voice crackle with unique life when recorded through cinema's means of audio reproduction. Loy's lovely voice is a trait she carries into all of her sound films, but no one responds to it, or is more deserving of its attentions, than Powell; on film, when they are together, Loy's voice is *for him*. Just as Powell's martinis prepare him for the extra dose of intoxication her presence will cause, Loy's voice is often pitched at a register intended most intimately for his ears. Like Powell's use of the cocktail glass, Loy's voice is both unbounded and individualistic, unrestricted by normative demands and socially adventurous, but still spoken at a pitch perfect for Powell's ears. Their interplay is at its most lyrical when Powell's lightly intoxicated way of striding through a scene combines with Loy's uniquely intimate way of addressing him through her vocal inflections. Her voice, further, retains a private intimacy, a sense she and what she says are only for him, even when the couple appear together publicly. No two other actors in this book blend the private and the public quite so effortlessly as do Powell and Loy.

A scene near the beginning of the first *Thin Man* film introduces us to Powell's handling of expressive objects and Loy's lovely lilting voice. Powell is preparing a martini at the bar. The camera tracks through a crowd of shuffling dancers to find him in the middle of his mixing. As played by Powell, Nick is delightfully sensitive to which drink is appropriate for which context—the martini he is making, he tells the waiter, is perfect for the Walston playing in the background. And the movement of Powell's body finds its own distinctive, contextually situated sway, taking the form of a kind of boomerang effect that carries Nick through his world. After pouring a glass, and placing it on the waiter's tray, Powell backs up a step, gently distances himself from the drink, and then nods to the waiter before drinking his martini with a pleasure that will return him, with the drink's promise of ongoing intoxication, to the playful rhythm with which he poured it. As Nick is indulging in this rhythm, the daughter of a former client, Dorothy, played by Maureen O'Sullivan, walks up to the bar. Powell turns around after O'Sullivan's approach, and his face comes close to hers—nearly an accidental kiss. "Hello," Nick says, with a tipsy interest in this woman from his past whom he cannot quite remember—the rhythm he has created through drink has made all things and people anew. So his first move is to invite her for a drink, so that she may share in his delight. For an ever so slight moment of narrative suspension, Powell's eyes look O'Sullivan up and down, opening up the possibility not so much that Nick will betray Nora but rather that he is willing to welcome this new woman into a flirty existence he shares with his wife. After all, it soon becomes apparent that Nick's performance in front of the bar is a preparation for the arrival of his wife, with whom he drinks best.

Loy's entrance is equally characteristic: we hear Loy's voice before we see her, as she shouts "Asta! Asta!" through the hallway of the hotel as her lovable fox terrier guides her toward Powell. Just as a tracking shot brought us to Powell, here again the camera, in tandem with a mischievous dog, guide Loy into the film, as she sheds Christmas packages and stumbles over Asta's leash. Her voice, so enchantingly declaring its presence on the soundtrack through protestation of canine movements, now, as Loy tumbles onto the floor, establishes its presence in a body possessed of, despite dog ahead, a kind of feline stealth, darting through scenes with glances and trills that claim her share of settings and situations ostensibly centered around her husband. The moment, in its sudden physicality, is a delightful disruption of everything audiences had come to expect from Loy in 1934. But the moment does not really prove that Loy had some sort of innate gift for slapstick comedy, suddenly realized all in one moment; she would never perform anything quite like this stunt again in *The Thin Man* series, and Nora is never again characterized as being quite so clumsy. What is really important to the moment is what happens afterward—how Loy echoes and matches Powell's earlier boomerang effect through her own expressive use of a prop and with her subtle and catty inhabitation of the scene. After composing herself after the fall, Loy gets up, notices Powell, and feigns surprise; Nora has known the entire time that Asta was dragging her toward Nick. She pulls out her makeup compact, and moves to use it to recompose her appearance after her fall. But this self-consciousness is a ruse; Loy is much too confident a presence to worry too much about appearance. Nora knows that it is not only her physical presence, but also the interior subjectivity signaled through her voice, that appeals to Nick. And so Loy asserts Nora's subjectivity, which must playfully vie with both dog and drink for Nick's attentions.

It is right that the dog, who jumps into Nick's arms after wiggling free of Nora's leash, should be linked more closely with Powell, for this is a dog who, in key scenes in the film's follow-up, *After the Thin Man* (1936), is established as a competitor for Nick's affections. Nora knows, then, that she will have to get at Nick by taking on the attributes of a more feline creature, as Loy conveys with her patented sidelong glance at Powell, her knowing attitude toward the ways Nick will attempt to bait her into playful quarrel. Powell tells the waiter that it is okay that the dog should remain—it is his. As an aside, he mentions that Nora is his, too, and that she may also stay. "You might have mentioned me first on the billing," Loy quips, the lilt on the final word in the line establishing her vocal tone as the primary instrument with which she will match Nick's own witticisms.

She matches him with drink, too, demanding the waiter catch her up with the six martinis she has missed while shopping. Dorothy has returned to Nick to say goodbye for the evening, and Nora wonders who this "pretty girl" was—but just as her interest in the mirror compact was mostly feigned, Nora does not take Dorothy seriously as competition. The question is meant as a volley toward her husband, an invitation to further playful patter. Nick returns with an ace, telling Nora hers is the only type for him—"lanky brunettes with wicked jaws." The catty irony the two characters share forms a knowing appreciation each has for the other's witty subjectivities.

As this look at their introduction in *The Thin Man* suggests, for Powell and Loy, courtship is not a prelude to a union but the playful lifeblood of the one already presently underway. In a book of philosophy entitled *Bearing Witness to Epiphany*, John Russon declares that this sort of ongoingly flirty marriage is a kind of ideal toward which all adults grasp, in the way it is able to return to the playfully open possibilities of childhood. Russon writes of marriage as the institutionalization of

> an epiphany of love, an experience of a reality that exceeds any self-conscious choice or action either of us has made. Indeed, marriage is as much a discovery of a new human reality as it is a decision made by the participants. In love, in marriage, we experience again something like the membership we experienced as children in family life. Here, however, there is a difference. Love and marriage are phenomena of the adult world, that is, of the world of individuated freedom that has emerged through adolescent erotic experience (88).

Martha P. Nochimson, in her discussion of Loy and Powell's pairing, divines much of what Russon sees as an ideal marriage in her reading of the "individuated freedom" these two actors achieve on film, writing of the pair's "spontaneous synergy, embodied vibrantly . . . [which] permits them to be direct and open about seemingly irresistible social pressures and thus to play with them rather than to be controlled by them" (87). The secret of this synergy, as Russon makes clear, is not its overt resistance to social pressure, but rather the way in which it is able to take shape within normative forms of married life. This sort of life is an outwardly acceptable social framework that, in *The Thin Man* series and various other Loy and Powell films, finds within the commitment of marriage a secret return to the eroticism engendering love, an ongoing context of desire in which love can flow in unpredictable ways. Octavio Paz notes a similar relationship between eroticism and love: "Love is attraction toward a unique person: a body and a soul. Love is choice; eroticism is acceptance. Without eroticism—without a visible form that enters by way of the senses—there is no love, but love goes beyond the desired body and seeks the soul in the body and the body in the soul. The whole person" (*The Double Flame* 32–33). Love transforms "the erotic object into a free and unique subject" (34). For Paz, in societies where love itself has become an ideology, one's polite attention to the subjectivity of her unique lover—the lover whom the senses has received, initially, as an erotic object, but then, a beat later, something more, a unique subject to whom one might commit oneself—takes shape as a courtesy, "a body of knowledge and a practice"—and "a way of life, an art of living and dying, an ethic, an aesthetic, and an etiquette" (34). It is a way of life, and a courtesy, that in Loy's and Powell's hands honors the subjectivity of the lover by responding to her, but which never forgets the eroticism, the delightful play of surface and body, that led one to become interested in that subjectivity in the first place. This delicate balancing act between a regard for the lover's interiority and a fascination with her physical way of being creates a pleasing aura of mystery between the characters Powell and Loy play, justifying James Harvey's claim that the two are "masters of the ambiguous gaze or glance" (178–79).

The ambiguity inherent in their work is evident in their performances together after both *Manhattan Melodrama* and *The Thin Man* proved successful in 1934, but it originates from their earlier work in the Hollywood studio system, films which serve as subtexts for the Nick and Nora roles. As Mark Winokur points out, before he became the gentleman detective in *The Thin Man*, William Powell's early career found him in a series of often quite unsympathetic, "interesting and villainous foreign roles" that implied an exotic ethnicity at odds with the more streamlined Anglophone persona of his performances alongside Loy (10). Perhaps the most interesting period of Powell's early career was in the early thirties, in which his earlier villainous persona blended with the more gentlemanly qualities of his later, romantic parts. Take, for example, Powell's dashing performances as gentleman thieves in films opposite Kay Francis (his most frequent onscreen lover prior to Loy)—*One Way Passage* (1932) and *Jewel Robbery* (1932), for example. Powell's most transgressive pre-Code role is *Jewel Robbery*, in which he plays a character known only as the Robber, who falls in love with a woman named Terri, played by Francis, whose husband's purchase of a prized diamond, the Excelsior, is interrupted by Powell's thievery. Powell will have to convince Francis of the greater pleasures offered by a life of crime, and he will do this by responding to her very physicality as if it were a charm worth stealing. The entire first part of the film, as if in endorsement of the Robber's efforts, establishes Francis as herself a jewel: we first see her luxuriating in a bathroom, playfully popping bubbles and flipping her soap out of the tub, all before being toweled off by the parade of servants that we have first glimpsed marching into Terri's mansion in the sequence's establishing shot. The whole sequence revolves around a bath she is taking to make herself glimmer before she herself acquires the glimmering Excelsior jewel; what she wants more is to *be* a jewel, one that might be robbed by the heart of a daring gentleman. When this gentleman does indeed show up to steal the very jewel Francis covets, it is also clear from Powell's performance that his character desires her as much as she desires the Excelsior—he is there to steal away her glimmering surface, the real jewel to be purloined. But Powell's robber, keeping things playfully on the surface of attraction, demands that his object of erotic interest take her own pleasure in his delightful performance of robbery. Watch how Powell, from the first moments of his entrance in the jewel shop, magically exchanges one object for another, as if to transition from his outward appearance as a gentleman to his activity as a thief, handing his hat, in close-up, to his partner, while his other partner opens the case from which Powell's robber will snatch a small pistol. And then how he approaches Francis, the only figure in the frame utterly riveted by everything he is doing. But she is more than a viewer; she is the jewel to be taken, and Powell, playing a thief who is himself a kind of prize, shows her through his performance that he is the thief to do it (figure 2.3).

Of course, Powell's attentions to Loy in *The Thin Man* and *Libeled Lady* (1936) amount to something more than his flirtation with Francis in *Jewel Robbery*. Yet Myrna Loy's own pre-Code movies—as odd as the actress herself sometimes found them (see Loy, on *The Mask of Fu Manchu* 75–76), in their persistent insistence that viewers accept a tomboyish redhead from Montana as an Asian villainess—frame Loy as herself a jewel, an object of erotic fascination. As her biographer Emily W. Leider points out, Loy, in these early films, was often cast as "a seductively sinister other woman, usually an Asian but sometimes Hispanic, mulatto, Gypsy, or Polynesian" (4). Loy's pre-Code roles include villainess Fah

Figure 2.3. William Powell and Kay Francis, bejeweled and besotted, in *Jewel Robbery* (Warner Bros., 1932).

Lo See in *The Mask of Fu Manchu* (1932), and *Thirteen Women* (1932), as well as her role as erotic object for lothario Ramon Novarro in the pre-Code film *The Barbarian* (1933)—in addition to a character we met early in these pages, the dyed-blonde Elaine in *Consolation Marriage*. In *The Barbarian*, Loy plays Diana "Di" Standing, a Western socialite visiting Cairo to meet her fiancé Gerald Hume (Reginald Denny). It is there that she meets Ramon Novarro's Jamil, an Arab guide who has an eye for Western women and for Loy in particular. Loy characterizes Di as a woman who would not be out of place in later screwball comedies, fretting about a lost schnauzer and begging her rich father and fiancé to pay for Novarro's Jamil, the man who has recovered the dog, to become her servant. What is different about Di, at least relative to the later Loy characters, is the explicitness with which she makes clear her desire for Jamil, citing his profile as the reason why she takes him as a new object of fascination. That he is objectified is certainly a sign of the film's troubling Orientalism. But in Loy's performance a more complicated play between objecthood and subjecthood is at work, one that takes her character's own objectification as a starting point for a play with subjectivity, and which indeed prefigures the more subtle figuration of eroticism and love in the later films with Powell. Where Di is able to take Jamil as her object, through exchange of money for services, Jamil himself finds Diana a trickier pursuit—a woman whose own delightful surfaces must be glimpsed, not directly, but through reflective surfaces, and whose interiority can only be reached through a play of voice and song. During a scene in which Loy and Denny discuss their impending marriage, Novarro's voice circles as a voice-off that, initially, sounds like non-diegetic music, and is only established within the story world once he appears onscreen and asks the lovers if they would like him to continue. Throughout the scene, Loy's Diana and Denny's Gerald discuss what is missing from their love life, beyond the presence of money and travel and exoticism—and the answer is clearly passion (or as Denny puts it, "romance, poetry, and all that sort of rot")—a passion signified not only by Gerald's lack of it but by the offscreen vocal presence of the swooning Novarro. Di is soon revealed to be the object of interest for Novarro's gaze; Jamil's desire becomes explicit the minute he reveals he has been the one singing the song scoring their conversation. This taking of Loy as object forms the film's primary motif, but it is a motif that eventually invites her character to take her own subjective pleasure in the erotic aura her presence generates. Later in the film Novarro will slink in silently, as Loy has Diana hook a garter on her evening lingerie, spying a look at her from another room through, first, the reflection in a bedroom mirror (figure 2.4), and then, a fuller glance through the

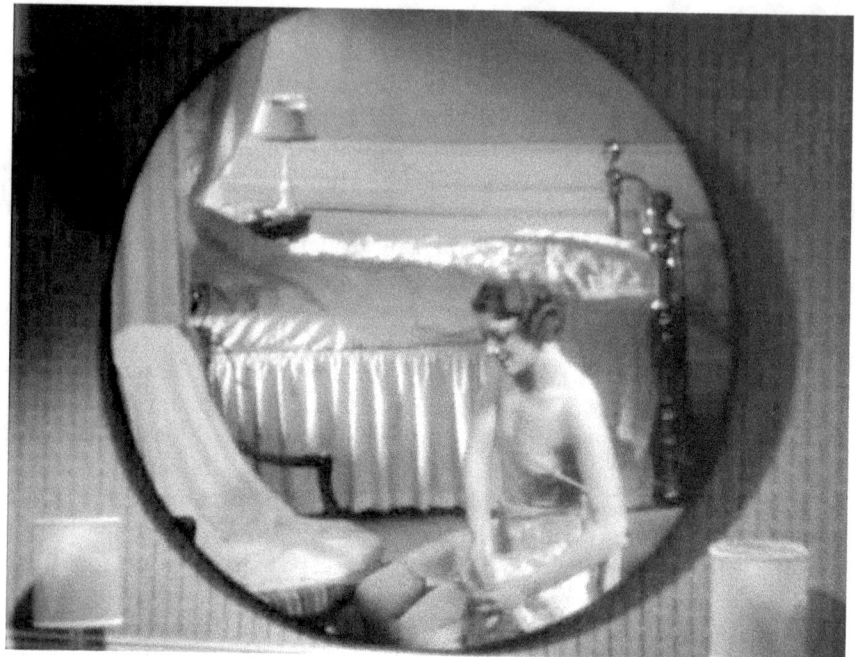

Figure 2.4. Myrna Loy in *The Barbarian* (MGM, 1933).

frame of a doorway, as Loy sings Novarro's earlier song to herself, the first moment in the film in which the actress's own lilting voice has space to take flight. And later, Jamil will abscond with her to a bath, inviting Di to indulge her senses in water and dressing her in a slinky slip—a moment that provides Jamil the opportunity to admire Loy, but which offers, more significantly, an opportunity for Di herself to discover, in fleeting moments, some semblance of subjectivity and desire through the power of her own eroticism.

All of this is to say that in this early film, Loy is positioned as an object of erotic fascination for both viewer and diegetic character, in ways that linger, as a kind of playful subtext, in her later comedies with Powell. But in this positioning, notably, she is not reduced to an object but rather, through the performance, makes clear the extent to which her own characters take subjective delight in their own erotic power of presence (a presence and enjoyment that the narratives of films like *Fu Manchu* and *Thirteen Women* punish, but in which something like *The Barbarian*, in moments, allows her character to indulge). That Powell has shown himself adept at appreciating the glimmering surfaces of his co-star in the earlier films with Kay Francis, and that Loy possesses a subtle power to turn her own erotic surface into the unfolding sign of a complex inner life, remains as an undercurrent in the playful comedy they create in *The Thin Man* series. Nochimson recognizes that the remembered residue of these earlier characters implicitly betrays a certain degree of unregulated sexiness in the later films the two actors made together, finding in Loy's "suggestion of feline cruelty and willfulness that lurks under her wifely smile" and Powell's "ruthlessness and sensuality of the gap-toothed Snidely Whiplash leer" a "double sense of domesticity and kinkiness [that] gives an electric charge to the comic panache of Nick and Nora juggling the categories of respectability" (103). This "electric charge" is, I think, a sign of the ongoing ability of Nick and Nora, and Powell and Loy, to respond to one another as erotic objects, as if informed by the performances of their earlier pictures—while at the same time never losing sight of the interior life that their modern form of courtly love, and love's courtesy, has cultured them to appreciate.

Most striking, though, about Powell and Loy's characterizations is not only the suggestion of ongoing erotic life coursing through a marriage, but the willingness of Nick and Nora to situate this harmonious interplay within a larger social world. Both *Jewel Robbery* and *The Barbarian* are intimate films, in which eroticism is conceived as a mostly private affair. But *The Thin Man* opens up Loy and Powell's performed love to a social form. If the opening scene in *The Thin Man* sketches the appreciatively ironic regard each of these lovers has for the other's subjectivity, later scenes, all occurring in their New York apartment, will establish the more purely physical and erotic attraction each delights in with the other, while at the same time remaining creatively responsive to the various denizens of the social world forming the backdrop for their play. These scenes let the two actors crackle with a charge familiar from their earlier pre-Code movies—but without reducing either to solely an erotic object, precisely because the eroticism involves both subjective feeling and a social interaction beyond the couple.

Later in *The Thin Man*, we join Nick and Nora as they orchestrate a dinner party for a group of friends. The friends are mostly Nick's—hoods he has sent to the joint, who have become friends after their sentences. That Loy should be an object of delight for many of these hardened men is no surprise, yet Powell's and Loy's movements throughout the scene, and the way in which their movements and gestures create rhythms in conjunction with framing, camera movement, and cutting, suggest that Nick and Nora remain always one step ahead of their party guests in their intimate yet still socially theatrical play of subjectivity and erotic surface. "I can look at a pretty girl, can't I?" one of Nick's friends says, offscreen—yet all he can do is look, because Nick and Nora possess the scene's more intimate connection. With the camera framing Nick in a medium-shot, through the internal frame of the kitchen door, he prepares to bring a tray of drinks into the living room—this party is already underway. As Powell begins his stride into the room, Loy lovingly places the final drink on the tray, with both hands, as if to bestow an extra gesture of careful tenderness onto the very object that will enable Nick's continued merriment. During this moment, in which Loy holds onto the drink for a half-beat longer than she might have had Powell not already begun his stride into the living room, Powell has his character lean to his left to kiss her—bestowing love onto the woman who is his only worthy distraction from drink, and away from the eyes of the partygoers whose continued entertainment nevertheless remains the goal of his movement in the scene (figure 2.5). As Powell strides through the room, Van Dyke's camera pans alongside him in a long medium-shot, stopping at various intervals as Nick engages different guests in moments of social affability, reminding one guest, who reminiscences about his and Nick's

Figure 2.5. William Powell and Myrna Loy are the life of the party in *The Thin Man* (MGM, 1934).

past together, that the good old days are not gone by, but are rather happening now, in this delightful party.

The moment is a perfect example of a generous leading man in Classical Hollywood soliciting gems of performance from character actors and supporting players as he sways through a scene. The most memorable of these is the grin of missing teeth he finds in character actor Harry Tenbrook, whose hood remarks on the delightfulness of Nick's wife. "Thanks—I wanted you to see her," Nick remarks; "and I wanted her to see you, too." Powell's line, a clear illustration of the hierarchy of attractiveness dividing leading players from supporting character actors in Hollywood cinema, nevertheless also positions Tenbrook himself as a worthy participant in the theatricality Nick and Nora are orchestrating—an emblem of this couple's generosity. Nick's journey around the room never quite comes to a conclusion—the long camera movement continues to follow Nick as he walks behind the sofa, serving more drinks—but the film cuts, in the middle of his lyric, to Loy, joining Nora in progress as she serves her own tray of drinks to the same guests just greeted by Nick. Her gestures and movements rhyme with Powell's earlier, circular gait through the same portion of the apartment: she serves two more drinks to the hoods who had earlier reminisced with Nick; and she offers a drink to Tenbrook, who matches his earlier appreciative comment about Nora with "I certainly think your husband's great." Nora responds sardonically, the slight jump in Loy's voice as she utters the line suggestive of Nora's own ability to respond to what others say with social dexterity and clever humor: "I'm glad somebody does." As good as these times may be, and as great as Nick is, Nora lovingly cloaks her most intimate pleasure—the delight she takes in her husband—under a veil of social irony.

Where most detective films emphasize forward movement—through new spaces, and then into yet newer ones, with the greeting and interrogations of further witnesses and possible suspects—Loy and Powell often find themselves repeatedly circling around and moving to-and-fro within the same set of domestic spaces (living room, bedroom, dining room), especially when there is a social function to organize or maintain. Although Nick will eventually have to move forward, investigating various urban spaces later in the film after accepting the responsibility of investigating the case, the story bits revealed within those scenes always ultimately return Powell to the domestic spaces (such as the dining room at the end of the film, where the murderer is revealed) in which he will orbit Loy and she him. The party scene is a virtual template for this roundabout trajectory, with Loy and Powell's attendance to the various guests occurring in semicircles around the living room and with Loy and Powell occasionally following the other here or there in the same circular pattern. This manner of movement emphasizes both actors' command of space and ease within it, and at the same time suggests a degree of polite detachment from the various concerns of the partygoers, concerns which come to include the murder case itself. But it also announces that, for Nick and Nora, the space of domesticity (and its various responsibilities, including the investigation of the case) is not one which determines their actions but is rather a space the meaning of which arises from their coupled gestures and movements, movements always open to revision and new inhabitation with each new circular pass taken.

The film's murder plot is in large part emblematic of the various duties that sometimes place stress and strain on a marriage, even as the couple willingly accepts the reality of these obligations. Yet what matters in *The Thin Man* are the ways in which Nick and Nora respond to the evolving situation, the way they perform together within the unpredictable "human reality" that is, and which surrounds, their marriage. (Unlike Lombard and Barrymore, who want to transcend lived reality, Powell and Loy want to find new ways to live within it.) In a standard detective film, the plot might take precedence over performance, determining staging and movement. But Loy and Powell respond to moments of narrative revelation with vivid and often humorous expressivity, reminding us that what matters in *The Thin Man* is performance's relationship to plot rather than its mere illustration of it. Later in this party scene, Loy walks to the door, with a tray of four drinks in one hand, to welcome another of Nick's friends to the festivities. Characteristically, Loy opens the door and extends the tray of drinks to the guest behind the door before looking at him, emphasizing this gesture of social affability toward the encroachment of incrementally revealed plot information (the arrival of a new guest, the moving forward of the scene) rather than the information itself. Even when narrative information juts into the flow of the scene in a more salient matter, Powell and Loy redirect our attention to the pleasures that might be found around the edges of it. After opening the door, Loy goes to the phone to inform the concierge that the announcement of more guests is unnecessary. Rudely, a radio announcement, emanating from an offscreen loudspeaker, interrupts Loy's delightfully effervescent dialogue delivery with the flatly delivered fireside report of the "latest on the Wolf murder." The voice tells us that the dead secretary was once a gangster's girl, a piece of plot that will become important later. Cut to Powell, standing near the radio, his eyes darting to and fro for some object of distraction that will lead him away from the social responsibility emanating from the radio. Powell finds it, grabbing yet another beverage.

He is, however, twice interrupted in his drinking: first, by the ongoing voice of the radio announcer, whom an annoyed Nick is compelled to shut off; and then, another voice, this one altogether more pleasant and inviting, belonging to Nora, announcing the arrival of two reporters. Both Loy and Powell, however, redirect the two men away from story and toward intoxication and good humor: Nick, by joking that Nora is the "waiter," and Nora, by reminding the reporters the only case Nick is interested in is full of scotch.

These gestures of amiable sociability throw into relief relatively private moments shared between Nick and Nora. Where, in the party scene of *The Thin Man*, Powell's expressive handling of drink and Loy's lilt of voice welcome friends into their sphere of domestic pleasure, in other moments their performative traits take on more intimate qualities, reminding us that, in this marriage as in all successful unions, there is always a large remainder of private pleasure left over for the couple to enjoy after social gatherings have concluded. After the party scene, Nick and Nora lie in bed—in separate beds, per the screen custom of most of the thirties—Loy positioned screen right, Powell on the left, in a diagonally framed medium-shot, a lamp and side table between them. "Nick?" She asks her sleeping husband. When he doesn't reply, she tries again: "Nick-*ee*?" The "*ee*" appended to the end of his name after the question is asked a second time is not simply affectionate play with spoken language. Rather, the shift in vocal register—the high-pitched squeak in Loy's delivery of "Nick-*ee*?," which blends into the next part of her question, "Are you asleep?"—reminds us that however appealing and generous Nora's voice may be during a party with Nick's friends, its real purpose is to compel her husband's attention. And it works; Nick gets up and offers her a drink (she declines the offer, so he gets one for himself). But the voice also compels Nick to perform for her: she is waking Nick to ask him to take the Wolf case; she wants to see him work. Loy relaxes her hands behind her head, lying still in bed as she watches Nick totter across the room to pour himself a drink. She appreciates it so much, indeed, that she asks for an encore performance: after Nick wobbles back to bed, Nora decides she wants the drink after all, giving her the opportunity to delight once again in the sight of Nick pouring it (she never drinks an ounce of it).

As a film, and as a series, *The Thin Man* circles repeatedly around moments like this one, where Loy's Nora compels Nick's attention through the siren song of her voice, and where Powell obliges with comical play with objects. This is why viewers return to these films again and again, even after a first viewing has revealed the perpetrators of the various murders. However, as intimately as we seem to be positioned here, in the bedroom of a married couple, there can be no mistake that we do not really share, cinematically, in the intimacy of marriage in the same way that the characters themselves do. The emblematic shot in the first *Thin Man*, in this regard, comes early: after Nick finally decides to take the Wolf case, he takes Nora in his arm, calling her his "Dr. Watson," and the two skip away from the camera, and away from us, with a spontaneous little dance that nevertheless gives off the impression of a certain studied artificiality, as if this couple were used to spontaneity, as if their spontaneous moments still had a comfortable ring of familiarity to them. The entire *Thin Man* series revolves around the performance of what most romantic comedies keep secret—the matrimony lying beyond the happy ending, beyond the narrative conclusion of most films. But by taking this secret as its performative subject, *The Thin Man* cannot help but put the viewer at one remove from our attachment to actors; those moments we often enjoy when watching other screen actors perform coupledom, the occasional sense that we have spied something that perhaps one or the other individual, in their courtship, has missed in the other, is not present in *The Thin Man* films. The intimacy of Nick and Nora is complete. Like one of Nick's party guests, we are invited to delight in it for a time; and we are even allowed a peek at their intimacy that the diegetic guests themselves are not privy to. But when the time is right, we must take our leave, as Nick and Nora skip away to their own purely private pleasures. We are, as an audience, ultimately like the dinner guests Nick and Nora treat with such affability: privileged to enjoy their company for a little while, in a generous and affable blend of the private and the public. But ultimately, like their dinner party guests, we are shown the door.

Of course, although Loy and Powell are, as performers, perfect for one another in all of their films together, not all of their films are about harmonious marriages. Some of their films present an interesting disjunction between performative harmony and strained coupling. *Libeled Lady*, for example, raised the hackles of film censor Joseph Breen, who objected to what he saw as the film's cynical deployment of marriage as an ironic plot device (Leider 172–74). Breen, as usual, missed the point. In *Libeled Lady*, marriage, rather than being treated with disrespect, is seen, within the film's narrative, as an important enough institution to warrant discursive, social attention—quite a shift from *The Thin Man*, where marriage is a private affair, hardly grist for the society pages. *Libeled Lady* is the first of the films in this book to include the newspaper as a key narrative motif (anticipating *The Philadelphia Story*, in the next chapter), implying that the private affairs of the characters played by Loy and Powell are not only worthy of public attention but also (unlike the mostly private goings-on in *The Thin Man*) open to public comment. The newspaper motif, of course, appeared in numerous films of the era, operating as what James Chandler describes as "the spinning newspaper headlines that seem to be thrown out of the sentimental vortex" (127) of various scenes of supposedly private intimacy between two or more characters. *Libeled Lady* performs an interesting variation upon this device; rather than newspaper headlines only punctuating or simply "spinning out of" the emotional complications of the characters, the characters must give convincing flesh and blood to the headlines themselves, which have been written *before* performance's gestures embody them with living truth.

The plot revolves around Loy's character, Connie Allenberry, a wealthy heiress, who is falsely libeled as an adulteress in editor-in-chief Warren Haggerty's (Spencer Tracy) newspaper. Haggerty hires former reporter Bill Chandler (Powell) to arrange a fake marriage to Haggerty's long-suffering fiancée, Gladys (Jean Harlow); Powell will then trick Loy into turning him into an adulterer by being seen with him in public, with Harlow making a stink. All of this is aimed to render the newspaper's false story a true one. Of course, Powell falls in love with Loy, and in doing so ironically intervenes in the narrative the diegetic newspaper is trying to construct: although their romance does unwittingly prove Loy's Connie something of an adulteress (she has, after all, "stolen" Powell away from his fake marriage with Harlow in the film), it ultimately demonstrates the flimsiness of public discourse in light of the greater truth created by Loy and Powell's performative accord. After all, in *Libeled Lady*, words do not give meaning to emotions; performed emotions give flesh-and-blood meaning to words, as if public commentaries on romantic matters were merely a prelude to the private acting-out of love's meaning. Later films studied in this book will open up heterosexual love to discursive questioning, but *Libeled Lady* takes an ironic attitude toward the very idea of such discussion, poking gentle fun at the very idea of public reportage on romance by continuing to locate emotional truth in the lovers themselves.

Throughout *Libeled Lady*, the performances of Loy and Powell suggest this ironic attitude not only toward the narratives crafted by newspapermen in the film's story, but also toward the film's own plot. Writers on performance often frame acting choices in terms of narrative functions, an approach Cynthia Baron and Sharon Marie Carnicke endorse when they write that "actors' work contributes to the trajectory of the dramatic action" and other various narrative demands (45). But as Andrew Klevan reminds us, choices in performance can sometimes tell a different story, can reveal an alternative narrative hidden underneath or alongside the main narrative framework (*Film Performance* 77). Where both the Spencer Tracy and Jean Harlow characters have a goal to win by the end of *Libeled Lady* (Tracy, to successfully defend his newspaper against the threat of Connie's father to take it to court in a libel suit; Harlow, to finally win over the reluctant Tracy in commitment to marriage), Loy and Powell remain relatively detached from the newspaper plot of *Libeled Lady*. The Powell character is reluctant to accept the deal to trick Loy, and Loy's Connie Allenbury treats the libel suit (the film's main plot device) as a minor annoyance. Indeed, Loy and Powell's characters in *Libeled Lady* are even more detached from narrative goings-on than they are in *The Thin Man* (there, detachment is compromised by Nick Charles's involvement with the case).

The rhyming positions and gestures of both actors in early scenes in the film (prior to the two characters' meeting) suggest their similar dispositions toward the demands of narrative. In Loy's first scene, her character's father (Walter Connolly) is barking into the phone at Tracy's character, informing him that he will not drop the libel suit. Loy is sitting on his desk, to Connolly's right. But Loy's heiress is hardly up in arms over the newspaper's false accusations. She is instead amusedly distracted, bouncing a tennis ball offscreen, the racket and ball jutting into and out of the frame. Then, a cut to the first long shot of Loy in the film, as the camera frames her from behind; she sits on her father's desk, bouncing the ball up and down until she loses track of it and it lands in front of her father. As she looks to her left for where it went, Connolly catches it, an endearing moment of father-daughter synchronicity that Loy commemorates, a beat later, with a playful tug on Connolly's ear. Loy's Connie likes to play, and Connolly's Allenbury, in catching the tennis ball and swiping her arm away, demonstrates his skill at matching his daughter's antics with his own. But Loy is ultimately the source of these playful gestures; her Connie is the one most willing to discard decorum, and perhaps even the five million dollars promised in the libel suit, in favor of play—a spirit confirmed a little later in this scene, when Loy nonchalantly lifts her sweater over her head, as if, in the words of Maria DiBattista, she were "shedding all the irritating encumbrances that go with her money" (100)—and as if she were willing to shed the irritating encumbrance of the narrative itself in favor of a fun game of tennis (figure 2.6).

The first appearance of William Powell in the film suggests a similarly detached regard for narrative business. Powell's character, Bill Chandler, has received an overdue bill from the hotel he is currently living in. Baron and Carnicke have described William Powell's characters

Figure 2.6. Myrna Loy, playfully disregarding plot, in *Libeled Lady* (MGM, 1936).

as "relaxed but self-possessed" (44), and that is certainly the case here: rather than conveying panic at the overdue bill, Powell characterizes Chandler as a cool customer, looking sidelong at the hotel desk before calmly walking forward, rereading the contents of the paper one more time, then folding the hotel bill discretely in his jacket pocket. The Tracy character approaches him from behind, arriving to pull Powell into the newspaper plot. But Powell's movements continue to direct the flow of the scene. As he walks forward, a step ahead of Tracy, and as the two characters quarrel over their contentious past, Powell hands a bill to a counter girl for a pack of cigarettes, an expressive prop he will use not only to deflect any possible suspicion of his having suffered financial hard times, but also to suggest his nonchalance toward Tracy's goal of persuading him back into the newspaper business. Powell continues to walk forward and away from Tracy, deflecting attempts to pull him into the plot by displacing our attention to a gesture free of narrative import: Powell picks up a lighter from a counter and lights his cigarette (figure 2.7). Powell pairs this gesture with an ironic regard toward narrative demands: he tells Haggerty he gave up newspaper reporting to work in the "intelligence department—I always did like contrasts," and

Figure 2.7. William Powell burning away the narrative in *Libeled Lady* (MGM, 1936).

then strolls into the dining room to have breakfast, which he prefers to Haggerty's "ideas." It is not that Powell is having Chandler avoid narrative entirely here; he is in fact working to establish a context in which he can become involved with the Allenbury plot on his own terms, terms that will allow him to be paid the amount he needs to continue living a life of leisure at this expensive hotel. Powell has his character achieve this aim by wielding a pair of props in the breakfast scene with Tracy: a document listing his demands for payment; and the hotel bill, which he tells Tracy is a lucrative contract for a book he plans to write on his sordid years in the newspaper business. After Tracy signs a contract agreeing to Powell's terms, he discovers that the book contract is an overdue bill—and that Powell's nonchalance regarding this offer of work was, in the face of the hundreds of dollars owed to the hotel, an elaborate put-on.

Powell's ability to mine props and dialogue for irony in *Libeled Lady* stands in some contrast to *The Thin Man*: where Nick Charles's wielding of drink makes him socially amiable (if still somewhat beyond the reach of supporting characters), in *Libeled Lady* Powell's Bill Chandler uses these props to stage a diegetic performance, a bit of fakery intended to fool others in his social world. This is precisely what leads Chandler to court Connie—to fool her, to stage a performance, to make phony the publicized libel suit. The trouble is that Loy's Connie knows right away he is up to something, matching him at every point with her own sharp sense of irony; indeed, Powell's confession, in the third act of the film, that he was hired by Tracy to trick Connie into giving truth to the newspaper story, is left entirely offscreen, reminding us that the union of Loy and Powell remains elegantly detached from the workaday concerns of the newspaper plot. In their shared scenes together in *Libeled Lady*, then, what we witness is not Powell tricking Loy into giving truth to the libel, but rather Powell and Loy developing, together, ironic strategies for remaining aloof from narrative, which often involves carving out a more private space within what is otherwise a public one. Of course, Powell's character must prove, first, that he can be as aloof as she, given that Loy, from her first moments onscreen, is already playfully ambivalent about the concerns going on about her. Later in the film, Chandler, then, will save Connie from deep engagement with social form—rescuing her from a pair of annoying socialites in a party scene. Powell guides Loy across the dance floor in a semicircle that matches the shape of Nick and Nora Charles's serving of drinks to their guests in the party scene of *The Thin Man*—only this time, Loy and Powell keep the attention of their characters firmly fixed on one another, as if the surrounding social world and all of the narrative gossip it contains were something to be kept at a distance. Connie, at this point, has no interest in Chandler; his sycophantic talk of fishing during dinner with her father has convinced her he is yet one more too-eligible bachelor on the hunt for her money. But Powell has Chandler deflect her wariness with sarcasm; when Connie anticipates the clichés Chandler will use to woo her—she knows all the lines, she tells him, including the ones where men tell her that her eyes look like emeralds and sapphires—Chandler distances himself from all of those unworthy suitors by telling her, with honesty, that her eyes actually remind him, instead, of "angry marbles."

    This sort of witty repartee is quite common in Classical Hollywood romances; in a sense, *Libeled Lady* prefigures the battle-of-the-sexes between Spencer Tracy and Katharine Hepburn. But where Tracy-Hepburn films such as *Woman of the Year* (1942), *Keeper of the Flame* (1943), *Adam's Rib* (1949), and *Pat and Mike* (1952) always engaged, on some level, with questions of gender, Loy and Powell remain in *Libeled Lady* as aloof from such social concerns as they are from the world of their diegetic surroundings. The film's most memorable scene—which takes place in a natural landscape, far from the prying eyes of society—is emblematic in this regard. Powell's Chandler has convinced Connolly's Allenbury that he is a master fly fisherman—he prepares for the ruse with Harlow in an earlier scene, in which Powell practices his casting on a hotel room curtain. He convinces Allenbury to invite him on a fishing trip with Connie, which gives Chandler the opportunity to crack the façade of the Allenburys' privacy and thus take the libel scheme a step further. The ostensible purpose of the fishing scene is for Chandler to win over Connie's confidence; if he is really a good fisherman, perhaps she can love him in earnest. The joke, of course, is that Connie already suspects Chandler can't fish; when she spies him yawning as the three march toward the stream (would an expert fisherman have trouble getting up early in the morning?), and when she expresses her doubt to her father about Chandler's claims at being an expert fly fisherman, Loy's sly smile and knowing glance betray the secret pleasure her character takes in watching Powell put on the ruse. The key prop for Powell in the sequence, however, is not the fishing line itself, but rather the hilariously amateurish guide his character hides in his backpack, *The Anglers' Hand-Book for Beginners*, complete with the illustrated piscine diagrams Chandler needs to even recognize the sort of fish he is supposed to be catching. Powell trips over a rock and lands face-first in the stream as he tries to read this book while fishing—and continues to fall repeatedly into the water as he chases the book as it floats away. Connie sees none of this; she only rejoins Chandler after he successfully (but accidentally) lands a gigantic walleye. In most movies, the moment would convince the heroine of the hero's skill, making him worthy of loving. And in terms of narrative, this is precisely what is happening in *Libeled Lady*: by catching this fish accidentally, Chandler gets a little closer to embodying the "truth" Tracy's newspaper wants the world to know about Connie by successfully inhabiting the persona he uses to trick her. But on a performative level, the film is more concerned with drawing Loy herself into the line of action: as Powell flails around with his line, trying to reel in the fish, Loy runs into the frame to help him, in long-shot, and, in her own flailing, looking for all the world a lot like a flopping fish herself. "The biggest, most elusive trout—you got him!" Allenbury exclaims to Chandler after they net it. But when the father places his hand on his daughter's shoulder as he speaks this line, we are reminded that Loy is Powell's real catch.

Moments of heightened physical comedy like this fishing scene are reminiscent of *After the Thin Man*, in which Nick and Nora furiously chase the dog Asta around the living room of their house after they discover he has eaten an important clue. Such moments take Loy and Powell beyond narrative, and push them into a privileged space, a private *mise-en-scène* carved out from social form, in which only the comic harmony of their physical and gestural interaction quite matters. These scenes also prefigure moments from *Bringing Up Baby*, in which Katharine Hepburn and Cary Grant chase a dog and a leopard around the Connecticut countryside. But the performances in *Baby* pivot around the narrative agency of the Hepburn character and the sexual ambiguity inherent in the subservient narrative agency of the cross-dressing Grant. By contrast, Loy and Powell remain aloof from social concerns, as if it were not simply this performative pairing, but the very idea of heterosexuality itself, which remained beyond question in their films. The perfection of their responsiveness to one another, its full attention to both the erotics of surface and the interiority of subjectivity, and the distanced space they carve out from the rest of society even as they (to a point) welcome it into their sphere with courtesy and politesse, throws into relief the more socially conflicted and existentially ambiguous qualities of love's performance in the remaining couples, threesomes, and quartets in this book.

3

"You Look So Silly"

Katharine Hepburn and Cary Grant in *Sylvia Scarlett, Holiday, Bringing Up Baby,* and *The Philadelphia Story*

My dear Sylvia, Linda, Susan, Tracy, dear all of you . . .

—Letter from Cary Grant to
Katharine Hepburn (May 29, 1984)

Someday . . . I shall write a book which shall catch what you caught in *Alice Adams*. When I do I shall regard myself as an artist.

—Letter from Tom Lennon to
Katharine Hepburn (August 7, 1935)

℮

FOR KATHARINE HEPBURN AND Cary Grant, there can be no state of final perfection. They are always on the move, alive with thought. Sometimes, they are thinking about gender identity, as when Grant puts on a woman's dressing gown in *Bringing Up Baby* (1938) and declares, with a giddy jump, that he has "gone gay all of a sudden!," or when Hepburn dresses as a boy in *Sylvia Scarlett* (1935). Their flights of thought more often emerge through forms of subtle physicality: interiority takes

Figure 3.1. Cary Grant and Katharine Hepburn, looking so silly in *Bringing Up Baby* (RKO Radio Pictures, 1938).

on physical form when, in *Holiday* (1938) Hepburn clutches at a champagne glass with a "repressed anger" (Naremore, *Acting in the Cinema* 85) at her conservative father, or, in *The Philadelphia Story* (1940) when Grant grabs at a set of candles as if they formed a church organ, his rendition of a wedding song the expression of a healthily ironic attitude toward the ritual of marriage, having lived through a failed one himself.

Rather than ever finally settling into a vision or ideal of the perfect couple, Hepburn and Grant always live, in their performances together, in the middle, swaying to and fro across a ceaseless play of ideas and emotions. Psychologist D. W. Winnicott locates the origins of this kind of creative, adult play in the original engagement with "transitional objects" children frequently experience, playthings that, for the developing child, appear as first, immediate connections to the adult, symbolic world (*Playing and Reality* 3–4). These objects are in-between the subjective world of the child and the objective world of objects and symbols to which the child has yet to be fully introduced. By encountering the object as a part of ongoing play, the child's eventual life within the symbolic world of adults retains the creative imagination of childhood. For

Winnicott, play thus remains important even after the child has become an adult, for in play we enjoy the healthy experience of "living creatively," inheriting the symbolic world of our culture in order to playfully refigure its future in our present (101).

In words that more directly pertain to the playfulness of Grant and Hepburn's film performances, but which echo Winnicott's thoughts about the transitional quality of play, Andrew Klevan, in his essay on "in-betweeness" in various moments of cinema, points to moments in *Bringing Up Baby* that delay narrative significance through performative play with rhythm and pace (see Klevan, "Expressing the In-Between"). One such moment: Hepburn's character in *Baby*, Susan Vance, breaks a heel. Instead of seeing in this accident a disruption of plan, she weaves this potential discontinuity into her own form of playful ongoingness, using an apparently useless object stripped of its instrumental and symbolic value (a woman's heel, made for walking) to her own ends: that of simply *keeping her going*. As Klevan writes, "Indeed, she is, for as long as necessary, impervious to interruption . . . She stands in front of David, [Cary Grant's character], continues to bob up and down . . . He shouts 'Stop,' and tries to restrain her by putting a hand on her shoulder, but as he releases it, she just pops up again. Each time the bobbing motion brings her face to face with him . . . Finally, she does stop, but not before she naughtily sneaks in a jerky, yet subdued, bob, irregular in rhythm, like the final shuffle of a child's mechanical toy insisting to be wound up again" ("Expressing the In-Between"). Hepburn in *Baby* knows so well the playful, performative potential of refashioning instrumental objects into "transitional" ones that she becomes, as Klevan himself suggests in his language, something of a bobbing wind-up toy herself, always giddy to be "wound up again" (figures 3.2 and 3.3).

Figures 3.2 and 3.3. Wind me up again: Cary Grant and Katharine Hepburn in *Bringing Up Baby* (RKO Radio Pictures, 1938).

Taking my cue from Klevan, and keeping in mind the potential transitional quality of expressive objects as suggested by Winnicott, I see this playful in-betweeness—a play that rightly snubs rigidly defined norms of gender, sexuality, and character psychology—to be the hallmark of Grant and Hepburn's work together. Rather than settle for one swooning moment of romance, Hepburn and Grant are always breathlessly on the move toward the next moment of connection, constantly splintering, through the vivid dynamism of their movement, every moment of connection, every gesture toward institutionalized coupledom. The emotional, erotic, and psychological unity lying behind every shot/reaction shot in Hepburn and Grant's screen appearances together is eventually shattered by the delirious, always ongoing movement of Hepburn and Grant across the screen between these various moments of connection, as the couple move on to the next bit of playful business, the next refiguration of the symbolic world they have inherited and to which they are now active, disruptive contributors.

Cary Grant and Katharine Hepburn first appear together in George Cukor's *Sylvia Scarlett*. Grant's Jimmy Monkley is a confidence trickster who fools the middle class out of their money. Monkley meets Sylvia after she flees from Paris to London with her father—he's on the run from the police, wanted for embezzlement. To sneak under the radar, Sylvia dresses up as a boy—eluding detection through androgyny, by becoming Sylvester. Thus, even more than Monkley, it is Sylvia who is committed to extending this playfulness into the texture of everyday life—first as a means to survive, but then, as the film goes on, to inhabit a different style of living. While Monkley tends to "bracket" his put-ons in the context of whatever trick he is currently playing—tricks that are as exploitative of the working class as they are the wealthy—Hepburn crafts Sylvia/Sylvester as more adept at playing with the definitions people and objects hold. In the film's second act, Monkley teams with Sylvia's father Henry (Edmund Gwenn) to steal "plenty of sparklers"—or expensive jewelry—from the home of a wealthy family presently out of town. Monkley's plan is to pose as theatrical agents who trick a Cockney maid, Maudie (Dennie Moore), into wearing them during a fake singing audition. Monkley assumes the role of "director" here, instructing Henry to hold his hat as a theatrical impresario might and leading Henry and Maudie upstairs to change their clothes into evening wear (and for the maid to put on the "sparklers" the duo mean to steal). Hepburn's "Sylvester" is, initially, excluded from these proceedings—she very nearly spoiled their last trick, so Monkley wants nothing to do with her. This will not stop Sylvester, though, for he finds an alternative entrance, catching the maid's attention through a bedroom window. Later, while Monkley is swiping the jewels from Maudie's neck during a kiss, Sylvester gets slowly drunk, lying down on the floor (in a languid pose which recalls a similar posture Hepburn strikes in her first film with Cukor, *A Bill of Divorcement* [1932]), muttering about "the sea," and raising his hands to the sky, as if imagining a different kind of scene in her mind's eye.

While Grant's character is busily trying to bring the narrative trajectory of the sequence to its conclusion, Hepburn the performer takes beautiful advantage of this moment of "in-betweeness." After Maudie realizes the jewels are missing from her neck, she scrambles around the room looking for them. As she does so, Hepburn bounces backwards on the head of a bearskin rug, encouraging Maudie to "dive for them—they've gone back into the sea!" while she performs a mini-dive off the dead bear's head. In her refusal to take seriously the maid's concerns over the lost jewels, and in her imaginative suggestion that a fetish object of the upper class should return, in playful appropriation, to its proper home on the ocean floor, Sylvia shares Monkley's own anti-bourgeois attitude. But she is more sensitive toward the fate of the poor maid that they have fooled—she knows the maid will be fired if the jewels go missing, so Hepburn has Sylvester direct the scene toward a more inclusive conclusion, inviting Maudie to join the troupe on their adventures. Throughout the scene, Hepburn reveals her character as a more playful performer than Monkley (if not Grant himself), seeing beyond the ostensible goal of the scene—to swipe the goods—and finding instead the opportunity to re-imagine a prop as a diving board and the floor as the sea.

Hepburn's playfully associative performance not only refashions objects in her mind's eye, effectively returning fully symbolic, adult objects to a pre-symbolic "transitional" state, but also plays with objects and ideas from previous scenes, reformulating them breathlessly into new ones. She describes Monkley, her father, and herself to the maid as "three bad eggs—and we were all *broke* this afternoon—*into a bowl*—or was it on the rocks?—yes, on the rocks, where the clean sand is, and sparkling water. . . ." The breathy inflection of the dialogue, and Hepburn's hand gestures, here refer to the three rotten eggs she broke in an earlier sequence, while trying to make breakfast, associating those discarded objects with her future goal—to shed the trappings of the bourgeois en route to the utopic rocks of the seashore. A beat later, after disclosing the ruse to the maid, she stands on the edge of the couch as if it were the mast to a ship, bidding fond adieu to those "clean things"—the jewels which, through her revelation of the ruse, she has already metaphorically tossed into the sea of her imagination. Hepburn then has Sylvester throw himself at the wallpaper decorating the wall of the room—wallpaper, appropriately enough, depicting a wide body of water and a flock of seagulls, bereft of the artifacts of the bourgeois class she has rejected. Sylvia perpetually redefines, and then redefines again in the next moment, her gendered placement within the performative world. And this is only one dimension of her generously playful attitude toward all objects, people, settings, and words in the world. It is as if her newfound and liberating ability to play in her performance of gender might itself liberate the world around her from its own settled definitions.

In the second half of the film, the troupe, having reconceived itself as a traveling circus, partially realizes Sylvia's vision in the previous scene, setting up a shanty near a seaside resort where Sylvia will eventually meet and fall in love with a bohemian painter. Hepburn, having already refashioned external objects and settings in the first half of the film, now turns inward, her various costume changes signaling the ongoing evolution of Sylvia. After interrupting a performance by the troupe, this painter, Michael Fane (Brian Aherne), invites the troupe home for a meal. While Monkley, Harry, and the maid enjoy a drink, Sylvia marvels Michael with her gymnastic pirouette on a pair of gymnast rings (an exercise designed to demonstrate a boy's upper-body strength). Sylvia, balancing upside-down on the rings, seems about to reveal something— "I'm not—"—before she is interrupted by the arrival of Michael's Russian girlfriend, Lily Levetsky (Natalie Paley). Annoyed with Lily, Sylvia creates a ruckus during a meal and the entire troupe is kicked off the estate—although Sylvia later returns, still dressed as a boy, to deliver apologies. Michael forgives Sylvia—now Sylvester—helping him up to a bedroom through the open window. Hepburn bounces into the room, positions herself in the middle of the frame, and straightens the fit of her blazer, reaffirming Sylvester's self-presentation as a "boy" before, a beat later, raising her arms to her torso in a gesture that means to begin the explanation of her "true" gender identity. She is in love with this man, so, now, if perhaps only for a moment, she wants to reveal herself as a woman. But Michael interrupts her again, moving for a drink while he complains about Lily and womanhood in general. Still, he says, he cannot resist a pretty girl—and Sylvia once again spies an opportunity to tell him she is a woman, wrapping her hands around a small statue of a naked female figure resting on Michael's mantle. This gesture is charged with ambiguity: Is Hepburn's cradling of the naked figure a sign of her true identity of "woman," or a rather more complex expression of her own desire, which might alight as quickly to the figure of a woman as to Aherne's rogue painter? After all, earlier in the film,

Maudie has planted a kiss on Sylvester's lips, and a naughty elision after the moment implies that perhaps the two of them enjoyed more than just a peck. And the figure on Michael's mantle bears no resemblance, with its shapely hips and large bust, to Hepburn's slender figure; if she is about to reveal a kind of womanhood, it will not be one which takes on this statue's shape. All of these ideas work together to suggest that Hepburn is trying to carve out an identity for her Sylvia that eschews available pre-articulations, one that cannot wholly refer to preexisting symbols representing womanhood for its shape and movement, and one in which a desire for Michael, this particular man, does not involve any acceptance of socially existing heterosexuality as parameter for play.

Later, Michael invites her to return to his estate for a sitting, wearing a "costume," in the hope that he might capture her in paint. Sylvia's costume of choice is a feminine sundress, which she has stolen from a group of swimmers near the seashore. But as Hepburn's performance conveys, this is no "authentic" revelation of identity; Sylvia's existence as woman is every bit a construction, every bit a performance. At the beginning of the sequence in which Sylvia returns to Michael's estate, Hepburn, in a long shot as her character announces herself to Michael, adjusts her hat, twirls in a circle around the room, and guides the palms of her hands along the sides of her chest, taking her own pleasure in her newfound physicality, which, although now outwardly feminine, is no less a "costume" or a disguise than her earlier posturing as Sylvester (figures 3.4 and 3.5). Upon discovering Sylvia in her dress, Michael delights in it, but in a way that serves to marginalize, rather than celebrate or share in, the pleasure Sylvia has discovered in her newfound self. He describes the tomboyish woman in front of him as a "freak of nature" and a "crowing hen." As he orders her to sit, Hepburn does so with her

Figures 3.4 and 3.5. Katharine Hepburn, taking pleasure in her performance, in *Sylvia Scarlett* (RKO Radio Pictures, 1935).

legs spread forward and apart, as if she were drifting back into Sylvester in implicit response to Michael's phobic attitude toward the complexly unfolding human before him. Andrew Britton, in his study of Hepburn, reminds us that what was challenging about Hepburn's star persona—what, perhaps, remains challenging about it in the present-day landscape of contemporary Hollywood cinema—is its "physical strangeness, which, in Garbo, the face recoups," but which "re-emerges in Hepburn's face as a disturbing impediment to complete possession of the image" (30). As Hepburn shows us in this scene from *Sylvia Scarlett*, however, it was the entire complex of her performative range—her way of sitting, of moving, of delighting in the unconventional eroticism of her body—that denies us (and Aherne's painter) any fixed image. "What is so funny?" Sylvia asks. "The way you stick out your legs," Michael responds. "Well, I didn't ask you to look at them," Sylvia responds, the line encapsulating how far the character has progressed beyond preconceived erotic limits through her playful attitude toward identity and behavior. Sylvia's own desire stands in autonomy from Michael; at the height of the scene's emotion, the film cuts to a close-up of Hepburn, unmatched to any corresponding reverse shot of Aherne, suggesting that Sylvia's desire remains very much her own possession, above and beyond any social connection that might be possible in the world of the story.

❦

If Cary Grant is mostly a witness to Hepburn's gender-bending in *Sylvia Scarlett*, in their next film under the direction of George Cukor, *Holiday*, it is Grant who makes the most immediate impression onscreen. Grant's performance in *Holiday* makes reference to the actor's performative past in vaudeville theater through a somersault act he performs at various moments throughout the film. Grant plays Johnny Case, a successful entrepreneur working his way up from out of the working class. Case plans to marry a woman he has met while on holiday, Julia (Doris Nolan), the daughter of the wealthy Seton banking family. When he tries to explain his love for Julia to his friends, an older scholarly couple named the Potters (Edward Everett Horton and Jean Dixon), Case does not identify Julia by name or occupation. Instead, Grant conveys dreaminess, gazing at the ceiling, admitting his inability to describe his lover with any accuracy; he can only conjure, in his mind's eye, an image of "those dimples when she smiles." James Naremore argues that the central weakness of *Holiday* is its lack of a "plausible reason" explaining why Case "should be interested in Julia in the first place" (180). But the incongruity of Case's attraction to Julia serves to make

Hepburn's appearance as Linda Seton, Julia's more free-spirited sister, something like the true manifestation of the daydream Case conjures in his discussion with the Potters, an actual manifestation of the girl he thought Julia was during their holiday together—"sweet, intelligent, the perfect playmate." Of course, in place of "those dimples when she smiles," Case will find in Linda a more challenging angularity. But for the moment, Johnny shakes off the Potters' concern over these plans of marriage, as Grant exits the apartment with a playful somersault that ends the scene.

The moment serves not only to illustrate the character's willingness to brush off the threat of bourgeois entanglement with a quick flip, but also to remind us that Grant's physical dexterity is every bit the match for Hepburn's athleticism. Of course, this would have been no surprise to audiences in 1938 who had seen their earlier film together, *Bringing Up Baby*. But where in the Hawks screwball comedy Hepburn is always one step ahead in her speed and movement, in George Cukor's *Holiday* the two are on an even keel throughout, matching one another move-for-move in a kind of comedic ballet. This matching of physical and gestural wits makes clear, long before either character is willing to articulate it, that Case and Linda belong together.

Later, Johnny arrives for the first time at Julia's home. Unaware of the Seton family's wealth, he has not anticipated a mansion; and, as the butler guides Johnny into the main room, Grant characterizes Johnny's need for adjustment through a self-conscious, sidelong glance at the butler's shoes, mimicking the rhythm of his walk as he tries to adapt to the physical context of his new surroundings. David Thomson has observed that as an actor, Grant's "most consistent quality is a diffidence or reserve to the events of his movies which gives immediate impression of a real intelligence meeting those events not in a predetermined way but with a flexible novelty of experience" (125). The first scene in the extravagant Seton home supports this assertion. Immediately after adjusting to the butler's way of walking, Case strides into an even bigger room, with two parallel, curving staircases. Grant heads for the right staircase, quickly readjusting his route once he realizes the servant is taking him to an elevator hiding behind it! Marveling at the bejeweled ceiling and works of art that surround him, Grant nearly bumps into a terracotta statue. Contemplating the Seton wealth surrounding him, he realizes he has lost track of the butler, and does not know which way to turn. Shouting "hey!" in search of his guide, for a moment Grant turns to the statue itself, as if the butler had become frozen like a statue or as if the statue itself might spring to life to guide him to his destination. Indeed, the Seton home is a place where one might become frozen and dull—but, in the presence of a Grant (or, later, a Hepburn), it can also again be a place where objects once more come alive.

Grant's ability to have his characters meet events in a flexible way is part of what makes *Holiday*'s insistence on the motif of Case's repeated somersaults—which express a pre-articulated, pre-determined philosophy of brushing off the bad things in life with a whimsical physical feat—rather odd; after the butler leaves Case alone to wait for Julia, Grant will perform another of these somersaults after wandering into yet another opulent room, as if he could dismiss his discomfort in this wealthy home with a quick flip. But the Case character will soon learn that he needs more than a somersault to extricate himself from marriage to Julia, and this knowledge comes, in part, through his ability to respond to Linda, who matches his physical dexterity with her own open-ended responsiveness to life. Nevertheless, Hepburn's character, Linda Seton, does not quite educate Johnny Case in *Holiday*, as her character does in *Bringing Up Baby*, where her Susan Vance will teach Grant's David Huxley how to have a good time. Instead, both Johnny and Linda express their rejection of the stuffy Seton way of life in parallel ways, not only through the ideas they share through dialogue but through a series of physical and gestural rhymes.

After Julia and Johnny leave for the morning, Linda bounds up the staircase to prepare her sanctuary, a preserved playroom from her childhood, for Johnny's lunchtime return. The moment affords us an opportunity to watch Hepburn bound across the screen in long-shot, darting up the stairs in a way that perfectly expresses what is, in the context of her father's stuffy and proper mansion, her character's own endearingly awkward enthusiasm. When Case returns for lunch, and is guided by the butler up to the second floor, Linda beckons him to join her in the playroom. The scene is the first opportunity for the actors to develop sustained rhythms between their performances and between their characters, and is beautifully described by James Naremore:

> When Grant enters, [Hepburn] is munching an apple . . . holding it out in a friendly gesture. This ingenious piece of business . . . serves to mock the Seton family values: while everyone else is stiffly putting on a front at Sunday services, Johnny and Linda behave with childlike informality, the apple evoking an Eden where women are healthy rather than sinful. Grant accepts the fruit and walks around, his back to us, while she stands chewing and regarding him. The dramatic pause gives her time to swallow, and because the scene involves polite dialogue and several camera setups, neither character

tastes the apple again—Grant merely holds it, preoccupied with the room. After a moment Hepburn picks up a cigarette and thoughtfully taps it against a box, as if considering how to begin. She keeps the cigarette unlit, using the incomplete action to show Linda's pleased response to Johnny's interest in the surroundings. (185)

As the scene goes on, Hepburn, guiding Grant through this storehouse of childhood memories, denotes parallels between the surface of her favorite toys and her own bodily surface, as in one moment in which she poses with her favorite toy giraffe, the pose playfully paralleling the length of the giraffe's face with Hepburn's own angularity. (This play with the giraffe is not in the final version of the script. It appears to be Hepburn's own delectable invention; see Stewart and Buchman 29.) And she takes pleasure in watching Johnny ride a child's bike, smiling beamingly as she kneels on the surface of a gym mat as he goofs around. The rapport between the two of them in the playroom emerges from their shared willingness to engage with transitional objects from childhood as a means of living and expressing creatively. But Hepburn is also careful to characterize Linda as protective of her feelings, resistant to too easily expressing herself in, or giving herself over to what is, after all, her father's home, a patriarchal social form; so she is restrained in her willingness to share her emotions with Johnny until she is sure her sister is not the right woman for him. After Johnny wheels the bike up to a painting easel, the canvas resting upon it covered with a cloth, he wants to see what lies underneath, assuming it is a painting by Julia. Linda prevents him from doing so, standing in front of the canvas as if to guard it and lifting her cigarette (now lit) to Johnny's torso, effectively substituting her sophisticated, slightly cynical present-day self as a barrier to the girl she was in the past, the girl who made the paintings.

As this scene suggests, Johnny and Linda connect through an intertwinement of both mind and body, expressed most notably in a later playroom scene, occurring while an elaborate engagement party for Julia goes on downstairs. The scene is a culmination of the physical and cerebral sympathies Linda and Johnny have felt for one another, but have so far been unable to express. Joined by the Potters and Linda's brother, Ned (Lew Ayres), Grant explains his character's aim to live off his stock market money for a while in order to discover what he is really working for. Hepburn expresses her character's alignment with Case's philosophy of life in physical terms, effortlessly stepping over the back of a couch to pour a drink and to position herself, in the scene's blocking, for Grant's eventual arrival by her side. A little later in the sequence comes "the feat of acrobatic skill," the gymnastic performance confirming, in physical and theatrical terms, that Linda and Johnny are perfectly suited for one another. The two of them, as James Naremore has written, "step onto the back of a couch, pushing forward with their feet so that it tips and carries them into the air like dancers"—and then "Grant lifts Hepburn onto his shoulders, where she stands like a brave, giddy amateur, holding her long skirt in her hand" (189). But the acrobatics are not only a way for Hepburn and Grant to show off their star qualities; they also serve as a way, within the space of the home, to expressively, and surreptitiously, disrupt pre-articulated social form. Nevertheless, despite this derring-do, the characters are not quite ready to explicitly articulate their love for one another—not fully ready for the alternative and improvisatory vision of life their acrobatics represent. Immediately after Grant (holding Linda's cherished childhood giraffe toy) suggests that the two perform acrobatically together, for example, Hepburn has Linda raise her hand to her heart, a sign of the emotional impact their acrobatics have had on her, an emotion that Linda nevertheless quickly hides beneath a veneer of performative self-consciousness and social decorum (figure 3.6).

Figure 3.6. Cary Grant, with Katharine Hepburn's treasured childhood toy, in *Holiday* (Columbia, 1938)

As this scene suggests, a verve for life in the existentially deadening Seton mansion can only be rekindled in Linda's playroom, and even then only after those stifling elements (her father, stuffy family friends, Julia) have been expelled from it. In the New Year's Eve scene, a heated argument between Linda, her father, and Julia about Johnny's decisions regarding his future way of life interrupts the playroom party. After the dust settles, everyone leaves besides Linda, who returns to the playroom in melancholy. A beat later, Johnny joins her in her solitude. Cut to a long shot of the playroom as Hepburn walks to an old music box on the left side of the frame, winding it up to play a Strauss waltz. "You better run on down, now, don't you think?," Hepburn says as she senses Grant walking from the right side of the screen, the space between them wide enough to provide a view of the trapeze, drum set, piano, and other playthings stored behind them. But where their earlier use of these playful, "transitional" objects was intended to creatively reimagine a life in the symbolic world they have inherited (literally so, as the playroom contains objects, such as her mother's self-portrait, which Linda has inherited from her parents), those props from childhood now stand unused, as if waiting for Linda and Johnny to rediscover creatively imaginative ways of wielding them.

After a moment, she invites him to join her in a waltz to the music-box Strauss (its nursery-room timbre accompanied by the sound of Johnny and Linda's footsteps against the floorboards, in a playroom that, just a few minutes earlier in the narrative, was so full of acrobatic life). Case tells her that he feels as if there is a "conspiracy" against them. She wonders what that might be. He responds—"vested interests"—and she responds in turn with a hushed, sensitive "I know," as if to suggest her purpose in this dance is not to have Johnny confirm Julia's unsuitability for him (something she, by now, already knows), but to draw him closer toward that knowledge. After a moment, Grant stops the dance, wondering aloud if Julia might be right in her outlook on life. Although momentarily stopped, Hepburn and Grant continue to hold hands, raised upward; as Grant speaks, he clenches Hepburn's hand a little tighter on each syllable in his words, with Hepburn then pushing her palm into his and her body toward him, as if her character were the last life support of the future plans Johnny now finds himself doubting. That's enough, for now, to inspire Johnny to start dancing again. As they continue to twirl around the room (progressing slowly toward the playroom's window), Linda shares her own doubt, the feeling that perhaps the importance she had ascribed to the engagement party, and thus her sister's feelings, was misplaced. Grant, at this moment, looks into Hepburn's eyes. Grant approaches her for a kiss, but Hepburn ends the dance and moves over to open the window as the first verse of "Auld Lang Syne" resounds from downstairs. As the wind blows in from the outside like a breath of fresh life, Grant leans in to kiss Hepburn on the cheek. The first genuine, mutually acknowledged expression of blooming love between the two characters has occurred in the playroom, full of the transitional objects that allow Linda to begin to imagine some future life apart from her father, and by the window which opens out onto the society in which their relationship will eventually bloom, away from the privileged space of the family mansion which has held it back. She accepts Grant's kiss, but, for the moment, prevents it going any further, pushing Johnny gently away and telling him to go downstairs. Now, Hepburn raises her hands to her heart again, a gesture not only of the feeling for Johnny residing within Linda but also of the modesty she intends to cloak around this love until Johnny breaks off the engagement with her sister and leaves the Seton home.

And once Johnny does this, *Holiday* can end, with a cruise ship carrying Linda and Johnny away from the stuffy other Setons. As Thomas Schatz reminds us, in screwball, the final embrace is often "treated offhandedly, like an afterthought" (162). Most viewers will infer that Linda and Johnny will marry, although the presence of the Potters on the cruise ship in the film's final scene reminds us of an alternative adulthood, a potential model for Linda and Johnny's own future together. Andrew Britton suggests that Hepburn and Grant in *Holiday*, standing as they do for a kind of play resulting in a "more free and pleasurable culture" with a "redistribution of power within the couple" renders the idea of marriage, in fact, "socially impossible" (7). In other words, in *Holiday*, our couple expresses intimately and privately what is ultimately irreconcilable with the social form surrounding them. The performances of Hepburn and Grant in *Holiday* shatter bourgeois convention, but their union at the end of the film remains beyond the grasp of any bourgeois audience still invested in those conventions. It is right, in fact, that the kiss should take place on a cruise ship. The challenges their philosophies of life present to the society in which they live leave them, at the end of the film, in search for a new society, in love and afloat to a different, alternative future.

❦

If both *Sylvia Scarlett* and *Holiday* position the Hepburn and Grant characterizations as a challenge to society through the way they reform conventional culture through their creative sense of play, *Bringing Up Baby* pushes this creativity even further through the figure of Susan Vance.

This Katharine Hepburn character makes play, and in-betweenness, not something that occurs as a result of temporary cross-dressing, as in *Sylvia Scarlett*, or as an event consigned to a small playroom, as in *Holiday*, but rather a total and radical philosophy of life, a way of being. Her speed of movement compels the Cary Grant character, and indeed the audience, to just *try* and keep up. To win Grant, her object of desire, Susan will employ what Maria DiBattista terms "evolutionary madcap," executed by the sublimely athletic Hepburn as "a series of pratfalls that would do the most seasoned farceur proud" (196–197). As Susan chases after David, and impels David to chase after her, across golf courses, night clubs, front lawns, countryside, jails, stables, and city streets, she demonstrates unmatched physical prowess, adapting to unexpected terrain (a deep riverbed that she imagines is shallow, a rocky hillside down which she falls, a wild leopard that she assumes is tame) with a breathless ability to adapt in an instant. As Alex Clayton points out, when Susan Vance falls or stumbles, it only confirms the film's own commitment to her speed of life, for "while her numerous accidents in the film . . . all result from a certain misplaced confidence, the film is less interested in scoffing at such assurance as it is in savoring her response to the mishap . . . Far from being fazed by such setbacks, Susan reacts with spirited, if capricious, resolve" (149). The film she is in—which, as V. F. Perkins has written, is imbued with a spirit of irrationality that is in fact the norm in a Howard Hawks screwball comedy (68)—is the perfect sympathetic context for her spirit and her resolve.

For the loving viewer of Hepburn, though, there will be a slight difference between one's line-of-sight and the vision of the Cary Grant character in the film; although viewers are narratively positioned in a way which parallels archaeologist Dr. David Huxley's own bafflement at being sucked into the vortex that is Susan Vance, lovers of Hepburn as actor take delight in having eye, ear, and heart challenged by her pulse-racing movements. And lovers of Hepburn know from the beginning what David Huxley doesn't yet: that she is going to move—that she is going to move very fast—and that we're not always going to be quite sure exactly where she's taking us (even when we've seen the film several times, we delight in renewed surprise).

The first meeting between David and Susan occurs on a golf course. David is there to convince wealthy Mr. Peabody (George Irving) to award one million dollars to his proposed dinosaur museum. The film joins David in a steady tracking shot as he and the lawyer stride toward the latter's golf ball. Mr. Peabody then stops, prepares to take his shot, and informs David he doesn't enjoy talking business during a golf game. David is not exactly out of place on the course—he finds his golf partner's ball before the lawyer does—but he is uninterested in the game itself, clearly using the golf session as a business opportunity. That David is focused on an overarching goal rather than the present moment of play is suggested by Grant's performance; after Mr. Peabody suggests he stop talking business and go find his ball, Grant's stuttering walk out of frame, his continued gaze upon the lawyer's ball rather than his own, and the first uttering of what will be a recurring bit of dialogue ("I'll be with you in a minute, Mr. Peabody!"), all indicate David's difficulty in moving from his stiff focus on work and ambition to the freer context of play. When David walks to find his ball, he spies Susan Vance for the first time, and a corresponding long shot of Hepburn selecting a club from her caddy and preparing to slice what is in fact David's hooked ball establishes the golf course as a setting in which this sublimely athletic creature is in full comfort. Cut to a closer shot of Hepburn as she prepares to whack at the ball; in the same shot, Grant walks up to reclaim poor David's golf ball. After she swings, she twirls around to David to tell him she forgives him for interrupting her shot because it ended up being a good one—the rules are less important to Susan than her ability to adapt, in a breath, to whatever interruptions might emerge around her. But David is not quite yet her focus: twirling around again and then striding out of frame, her focus for the moment is on the golf ball, both Grant and Hawks's tracking camera following to keep up with her.

I am amused by a question, while repeatedly watching and attempting to adjust my eye to the rhythms of Hepburn as Grant tries to keep up with her here and throughout *Bringing Up Baby*, a question that I am convinced is impossible to answer in conventional terms: When does Susan fall in love with David, exactly? Unlike clichéd love stories, which tend to converge their characters' love in what Naremore, following Stanislavski, might call an "acted image" (72–73), Susan's love for David happens not in a "moment," but is the gradually emerging product of several moments Hepburn strings along breathlessly. After locating her ball on the green, Hepburn sinks the putt (in a single long shot, confirming the scene is a product of the actor's athletic grace, rather than tricks of editing; see Mast 142). After doing so, Grant bounces on his tiptoes to reclaim his ball—"oh my, this is so silly," he utters—a few steps ahead of Hepburn before she quickly reclaims her place next to him with quick stride. This is one of a handful of moments in the film in which *Bringing Up Baby*'s continuity editing is not quite up to the challenge of keeping up with Hepburn; after she runs to join Grant at the hole in a long shot, the film cuts into a closer medium shot in which Hepburn is two or three steps behind where she was in the immediately preceding long shot, as if her speed were too much for the wheels of classical continuity. The efforts of the film itself to adjust its rhythms to Hepburn's way of walking mirror David's efforts to keep pace with Susan, an effort that is as cerebral as it is physical. Susan's performative irrationality has a fully rational basis, exemplified in her responses to every bit of evidence that David tries to put at her that she has mistaken his ball for her own: she knows full well that her golf ball is David's Cro-Magnon ball, rather than her PGA; she knows that David is not simply lost on the golf course, but is trying to recover his ball; she knows that David has no interest in the skill of her putting when she emits a triumphant "Ha!" upon seeing her ball fall into the hole. That she knows all of these things without precisely caring about any of them is conveyed as much by the dialogue (when David points out the circle on the ball, proving it is his brand, Susan quips: "Well of course it is. Do you think it would roll if it were square?") as it is by her tendency to slip quickly out of frame while David is still focused on some object within it. For example, when Grant caustically asks her if he can take his ball with him, Hepburn hands her club to her caddy—this game and that object having served their purpose in temporarily delighting her—and quips that he can, only if he promises to return it to her afterward. Susan moves so fast, it is perhaps only when she realizes David is able to keep up with her that her love for him begins.

David will have to do more than just be fast; he will also have to adjust to Susan's lack of social decorum about property. Before the film is over, she will steal a handbag, two cars—one of them twice—and a wild leopard. She cares not about who "owns" objects, but only about what pleasure particular objects might bring her for a moment, how these might serve as temporarily useful playthings. No other character we will meet in this book so beautifully and so chaotically refigures the social world around her with expressive gestures and movements driven by her own playful desire. (Where Linda in *Holiday* often holds emotions close to her vest, Susan declares them with glee.) She treats all of these objects and vehicles as "transitional" phenomena, using them to her ends but then discarding them before they can induct her into the dull, symbolic world of adult propriety. Christopher Bollas writes that objects in life lead us to become "substantially metamorphosed by the structure of objects; internally transformed by objects that leave their traces within us, whether it be the effect of a musical structure, a novel, or a person" (59). But as Hepburn's performance everywhere suggests, Susan stops short at allowing any object or person full internal transformation of her inner life: she is already overflowing with vitality, and the objects around her serve primarily to enable her screwy ends, and are tossed out once these ends have been achieved.

Her second meeting with David, in the Ritz Plaza scene, deepens our understanding of her playful use of objects. David has shown up at the Ritz to look for Mr. Peabody; before he spies Susan, he is already the picture of clumsiness, struggling to retain proper decorum after dropping his top hat in front of a pair of coat check girls. A cut to Susan establishes her in the same space as David (although he has not seen her yet). She is listening attentively to a barkeep, teaching her how to perform a trick with olives. It is one of the few moments in the film in which Susan actually takes instruction from another person in her creative wielding with objects (her acute sense of the potential playfulness of any object is otherwise inherent in her being). But Susan is not a docile, submissive student; Hepburn's performance—fluttering hand gestures as she beckons the barkeep to continue with his demonstration; impatient nodding as he works through each stage of the trick—suggests both her careful attention to his instruction as well as her overflowing pleasure, her desire that he get on with these delights so she can try them out. After the barkeep's olive demonstration, she waves her hands around in the air giddily, as if to clear the space for her own attempt at the feat (which will, of course, be more fabulous than anything this unassuming bartender has ever seen before him!). Now, she goes through the gestures she has just been taught, not in order to please her teacher but to please herself, as if what she were about to do with the olives were now *her* trick simply through her attempt at doing it. And so, she flips the olive up into the air and it ends up not in her mouth but rather, on the floor, to provide the cue for Cary Grant to enter the scene, slip on the olive, and fall on the floor in a pratfall reminiscent of the best silent comedies (figure 3.7). Susan is about to apologize, but then she sees it is David. "Oh, hello," she says, mischievous fluttery in her voice; "you're sitting on your hat!," she announces, as if conveying new information the hard floor's impact on Grant's posterior did not already confirm. "That's silly," she says, relinquishing ownership not over the act of dropping the olive, but its result. When Susan Vance creates a whirlwind, she takes authorship only over the whirlwind itself, not the responses of others to it. Everyone else will have to adapt to the situation she creates. "You can't do that trick without dropping *some* of the olives; it takes practice," she says, keeping the trick itself her priority, above and beyond its consequences.

As Grant's movements confirm as the scene goes on, David tries to adapt to Susan by endeavoring to get away from her. He will attempt to do this throughout the film, but will repeatedly be drawn back into her orbit. After David's pratfall, he leaves, but Susan continues to follow him. He tries to shoo her away; she stops at the table of a psychiatrist and reaches down to grab an olive while keeping her gaze firmly planted

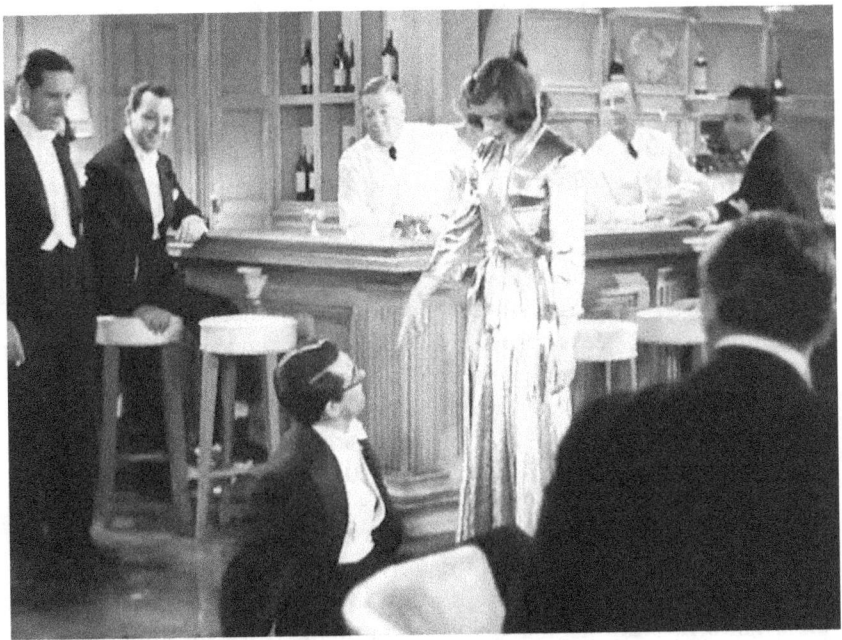

Figure 3.7. Cary Grant, and the knowledge the hard floor provides, in *Bringing Up Baby* (RKO Radio Pictures, 1938); Katharine Hepburn looks on.

on David. She continues to practice her olive trick (still failing, with the olives dropping away from her mouth after she slaps them up from her hand), as if to suggest her pursuit of and possible relationship with David will only be worthwhile if she is able to continue to play her games while doing so. She is momentarily distracted—more precisely, distracted from her earlier distraction—by the psychiatrist, who talks to her about the "love impulse" in men, which, he says, "very frequently reveals itself in terms of conflict." Of course, she takes this diagnosis as a sign of David's subconscious desire for her! Susan's manipulation of the psychiatrist's meaning (the verbal equivalent of her play with the olives) transforms itself into more mischievous play, this time with a handbag she swiftly purloins from the doctor's table. She glides over to David, who is sitting and waiting for Mr. Peabody, with the giddy news. "You know why you're following me? You're a fixation!" As she informs him of this fact, Hepburn's face radiantly expresses Susan's confidence in her new, goofy knowledge. A beat later, she recognizes the purse she's grabbed from the doctor's table isn't hers; she hands it to David, in full knowledge of the chaos this will cause when he, after growing impatient waiting for

Susan to return for her purse, tries to walk over to the bar to return it to her and is found with the purse by its rightful owner, the doctor's wife. As this kerfuffle commences, the film cuts to a medium-shot of Hepburn standing gleefully with the barkeep, aglow with her success in finally performing the olive trick successfully—"I did the trick! I did it once!"—before turning around to witness the real spoils of victory her conquest over the olive has awarded her, the chaos it has generated in poor David's life.

Central among the many striking things about Katharine Hepburn in *Bringing Up Baby* is that her Susan Vance, throughout this string of chaotic events, seeks repetitions with a difference, stringing Huxley along as she enables the happening of a variety of screwy situations (a lost ball in a golf course, a torn dress at a nightclub, lost clothing which forces the Grant character to cross-dress, a lost leopard in a countryside, role-playing as a gangster's mole in a county jail). All of these nutty goings-on serve to extend the time she is able to spend with David and work to ultimately convince him of his love for her. Flirtation, after all, is all about exploring time, and deferring the moment of institutionalized commitment. Susan, perhaps more than any other character in this book, takes flirtation as her only commitment. If his de-sexed devotion to profession constitutes David Huxley's duties, Susan Vance, once she meets David, works to create a context that preempts obligations, carving out flirty time for unrealized possibilities. It should also be noted that David himself, despite his outward stoicism, takes the shape, throughout the film, of a "less familiar possibility" to her. Indeed, the intensity with which Hepburn gazes at Grant in this film (figure 3.8) suggests Susan has never quite met anyone as alluring as Dr. David Huxley, despite the fact that he seems rather blind to his own allurements. So although the scenes analyzed above suggest that Susan moves very fast, she moves fast not simply to get through moments with David. In ways that again reminds us of Adam Phillips's theory of flirtation (explored earlier in this book), Susan seeks perpetually to extend the time she has with David further and further, flirting with him until he comes to recognize the pleasure he might also take in doing the same with her. But to do this she must always remain one step ahead of David, ready always to stage a new scheme or chaotic disruption of plan that will keep him close.

Much commentary on the film has pivoted around the various objects Susan wields in these various disruptions (a golf club, a golf ball, a dinosaur bone, a cigar), and the double entendres these objects seem to carry throughout the film. But repeated viewings of the film make the sexual meanings less interesting than the way Susan wields them to create a temporal space in which she may continue to flirt with her

Figure 3.8. Katharine Hepburn, gazing radiantly at Cary Grant, in *Bringing Up Baby* (RKO Radio Pictures, 1938).

object of desire. So, as we have seen, although Susan makes great use of all these objects, she would no doubt be somewhat bored with the effort of so many critics to interpret their coded sexual meaning. She already knows that meaning, and as if to signal that her interest lies not in the metaphors for sex the objects carry but in the sex itself promised in a potential future with David, she discards the objects as quickly as they have proved useful to her desire to keep David close and in pursuit, as if she were suspicious of any finally interpretative or symbolic meaning her continued use of the objects might confirm. The objects are expressive only of Susan's ongoing desire to flirt, and then flirt some more. And they are important only insofar as they are useful to the context that Susan is able to create from out of them.

Bringing Up Baby declares the love of its central couple, then, not through a ritual at the end of the film (such as a wedding), but through action, through the repeated confirmation that the hero is in fact willing to join Susan in the open-ended context of adventurous flirtation that she creates. It is the kind of action that contains a mutual acknowledgement of the other (Hepburn and Grant never vie for sole performative possession of the frame as Lombard and Barrymore do in *Twentieth Century*), and the kind that never settles into a final image of settled, harmonious coupledom (as Loy and Powell finally do). Further, that David ultimately assents to Susan's vision of life is not suggested by anything he says—he does not admit that this day he has spent with Susan is "the best of his life" until right before his beloved brontosaurus comes crashing down in the film's final scene—but by David's incrementally increasing ability, as the film goes on, to match Susan's screwy movements through the landscape as he searches for a dog, a dinosaur bone, and a leopard. He, in effect, becomes a screwball. Love follows.

❦

If Susan educates David in *Bringing Up Baby*, the situation is reversed in the final film pairing Grant and Hepburn together, *The Philadelphia Story*. Hepburn's character in this George Cukor film, wealthy heiress Tracy Lord, has divorced C. K. Dexter Haven (Cary Grant); it is implied that his alcoholism is one reason for their break-up. She has new plans to marry George Kittredge (John Howard), a member of the nouveau riche. Dexter has plans of his own; he employs two journalists from Spy Magazine, writer Macaulay Connor (James Stewart) and photographer Liz Imbrie (Ruth Hussey) and brings them to the Lord mansion, with the intent of spoiling the Lord-Kittredge wedding all while convincing Tracy he is still the man for her. Dexter is still in love with Tracy, not because he has learned to overlook what he takes as her central character flaw—her inability to tolerate the flaws in others or in herself, clearly exemplified in her attitude toward both Dexter's drinking and her father's own philandering—but because he now believes *she* has the ability to realize this is a flaw, and that she will be able to, with a bit of work, live with the shortcomings of others and herself, that is, to be "human, a human being," to take full possession of her life, her sexuality, and their possibilities.

It should be noted that George Cukor tells this story in a style that is not all that different from that of Howard Hawks: a preferred emphasis on long shots with cut-ins to close-ups emphasizing gradual evolutions in character relationships. Where Cukor and Hawks differ is the ends to which this style is directed. As V. F. Perkins points out, where Hawks creates alternative worlds in his comedies, worlds imbued with the irrational, skewed visions of the characters themselves, Cukor places his figures in a more naturalistic world, in which expressive idiosyncrasies of character play against a more normatively and rigidly defined social landscape that tends to resist their interventions (68). In terms of the performances, the distance between *Bringing Up Baby* and *The Philadelphia Story* is also felt acutely in the actors' use of objects. Where Hepburn has Susan Vance discard transitional objects before they can become fully part of an adult social world, objects in *The Philadelphia Story* linger and loom, their presence and their use by the players suggesting a complete entanglement between the expressed psychologies of the characters and the symbols of the social world in which they live. A brief overview of the salient objects that appear in the film is enough to suggest their fully developed symbolic value and the failure of the characters (Tracy especially) to imagine new, playful uses for them. There is Dexter's wedding gift for Tracy and Kittredge, the miniature model of the *True Love*, the ship that once symbolized the love Dexter and Tracy enjoyed in their first marriage, and which Tracy admires after diving into the Lord mansion pool. As she wades in the water, she holds the boat in her right hand, speaking to George of its past significance in her life; but she cannot quite bring herself to play with it (thus failing to find any new playful, pre-symbolic use of it), so it floats out of frame. And then there is the camera Liz Imbrie brings to the mansion, to take pictures of the wedding and thus open the private world of the Lords onto the public. The camera is, as Robert B. Ray has pointed out, an Argus C-3 Rangefinder, one of the first affordable 35mm cameras, and in the frame of the film a sign both of Liz's artistic frustration (she would much rather be a painter than a photographer, but, of course, needs to pay the bills) and Tracy's "frigid virtue," which does not take kindly to being extricated from her aristocratic perch through this mechanical means of reproduction (see Ray 87–89). And so she destroys it, intentionally tipping over the patio table, onto which Liz has unwisely placed the camera while reaching for a drink, and in doing so removing the object from her world rather than finding a playful new use for it. There is also Macaulay Connor's book of poetry, a failed stab at artistic immortality that Tracy, after reading it at the public library, takes inspiration from; she offers Macaulay the financial support he will need to write another one, patronage that Stewart's character rejects as old-fashioned. Perhaps the only objects in the film that are in any sense "transitional," that retain a sense of play in their warding-off of the already articulated symbolic world of proper adults, are the champagne glasses that, later in the film, assist in getting Tracy and Connor slowly drunk and free of inhibition.

If these objects are a sign that Tracy Lord has forgotten what Susan Vance knew—that is, how to imaginatively play with the world around her, which is one way to be a "human, a human being"—Cary Grant's Dexter remembers, and his role in the narrative is to teach Tracy what her life might possibly become again. Within the intertext formed by the films in this chapter, this education emerges from Dexter's remembrance of what past Hepburn characters have demonstrated (and perhaps, at the earliest moments in their courtship, what the Tracy Lord character used to be), that is, a playful and vital engagement in life and a rejection of already established ways of thinking and acting. Andrew Klevan regards Grant's characterization of Dexter as a "presence hovering on the edge of things, interfering vividly and yet influencing indirectly" (*Film Performance* 39)—existing in a state of in-betweeness to where Dexter would like to return Tracy, a liminal position on the edge of polite society rather than one fully immersed in the symbols and pretensions of its falsely adult world. Grant's various gestures, expressions, and positionings, throughout the film, suggest his marginal relationship to the social world into which he is intervening. In Grant's first appearance, he is following Connor and Liz through the hallways of Spy Magazine. Grant has a sly way of slipping into this scene, suddenly there, in the background, on the right side of the frame after Stewart and Hussey have already been established in its center, and then disappearing just as quickly out of frame after Stewart and Hussey walk into the managing editor's office. Later, when Grant arrives through the back entrance of the Lord family mansion to interrupt Tracy's wedding planning, he does so without virtue of an establishing shot, slipping into the room with Tracy's sister, Dinah (Virginia Weidler), much to Tracy's consternation. He will proceed to interrupt moments like this throughout the film, standing on the margins of scenes (as Klevan puts it, "waiting in the wings" [*Film Performance* 38], in the theatrical sense) in order to gently guide the events in a direction he prefers, toward a reunion with Tracy.

But Cary Grant can only "slip" into scenes so much: no matter how liminal a shape he takes as he pops up into spaces here and there throughout the film, he is still Cary Grant, and our attention remains fixed on him even when his performative placement is subtle and indirect. Tracy herself subconsciously seems to be drawn to his orbit, as Hepburn's movements in her second scene with Grant in the film suggest. After Dexter interrupts Tracy's wedding planning, Hepburn approaches Grant from the right side of the frame, as if to indicate her ownership over space into which he has, uninvited, presented himself. Grant then returns the favor, moving toward Tracy, as Hepburn backs up to the edge of the frame and closer to her original position in the scene. The tracking camera then moves out to a longer shot to incorporate all of the characters in the scene (Tracy and Dexter; Tracy's niece, Dinah; and Tracy's mother), but the emphasis is still on the space between Grant and Hepburn, the composition separating Dexter, Dinah, and Mrs. Lord, grouped together on the left side of the frame, from Tracy, who stands alone on the right side. Hepburn—watching, for a moment, the embrace Dexter and Dinah form around Tracy's mother—isolates herself further, fiddling with a few wedding objects while making caustic comments about Dexter's alcoholism. If the dialogue suggests past reasons for the failure of their marriage (Dexter's drinking), the positioning of Hepburn in the scene confirms the ongoing emotional distance caused by the failures of the past. But Grant works to draw Hepburn back to him. As she makes out to leave the room, Grant follows her to the door, momentarily eliminating the space between them. After Grant walks back to the center of the room to rejoin Dinah and Mrs. Lord, Tracy follows him and keeps close, even as the quarrel between them continues. Hepburn, standing above Grant, punctuates her role in the spat with a disdainful gaze down. But he has seen this look before, and he is committed to the idea that, in the new relationship he envisions for them, it will have no place: "No, you're slipping, Red. I used to be afraid of that look. The withering glance of the goddess." This withering glance keeps Tracy at the center of her world, in the position of virtue that gives her power, and turns our earlier sense, from *Bringing Up Baby*, that she orbits around Grant on its head. With this look, she bids him to orbit around her, as the virtuous goddess who Dexter will work to bring down to earth as the film goes on.

Although Dexter and the various other men in the film may refer to Tracy as a goddess, this does not mean Hepburn's performance is itself stilted or still. Although not nearly as demonstrative of her lithe athleticism as her portrayal of Susan Vance in *Bringing Up Baby*, her turn as Tracy Lord in *The Philadelphia Story* is nevertheless full of dynamic gestures and movements. In her first appearance in the film, she reclines on a sofa, propping herself up with her left elbow while she puts the finishing touches on her wedding reception menu. Dinah sits to her left. She asks her mother, who stands in the background, how to spell "omelet." Mrs. Lord confirms the spelling. "I thought there was another 'l,'" Hepburn responds, prolonging the intonation of "l" with her drawl while she swings her right leg around Dinah's head as she prepares to get up, contorting her body into a corporeal "l" that in effect substitutes for the extra letter Tracy wanted to add to the word (figure 3.9). This movement is another fine example of a Hepburn character, through her qualities of performance, taking an obstacle established by socially agreed-upon rules (in this case, a letter in the alphabet) and transforming it through a creatively expressive movement.

But where Susan Vance moves breathlessly forward, out of frame, into the next moment of orchestrated chaos, Tracy keeps near the center of the frame, in the middle of things, secure on her perch. Hepburn's most memorable movement in the film may be her graceful dive into

Figure 3.9. Katharine Hepburn, writing with movement, in *The Philadelphia Story* (MGM, 1940).

the pool in a later scene. The moment affords us another opportunity to admire Hepburn's athletic prowess in long-shot, but to significantly different ends than in earlier films with Grant. The pool itself is firmly located at the center of the Lords' world. The difference between Hepburn's way of moving through Hawks's world in *Bringing Up Baby* and her way of moving through Cukor's world in *The Philadelphia Story* is a question, ultimately, of her character's relationship to surrounding context. In *Bringing Up Baby*, Hepburn embodies Susan as a woman always moving forward, kinetically shaping her life as one imbued with movements and gestures prepared to adapt to whatever obstacle or change the world around her throws in her way. In *The Philadelphia Story*, Hepburn's dynamic physicality and her character's skill at responding to the contingencies of the world, by contrast, nearly always keeps her in the center of the frame. Her dive into the pool generates cinematic ripples across a series of visual centers: Hepburn's centered position, in the frame, between the statues surrounding the pool (themselves symbols, perhaps, of her own frozen virtue) and Cary Grant; through the way the tracking camera keeps her centered as she nimbly tiptoes to the diving board;

to the circles of ripples created in the pool after her body breaks the surface of the water; and to her centered position, in the pool, in the bottom-third of the frame after the dive (figure 3.10). Without sacrificing an iota of her own performative vitality, Hepburn situates Tracy at the center of her aristocratic world. If her performance in *Bringing Up Baby* is centrifugal, always breathlessly moving onward and outward, in *The Philadelphia Story* it is centripetal, characterizing Tracy as a woman who likes to keep herself positioned on her pedestal, centered so as to be admired.

Dexter, of course, will eventually find a way to wrest her from that perch at film's end, toward something more closely resembling (in character if not in kinetic speed) the centrifugal life of Susan Vance in *Bringing Up Baby*. Yet Grant's presence in *The Philadelphia Story*—on the edge of things, slipping into the narrative here and there—also opens up a space for another character to try to win over Tracy: Jimmy Stewart's Macaulay Connor, an ambitious middle-class writer who is reporting on the Tracy Lord marriage, begrudgingly, for his newspaper's society pages. Connor would prefer to be a serious writer of serious books.

Figure 3.10. Katharine Hepburn, in the center so as to be admired, in *The Philadelphia Story* (MGM, 1940).

Tracy has glimpsed some of that serious work, earlier in the film, checking out Connor's sole volume of poetry from the public library. His writing has moved her, and she tells him so. After this initial connection, in a scene by a pool later in the film, free from the presence of Dexter, the two become inebriated enough to flirt with guards let down. This brief, intoxicated courtship is the first time in our story of love's performance where the central couple will be significantly threatened by an outside force. But what Tracy learns about herself through Connor's affections paves the way, eventually, for her reunion with Dexter at the end of the film.

Much of what we come to know about each character in this sequence, and thus much of our regard for the various things James Stewart and Katharine Hepburn are performing in this moment together, is bound up in shot-reaction shot editing patterns structuring the sequence, and the way the actors embody these frames. Connor and Tracy are drinking champagne, slowly getting drunk. Tracy is teasing Connor about his intellectual pretensions, referring to him repeatedly, and condemningly, as "Professor." The conversation proceeds into a lightly intoxicated argument, unfolding in mostly long- to medium-two shots, until a crucial moment in which Connor declares his love for her, motivating closer shots and reaction shots. "There's a magnificence in you, Tracy," Stewart says, his arm raised as if to give a lecture. But now, for the first time in the sequence, we cut to a luminous close-up of Hepburn-as-Tracy. Her head raised upward, initially, at a haughty angle, Tracy's eyes then dart up and down, shyly, in a counterpoint, as finally she admits self-consciousness in an attempt, perhaps, to bring Connor's words down to a more human level. But cut to a reaction shot, equally close, of Stewart-as-Connor: his eyes open, his mouth slightly agape as deeper tremors of love vibrate within him—Connor's regard for this woman cancels out every attempt she has made to humanize herself. And in bestowing upon her this complete regard, Connor is moving away from his own haughty, professorial posturing, and will now declare his love for her as a man free of restrictions of class and position.

Tracy, though, tells him it is getting late, and time for each to retreat to their separate bedrooms. As she walks away, cut back to a two-shot. Stewart raises his arms, still gazing at her, and begins talking. This stops her in her tracks, although she is still facing away from him:

> CONNOR: The magnificence that comes out of your eyes and your voice and the way you stand there and the way you walk . . .

Cut from the two-shot to a close-up of Connor (figure 3.11) as he continues to play the troubadour, his intensity becoming almost ferocious as he now spits the words:

CONNOR: . . . You're lit from within, Tracy . . .

Cut to a corresponding close-up of Tracy (figure 3.12), the passion of Connor's words finding their palpable equivalencies in her own affections, as she looks offscreen, perhaps imagining what the words might really mean. Although she is facing away from him in the blocking of these two shots, it is almost as if—and *especially* as if, if we have felt the words Connor is speaking as intensely as Tracy herself feels them—this vision of Tracy is a creation of Connor's words, rather than another human being toward which Connor is gazing in actual space. Connor is here fully complicit with Tracy's own efforts to center herself as an unreachable ideal in her world. He continues:

CONNOR: You've got fires banked down in you . . .

Cut back to Connor, as he continues; Tracy must have lit fires in him, as well, for Stewart now jerks his head to the right as if in response to an unexpected vibration in his words:

CONNOR: . . . Hearth fires and holocausts.

Cut back to Tracy. The intensity of Connor's words have now made her uncomfortable on her perch. Her hands clasped together, she slowly

Figures 3.11 and 3.12. Hearth fires: Katharine Hepburn and Jimmy Stewart in *The Philadelphia Story* (MGM, 1940).

begins to pull herself off the pedestal Connor has placed her on, turning to him, wrenching him free of his fantasy, and showing him the face of the woman she actually is (she is still, however, centered in the frame). Then, a cut to a two-shot presents both characters facing one another, as Stewart has Connor reassure Tracy of her humanness, which has made her magnificence all the more remarkable. But now that he can see her—now that the fantasy of the shot-reaction shot, in which she was facing away from him, has ceased—he cannot quite re-attain such poetry, and descends to his own normality. "Why, has your mind taken hold again, dear Professor?" she asks. It has—and the fires, for a moment, die down again.

Connor works hard to keep Tracy centered on the pedestal she has kept herself upon throughout the film. However, Tracy begins here to slightly slide off her perch, to reveal more slippery gestures and movements indicating the humanity Dexter would so like her to discover. This is suggested in the idea that Connor, in his efforts to keep Tracy centered as his feminine ideal, actually misses quite a bit of what is admirable about Hepburn's presence in the scene. Not everything I want to say about what these two actors are doing here, not everything they have done which has affected me, is quite contained within the lines of character sight generated by their performances and communicated, to us, through the editing. Indeed, besides establishing Connor's own idealized vision of Tracy, Hepburn and Stewart generate gestures and movements that Connor cannot quite yet grasp. There is something, indeed, that escapes the line of sight established in the cutting-together of actor eyelines, something that must necessarily escape given classical cinema's tendency to block actors at slightly frontal stances, in ensemble shots, in order for most of the front part of the body to be facing the camera (see Naremore 24, 39). This is particularly true of screwball and romantic comedy of the 1930s and early 1940s, which often emphasizes the physicality and athleticism of its characters with long- and medium-shots that offer us views of performance that escape the vision of a single character, and which substantially inflect the usual pattern of continuity cutting; and it is particularly true of the films of George Cukor, the director of *The Philadelphia Story*, who films Hepburn, especially, with a sensitivity that seems to elude Connor here. (Indeed, this sensitivity toward her, and shedding of misogyny, is something we might say C. K. Dexter Haven, her ex-husband, is trying to achieve in his quest for their remarriage. If she needs to be cut down to size, he also needs to prove himself worthy of the considerable size she will still possess, and to which he will eventually have to soberly respond if their second attempt at marriage is to succeed.)

And, further, Stewart cannot see Hepburn in the shot-reaction shots I am discussing. She is facing away. So in the same moment as he creates an idealized vision out of his poetic words, what is more available to us than to Jimmy Stewart is the humanity of Katharine Hepburn's expressions, which, although still very much the center of her world, work to convey the mix of pleasure and trepidation in response to these hearth fires he spies in her eyes. For unlike Stewart, we begin, gradually, to see Hepburn as a woman here—the "new woman" Dexter would like to help her create, the new woman Stanley Cavell claimed was the creation of the most progressive of the screwball comedies (see *Pursuits of Happiness*, especially pages 16, 57, 65)—in all her ambiguity and ambivalence, as she faces us, away from him. Indeed, for a long stretch in this sequence, Cukor avoids shot-reaction shots entirely, preferring instead to show us Hepburn and Stewart together, in space; and because they are not always looking at one another in these longer two-shots, elements of their performance which have affected me escape the affections of the characters they play. For example, Connor knows Tracy is a swimmer, and has seen her move through space—but has he any knowledge, in this scene, really, of the way she moves? Is he aware of the way she glides, as if on air, across the grass and the porch as she moves to answer a phone (one of the few movements in this film in which she de-centers herself, gliding away from the center of the frame as the tracking camera works to keep up with her), and how she then turns, stating the obvious in slurred speech ("it isn't ringing anymore") in order to punctuate her movement across the grass with an endearing comical touch that has confirmed her character's newly discovered down-to-earth humanity? In the context of the present scene, I cannot say, for even though Cukor's tracking camera does its best to keep up with Hepburn, by the time it returns to Jimmy Stewart's character, who has approached the porch to pour another glass, he is looking down, preoccupied with his drink. Cukor's attitude toward the men in this film might be emblemized by the desire one gets to slap Connor for messing with alcohol while this enchanting human being lies in his purview, showing a gracefully centrifugal, more complexly human movement for the first time in the film. Cukor's camera, open to the intoxication of Hepburn's own lightly intoxicated movement, enables us to see even more of performance than Stewart's tipsy Connor can quite glimpse.

My viewing of this scene has thus surrendered itself to the way Hepburn moves in this sequence; and her performance has signaled a moving evolution in her character. I delight, then, not with the idealized vision of Tracy that Connor creates, but rather with the way Hepburn darts away, in concert with her most sensitive director, George Cukor, from the idealism that Connor betrays here, and from his desire to possess her, to continue to center her in the world, rather than love her, with all the new contingency and unpredictability that she has now discovered in her own movement. To admire the way Hepburn moves in this sequence is to break out of the limits of Connor's appreciation of her—while he is thinking about booze, Hepburn is getting the viewer drunk on the way she moves. It's enough to give us reason to question Connor's confidence that he is the man for Tracy, and that their potential union together might be anything very different from the stultified class he critiques.

Connor's temporary infatuation with Tracy not only misses what her devoted viewer beholds; it is also lacking the shared history Dexter has with her, and the promise of a new, alternative future a reunion with him holds. Because, after all, Cary Grant's C. K. Dexter Haven already knows all about the way Tracy moves. He has been married to her, and he knows her capacity to be human, even if she has presently forgotten it; he has lived with her, and with all that means. And so while the pleasure we take in watching Hepburn move in the above scene from *The Philadelphia Story* is enough to cement our own intimate and unique attachment to her presence in the film, Dexter's knowledge of Tracy ultimately goes well beyond ours; this knowledge is not entirely unlike that shared between Myrna Loy and William Powell in their various films, the knowledge that the intimacy shared between even the most socially positioned of married couples is still ultimately a private one. This was a knowledge shared in their past, as a presumably (once) happy couple. Dexter doesn't want to rekindle exactly that, however, because, whatever it was, it didn't work. What Dexter wants is to bring Tracy down to earth, but not in order to "cut her down to size" in the way Spencer Tracy will do so bluntly, two years later, in *Woman of the Year*. Rather, he wants her to join him, fully human, in the new adventure he spies for them in the space he has carved out, away from the center, just on the edge of polite society. As with many other comedies of remarriage, the permanence of the happiness Tracy and Dexter have found is ambiguous, as uncertain in its future as the makeshift wedding at the end of the film is as far from any "ideal." This is the proof of its reality, and its very human beauty.

❦

As a tandem, Hepburn and Grant blend individualistic distinction with collaborative fluidity. They play lovers who allow the individuality and distinction of the other to flourish in the space they presently occupy together. We may leave a Hepburn/Grant film feeling, perhaps, that the two characters aren't quite right for one another—as some of my students sometimes feel (and indeed, as no less a critic than Robin Wood feels; see *Howard Hawks* 64–65) when I show them *Bringing Up Baby*; they cannot quite believe a professional scientist like David Huxley would turn over his life and work to a madcap tornado named Susan Vance. I do not share their doubts about that film, but I do sometimes wonder if Linda Seton in *Holiday* is quite prepared to live for "peanuts" when she declares her love for Grant's Johnny Case. And in *Sylvia Scarlett*—their only film together in which they do not play lovers—their characters quarrel and bicker throughout. But this tension is one of the delights of their films; it is precisely because the two aren't exactly "perfect" for one another that the films remain so interesting. Hepburn was far too independent and self-assuredly beautiful to much care about any man's gaze, and Grant's suave, leading-man image must undergo a certain degree of mussing-up (in *Holiday* and *Bringing Up Baby*) or de-centeredness (*The Philadelphia Story*) before he can persuade us of his coupledom with Hepburn. Their very unique and at times contrapuntal personalities open the way for an appreciation of distinction and difference in a union, different in its details from the ideal established between Loy and Powell and less outwardly theatrical than Lombard and Barrymore. They are screwball's daffiest couple, full of vitality and life.

Part II

Noir Amour

4

Love's Possession

Dana Andrews and Gene Tierney in *Laura*

THE NOIR LOVER EXISTS IN A world of dream—she often appears as if she *is* a dream. Certainly Humphrey Bogart must have thought he was dreaming, on and off the set of *To Have and Have Not*, when he first spied Lauren Bacall. But not every noir performance makes this oneiric quality easy to detect. Gene Tierney and Dana Andrews, in Otto Preminger's *Laura* (1944), are also quite beautiful, but they lack, strangely, the inimitability and distinction of a Bogart and Bacall. The stoic Andrews, as working-class Detective Lieutenant Mark McPherson, is not as hard-bitten as other examples of the noir hero, such as Bogart or Robert Mitchum in *Out of the Past* (1947). Neither is he mysterious—his handsomeness is genial, his way of moving smart and pointed without being ostentatious or arrogant. Gene Tierney, meanwhile, exudes the sort of classy feminine presence Hollywood studios would work hard to cultivate in the 1940s—her appearance recalls Jennifer Jones and Hedy Lamarr, both of whom were offered the role in *Laura*, and both of whom turned it down (Behlmer 185). Neither Andrews nor Tierney capture the imagination quite as forcefully or as theatrically as, say, Katharine Hepburn or John Barrymore, and they do not seem quite as adaptable to a variety of narrative situations as Myrna Loy or Cary Grant. They also lack the genial aim of affability that welcomes others into their social sphere—think William Powell or Carole Lombard. Their appeal lingers in darker shadows.

Of course, Tierney and Andrews bring something to *Laura* the viewer would miss had they not been cast: their difference from the

Figure 4.1. Falling in love with a painting: Gene Tierney and Dana Andrews in *Laura* (Twentieth Century-Fox, 1944).

screwball performances we have just visited is not a lack. They only remind us that noir cinema does not belong to its players in quite the same way screwball so intimately belongs to Hepburn, Grant, Lombard, Barrymore, Loy, and Powell. In screwball comedy, the comically radiant gestures of the aforementioned actors effortlessly take the world around them as a proscenium for performance. Screwball comedy, created through a reliance on long shot and mostly unobtrusive continuity editing, enables the actor to become an imaginative participant in the film's synthesis of the public and the private worlds on display in any film's *mise-en-scène*. Noir actors create *mise-en-scène*, too—but it is a struggle, not always won. As Donna Peberdy has noted, the performer in noir is often regarded "as an inhabitant"—rather than a creator—"of the *mise-en-scène* . . . the noir actor takes on these moods [established by lighting, camera, cinematography] by default with cinematography and style creating meaning on behalf of the performer . . . it is technology rather than the actor that is deemed the author of performance in noir; cinematography constructs the effect" (319). Peberdy goes on to argue against this notion, yet many approaches to discussing noir still revolve heavily around emphasizing lighting, camera, and lens. Extensive studies of performance in noir cinema—detailed descriptions of gestures, movements, expressions—are relatively rare.

As a whole, critical literature on noir tends to sidestep extensive commentary on acting, eschewing a description of the performer in favor of exploring how deep-focus cinematography, low-key lighting, and sonic ambience situate the actor as a figure in a *mise-en-scène* full of threat and danger. Although useful recent work has begun to probe the way in which the actor's oscillations between reserved expressions and more ostensive performative signs contribute to and interact with the dynamic narrative patterns and stylistic contexts of noir films (see Baron, "Gesture Under Pressure" 18–20), in much of the literature on noir and performance, the actor is characterized as a minimalist, called upon to play enigmatic figures. Emblematic of this tendency is Foster Hirsch's essential piece, "The Noir Actor," in which it is written that the "performers most closely identified with the genre have masklike faces, their features frozen not in mid- but in *pre*-expression." For Hirsch, further, the noir actor "does not open up the frame, claiming screen space for himself, but plays close to the chest, remaining a figure in the noir landscape, one element in the film's overall composition . . . Actors who either overact, or who project a basically sunny disposition, appearing to be at ease with themselves and the world, are not noir material" (146). Although some conflation of actor and character is going on here—one can obviously imagine a noir actor being perfectly at ease with the world while playing a noir character at some odds with it—Hirsch's point nevertheless hints at the work the discerning cinephile must do to appreciate, to love, the noir actor for herself, her gestural expressivity cloaked in low-key lighting, ominous music, and claustrophobic framings taken as the defining hallmarks of noir style.

In the introduction, I suggested that loving actors, and understanding the love they perform, involves paying close attention to what happens to the totality of a film's space: what alternative form of life is signified by the love performed? How does the intimate and private share of a film's world, in other words, synthesize with the larger social world on display in the film, and perhaps transform the world in light of this new image generated by performance? Yet noir actors often play characters who find it difficult, if not impossible, to change their world through their love. As Edward Dimendberg has shown in his influential study of noir and modernity, the narrative space of noir films is itself subject to a complex tension between centrifugal and centripetal forces, in which characters are subject to, rather than in control of, urban transformations and dislocations (18). This placement of the actor within a heavily expressionistic style would seem to serve as something of an allegory for the complex positioning of the character herself in this conflicted space—the stylistic shape and tone of the space seems, if not always determined from the outset, too intricate or overwhelming for a single figure to grasp.

Gene Tierney and Dana Andrews form the perfect example of this particular sort of recessive noir couple: one that unites out of love, but which does not—cannot—inflect the space around them with new norms of living. In this, they also refract something, in their performances, about how love was actually performed in American social reality around the time of noir's emergence. In the first half of the twentieth century, courtship rituals in America, as Ellen K. Rothman has studied, became a matter of knowing how to move—that is, how to assume the movements the culture had already articulated, rather than inflecting movement with one's own personal way of playing. "'Catching' a mate," she writes, "had become a matter of wearing stylish clothes and knowing the latest dance step, rather than demonstrating certain attributes of character" (225). This emphasis on assuming the fashion of the time "made self-exposure a risky proposition," as Rothman goes on to note. The eschewal of ostentation or histrionics in the performances of Andrews and Tierney—and the way, at times, they give themselves over to a kind of blank (if still quite fascinating) stillness—captures something of the flavor of this fear of exposing one's distinctive, uniquely inflected self in normative American society. If American courtship revolves around masking one's own personality and gestural idiosyncrasy in favor of the fashion of the time, so as to be read by the person one is wooing as a "good mate" according to whatever norms pressure an individual at any given historical moment, the fashion of noir revolves around a deep sense of unease with this social mask one wears while wooing. Thus the revelation of actorly personality in noir performance expresses the character's own desire to inhabit social form with personality, inimitable presence, and something beyond what has become, in noir, a disabling and foreboding normativity.

What is a challenge for the characters within the films, I think, is also a challenge for the cinephile writing about them: just as the noir character struggles to transcend the threatening norms of an opaquely perceived social world, so too does the writer on noir contend with the fact that there is no longer anything particularly distinctive or transgressive about loving noir cinema. Noir itself, and the desire for noir, is now perfectly normative. Corey K. Creekmur gets at this idea when he writes that "love of film noir only retains a passionate intensity insofar as it continues to verge on a prohibited, illegitimate infatuation, even if the public view of this relationship increasingly resembles a socially sanctioned marriage" (67). Later, he intriguingly complicates this notion by suggesting that the cinephile's "love for film noir has an analogue in the behavior of characters in the films" (72). Creekmur here strikes at the dialectic of *noir amour*, a tension between, on the one hand, the illicit and the liminal, and on the other, the normative and the visible, existing in both the cinephile's love of noir and in the love performed by noir characters. In its status as an idea, first formulated by French critics, noir cinema pointed to anxieties in America during and after World War II, implying troubles in the American body politic Classical Hollywood cinema often ignores or represses. But love for and love within noir is also as perfectly typical, at least in the outwardly viewable, public forms it takes on, as marriage itself. After all, everyone loves noir (and even though no one called these films *noir* in the early forties, many of them were quite popular at the box office). *Noir amour* is an erotics tempered by the institutionalization of its object (within academia, and within Hollywood) and by the couplings we often find at the heart of their tortured and sometimes tortuous narratives, couplings that do not outwardly challenge the American shape of love in terms of either gender or sexuality. To love noir, then, would seem to open onto an exciting, hallucinatory danger that, paradoxically, has been fully institutionalized, a state of affairs that has tempered the more challenging effects of noir style in favor of carefully rehearsed scholarly debate, complete with normative ways of speaking and writing.

But perhaps the love of the noir actor, and the love performed by the actors one loves, cuts closer to the quick of the cinephile's quickened heartbeat. If the "external appearance" of love in noir is perfectly normative, as Creekmur suggests, it is only by digging into the internal tremors of love and desire—as conveyed through fleeting moments of poise, stillness, movement, gesture, and expression by noir actors—that we glimpse the more internally transgressive elements of life within the universe of this genre and its performative experience. After all, not much work on noir performance has been done—perhaps something that might strike our hearts still lies there. So perhaps the love of the noir actor, and the love performed by the actors one loves, brings us closer to what makes the cinephile's heart race in an experience of this otherwise much written-about genre. If the "external appearance" of love in noir is now perfectly normative, it is perhaps only by digging into fleeting moments of poise, stillness, movement, gesture, and expression by noir actors that we glimpse the interior elements of life within the noir universe.

But unlike, say, Katharine Hepburn and Cary Grant, who successfully refigure social norms of gender and sexuality, Gene Tierney and Dana Andrews—effective presences but relatively reduced in their expressive range, compared to many of the other actors discussed in this book—suggest a desire for a different future without ever quite changing the space of their present. In *Laura*, as Chris Fujiwara has written, their performances suggest that the "time in which the new can emerge" (48) belongs wholly to the characters played by Tierney and Andrews. But this "new" does not find shape within the narrative time of the film itself. Noir love, in this film, always looks toward the future, to a form of living that, in the present, in the treacherously surreal and dream-like world in which the characters live, remains unperformed, and perhaps unperformable.

In *Laura*, Dana Andrews plays a police detective, Mark McPherson, called upon to investigate the mysterious death of the title character, Laura Hunt, played by Gene Tierney. But is she really dead? The three chief suspects—journalist Waldo Lydecker (Clifton Webb), painter Shelby Carpenter (Vincent Price), and society woman Ann Treadwell (Judith Anderson)—all seem to think so. Yet Laura lives on, not only in the flashbacks conveying the information Lydecker is telling McPherson, but also, eventually, in a series of images appearing after our hero falls asleep (in a chair a few feet away from a glamorous painting of Laura, which he views) with a glass of brandy in his hand, images that feel precariously perched between reality and fantasy. It is in that liminal space, that space of limbo between wakefulness and dreaming, that Andrews and Tierney perform. And there, Mark McPherson and Laura Hunt fall in love.

Writing on noir often encounters the oneiric, of course. Even before noir had a name, surrealist writer Louis Aragon described run-of-the-mill Hollywood crime films with a language steeped in dreams, writing of their propensity to "raise to a dramatic level a banknote on which our attention is riveted, a table with a revolver on it, a bottle that on occasion becomes a weapon, a handkerchief that reveals a crime, a typewriter that's the horizon of a desk" (29). As James Naremore notes, "Aragon might well have been describing thrillers of the 1940s, which were perversely erotic, confined largely to interiors, photographed in a deep-focus style that seemed to reveal the secret life of things, and often derived from the literature of alcohol—a substance especially conducive of desire, enervation, euphoria, confusion, and nightmare" (*More Than Night* 18). Aragon here prefigures, in his focus on the photogenic qualities of American crime films rather than their detective plots, the argument French writer

Nino Frank would make twenty years later. In his thoughts on noir films such as *Laura*, *The Maltese Falcon* (1941), and *Murder, My Sweet* (1944), Frank locates the innovation of noir style in its focus on what he calls the "third dimension," deep textures disposing with the traditional detective film's focus on externally motivated action and soberly organized plot in favor of "facial expressions, gestures, utterances—rendering the truth of the characters" rather than using the characters as pawns in a mystery narrative (18). Frank goes further than to try to define a genre or a style (the two terms around which debates about noir frequently circulate); he is more interested in establishing noir's distinction, relative to the prestige pictures that win Oscars and middlebrow approval, its delight in the palpability of "meaningful glances" (19), and gestures, movements, and expressions, rather than overly studied shot compositions. (The reappearance of Frank's essay in an important collection of pieces on film noir, Alain Silver and James Ursini's *The Film Noir Reader 2*, in fact features a still image of one such meaningful glance, exchanged between Gene Tierney and Vincent Price in *Laura*, but perhaps the best images for Frank's argument come later in the film, when Dana Andrews, intoxicated by a painting of Tierney, dreams of her.)

To frame noir as dream-like, or in any sense "subjective," is tricky, however. Even though the genre's debts to Expressionism have been explored, it is nevertheless true that many noir plots revolve around external, rather than internal, action—on guns, on scheming and desperate bad guys, on private dicks prowling the streets for clues. And this is true of *Laura*, too; despite its ostensible presentation of a voiceover narration revealing internal subjectivity, Preminger's concrete, exacting visual style focuses more expressly on *external* action rather than tortured subjectivity. In this sense the film's reliance on internal voiceover is somewhat deceiving. The film is framed by the internal, diegetic narration of Waldo Lydecker, who pecks at a typewriter, in the film's opening scene, as we hear the story he is writing on Laura Hunt for the newspaper in his voice on the film's soundtrack:

> I shall never forget the weekend Laura died. A silver sun burned through the sky like a huge magnifying glass. It was the hottest Sunday in my recollection. I felt as if I were the only human being left in New York. For with Laura's horrible death, I was alone. I, Waldo Lydecker, was the only one who really knew her, and I had just begun to write Laura's story when another of those detectives came to see me. I had him wait. I could watch him through the half-open door.

This narration is only ostensibly about Laura; his narration is more about himself, "I, Waldo Lydecker," and the authority he possesses of her story. But the film's structure, far from expressionistically echoing Lydecker's story, casts doubt on what he says. Lydecker's words, beyond his self-absorbed focus on "I," are wholly unreliable in every point of fact. As Kristin Thompson has shown in her formalist analysis of the film (162–194), it is impossible to determine whether or not the story events in the film occur in reality or dream, given that the voiceover narration with which the film begins is voiced by a character who, it will turn out, cannot possibly have delivered it after the events we see unfold, since he actually dies at the end of the film. The only "reality" in *Laura* (a reality which, in fact, may be completely a dream) are the images Preminger presents to us, not the words his characters say. The dream in *Laura* exists not in interiority, or in voiceovers, but on the film's visual track, the concrete gestures, movements, and expressions that cut quicker to hidden desires struggling to achieve social articulation.

The opening sequence of *Laura* establishes Otto Preminger's cool, sustained directorial detachment, giving Dana Andrews room to roam—and time for us to begin to focus on the external behavior signaling his inner desires. The sequence begins with a complex tracking shot, passing from left to right across, first, a glass case storing prized *objets d'art*, and, then, a grandfather clock, an open window leading out onto a terrace (a space we will never otherwise glimpse), a sitting room framed with shelves of porcelain and glass objects, as well as books, framed pictures, and a personal gallery of masks. After catching up with Andrews's detective, the camera, after it comes temporarily to rest, registers McPherson's sidelong smirk in the face of all of these objects—a knowing glance that demonstrates, for Carl E. Rollyson, "an aesthetic sensitivity" (152) in McPherson that he otherwise keeps cloaked from the other characters. To engage with noir performance, as is already evident here, is to always engage with a character who is hiding, rather than ostentatiously displaying, his distinction. But now, something else catches McPherson's eye—the grandfather clock already glimpsed on the other side of the room. Andrews's movement prompts the first of several moments in the film in which the camera makes us aware, as Chris Fujiwara writes, "of offscreen space as not just, or even primarily, space, but as place: a place previously visited, to which we might return" (52). A return to a place often prompts a reckoning with some object we might have missed the first time in it—such as the strange glass vial that McPherson spies in the corner of his eye after moving over to the grandfather clock, an object mysterious enough for him to open the glass case and hold it in his hand. Already the camera has drawn attention to this object, in the first tracking movement across the room, but now it follows Andrews, in the same sustained tracking shot, as he moves over to take a closer look at the vial, passing our eyes over a place we have already visited but are now primed to watch carefully as a particular actor moves through it. If Preminger's camera repeatedly tracks across the same set of spaces it is not so much to reveal something viewers might have missed but rather to show characters, and in particular McPherson—a stranger to this environment—move across and within spaces already dangerously embedded in the memories of several other characters who have lived and loved here, one of whom might be a murderer. This is the screen world he will live in for the next ninety minutes, the world in which he will fall in love with Laura, who is perhaps no more real, no more a flesh-and-blood woman, than any of Lydecker's precious aesthetic objects.

It is telling that the first stroll this detective takes through the world of this film is through a living space decorated with delectable possessions, for Laura herself is treated as an object, a prize to be won, by the men in the narrative. It will be some time before Andrews actually glimpses Tierney, though—some time before Mark sees Laura. The first time he does, later in the film, while interviewing suspects Lydecker and Shelby for a second time, it is in Laura's apartment. The portrait of Laura (a photograph of Gene Tierney paint-brushed so as to look like a painting) looms above him. Lydecker is castigating McPherson, who lolls around the apartment with only professional interest, for calling Laura a "dame." Webb positions himself in front of the portrait and demands that Andrews look at it. "Not bad," Andrews says, in a casual way, his eyes cast in shadow, only glancing, and not gazing, at the portrait—although Preminger emphasizes the portrait for us, in a cut to a close-up of the painting above the mantle after Lydecker mentions it, the painting has yet to fully command McPherson's vision. His indifferent "not bad" is comical in retrospect, not only in light of the actual presence Tierney will project when she finally appears on the image track after twenty minutes, but also in relation to the depths of torment this painting, which McPherson regards now with disinterest but which he will desire and seek to possess, as the case begins to take its toll on him later in the film and as Laura's image begins to haunt his dreams.

McPherson will not just fall in love with this painting as he slips deeper and deeper in this investigation—he will seek to possess it, as Lydecker already appears to do in memory, by bidding it on it in an auction (not shown onscreen, but mentioned in the dialogue). It this possessiveness toward Laura that makes the achievement of Tierney's performance initially difficult to perceive. Her male co-star is playing a character who wants to own her image—to treat her like Lydecker treats his prized objects encased in glass, as a vehicle not only of his desires but as a means to raise himself above his station. (Throughout the film, McPherson is palpably irritated whenever Webb's character torments him about his lower-class origins; is the classy Laura his way up?) Tierney, indeed, sensed she was to play a possession, an object, a dream, in *Laura*, and was uneasy with it:

> The time on camera was less than one would like. And who wants to play a painting? (132) . . .
>
> I never felt my own performance was much more than adequate. I am pleased that audiences still identify me with Laura, as opposed to not being identified at all. Their tributes, I believe, are for the *character*—the dream-like Laura—rather than any gifts I brought to the role. (136)

Despite her hesitation over taking the role, Tierney's memorable achievement in the film reminds us that if male characters in noir occasionally take women as their objects, it nevertheless requires of the actress playing the object to have active talent, presence, and subjectivity.

Many of Tierney's films project her remarkable ability to reduce her ostensive range. She is capable of theatricality, evident in early films before *Laura*, particularly Josef von Sternberg's exquisite *Shanghai Gesture* (1941), as well as John Ford's *Tobacco Road* (1942). But in *Laura* and many of her other memorable films, she projects a stillness and coldness when the narrative calls upon her to play a character under the control of another. Still frames from a variety of Tierney performances suggest her ability to effectively poise for the camera, rather than ostentatiously convey interiority. Perhaps the most memorable of these moments occurs in John M. Stahl's noir melodrama *Leave Her to Heaven* (1945), in which Tierney comes quite close to embodying pure evil as Ellen Berent. Ellen is a spoiled socialite who, obsessed with a man, Richard Harland (Cornel Wilde) whose physical appearance echoes that of her beloved late father, orchestrates the death of a disabled boy, Danny, played by Darryl Hickman, who interferes with the complete attention Ellen believes she deserves from Richard. No viewer who has seen *Leave Her to Heaven* can ever forget the way Gene Tierney presents

Figure 4.2. Gene Tierney, in stillness, in *Leave Her to Heaven* (Twentieth Century-Fox, 1945).

Ellen, sitting on a raft, a paddle in each hand, not moving—and cloaked behind sunglasses masking her eyes as she watches Danny drown in the middle of a river (figure 4.2). In the commentary track for the DVD, Hickman himself (who became, years after the film's release, an acting teacher fully committed to the Method, and a popular writer on the subject of one's "full command" of character in performance) critiques Tierney's acting skills, pointing in particular to a scene in which Ellen suggests to Richard that he stop working and live off her inheritance as an example of her tendency to present or "indicate" feeling to the audience rather than fully inhabit it. But it is precisely the point of *Leave Her to Heaven* that Ellen is not possessed by anything that might resemble a coherent human psychology. We know the narrative motivations that drive Ellen, but no one, least of all Ellen (or Tierney, or Hickman), understands what drives her to realize those desires through the sadistically impenetrable act of watching a helpless boy die. And Tierney conveys this existential blankness perfectly through her achievement of stillness and poise.

Ellen takes direct and murderous control over her situation, but more often Tierney's own ways of positioning herself are in fact presented as ways of being posed and positioned by others, the films themselves (including those she made outside of noir) often raising the issue of how much agency Tierney and her characters have in shaping gesture, movement, and expression. In Jacques Tourneur's surreal Western *Way of a Gaucho* (1952), Tierney plays Teresa, a Spanish noblewoman who is rescued by Martin Penalosa (Rory Calhoun), a gaucho who has deserted his militia. Teresa's love for Penalosa is characterized by her willingness to be submissive: in her early scenes with Calhoun, after her character is rescued and the two hide away from the militia under the expansive shadows of trees, Tierney lies still for several minutes, listening demurely, as the gaucho shares his life story with her. The erotic presence Tierney establishes in the sequence is a product of her presenting herself in stillness to the camera while wardrobe (a torn white blouse, revealing an exposed shoulder) and off-camera effect (a blowing fan provides a mimic of wind blowing through her hair) complete the characterization. The most evocative image of Tierney in the film is found in the same sequence; as her character sleeps under the trees, the shadows of blowing leaves pass across her face and torso, suggesting the possession by forces beyond or above the character that so often characterizes the Tierney character's submissive position in the diegetic world.

Other films starring Tierney self-reflexively comment on the actress's ability to present gesture and effectively pose in frozen expression for the camera, and of the male characters' pleasure in fantasizing about those gestures and postures. In *The Razor's Edge* (1946), Tierney plays Isabel, a socialite who loves the wandering bohemian Larry Darrell (Tyrone Power). The film is based on a W. Somerset Maugham novel, and in this particular adaptation Maugham is also a character (played by Herbert Marshall). In one scene, Maugham and Isabel are discussing Darrell's impending marriage to the alcoholic Lucie (Anne Baxter), a union of which Isabel does not approve. Early in the scene, Tierney exhibits a relatively wide range of expressivity and movement, conveying the character's indignation through the raised volume and pitch of her voice and walking back and forth between Maugham (seated on the couch) and the fireplace mantle to convey her character's anxiety. Tierney overplays the scene a touch, gesticulating and raising her voice in atypically exaggerated ways. But the sequence eventually brings Tierney back to stillness. Maugham, settling Isabel down, comments that, despite her present anger, he always enjoys the sight of her. "Of course, your most fascinating feature," Marshall says, "are your hands—they're so slim and elegant—I'm always amazed at the infinite grace with which you use them. . . ." While saying this, Marshall's Maugham cradles Tierney's arm in his own, admiring her hands with his gaze (figure 4.3)—

—before he continues speaking: "Whether by nature or by art, you never make a gesture without imparting beauty to it." While speaking this line Marshall moves his right hand to the hand of Tierney's he is admiring, as if preparing to set it free (figure 4.4):

He goes on: "They're like flowers sometimes—," while raising the forearm as if it were the stem and the fingers petals (figure 4.5)—

—and then: ". . . sometimes, like birds on a wing," gently pushing the forearm back towards Tierney, as she herself watches the unfolding movement (figure 4.6):

Figures 4.3, 4.4, 4.5, and 4.6. Herbert Marshall and Gene Tierney, never making a gesture without imparting beauty to it, in *The Razor's Edge* (Twentieth Century-Fox, 1946).

These moments suggest not only Tierney's ability to pose in stillness for the camera; they convey her characters' frequent willingness to be poised and positioned by men—a thematic that will be interrogated in *Laura*. But where films like *Way of a Gaucho* and *The Razor's Edge* show us men positioning Tierney's characters in a social world that is presented as "real," *Laura* shows us the same occurring, first, in flashbacks prompted by the narration of one of her suitors, and then, in dreams. This is where the Tierney character can turn the tables, resisting her possession by men and instead inhabiting *their* dreams. But there is a further wrinkle. The analyst of performance courts complicity with the desire of these male characters to reduce Tierney and her characters to stillness. In order for the writer to convey what he has seen in Tierney's performances in these various films (and in *Laura* especially), he must freeze the frame, her ability to achieve stasis and poise conveyed not only in writerly description but also photographic stillness. The idea that Tierney is best "captured" not through (or solely through) a writerly description of gestures, movements, and expressions but rather through the inclusion of the still frame alongside text means that just as characters in the films come to be possessed by men, so too does the analyst freeze her motion so as to affix a critical quality to her in his text. This, of course, is true of the inclusion of a freeze frame in any text on film acting, but it is an idea that calls for explicit comment in writing on *Laura*, which thematizes the possession of its leading lady's stillness. In including still images, the writer on film cannot retreat from the responsibility of writing words about that stillness, about how that stillness affects him. This subject of capturing the mood of stillness when a performer poses immobile is one on which William Rothman has written eloquently: "Nonetheless, frame enlargements, however evocative, do not in and of themselves complete the task of *capturing* such moods. To accomplish this, the writer has to find words to say, for example, what the mood is that this face is expressing at this moment, what the thoughts and feelings are, or may be, that are at once coloring her mood and being colored by it" ("Silence and Stasis" 107–108). In effect, the cinephile finds his way out of complicity with the freezing of Tierney's agency by describing his own moods when she is so frozen; in so doing, he lets the moods expressed by Tierney in stillness inhabit dreams (his, and perhaps those of the reader). This is where a cinephilic reckoning with the effects of performance in *Laura* has strange parallels with the experience of the Dana Andrews character in the movie. Just as Mark McPherson, with the help of drink, lets the image of Laura inhabit his dreams, so too can a cinephilic attachment to the performances in *Laura* teach us how the cinephile might eschew possessing the beloved figure and instead allow her to possess him.

But while Andrews can craft his characterization of McPherson as a man who stands at some degree of controlled, patient remove from the baiting of Lydecker, Tierney cannot: from the very beginning of the film her character is framed and possessed by others, not only within the painted portrait adorning the film's title sequence, but also within the narrative frame of the flashbacks. Lydecker narrates her first appearance. Preminger's camera tracks toward the table in a café, where he sits with McPherson. Lydecker is recalling his first meeting with Laura—this is the table they used to share. As Webb speaks, he gazes away from Andrews; Lydecker is mesmerized by a memory of Laura about to become manifest for us on the film's image track. Our first glimpse of Tierney, after the dissolve to Lydecker's recounting of the past, is as she faces away from us, as her girlfriends urge her to go speak to the great journalist. Lydecker, in this memory, sits at the opposite end of the room. Laura is about to approach him because he might be a good subject to endorse a pen in the ad campaign she is designing. Tierney is modestly dressed, in a fashionable hat and suit, conveying the look of a working woman, a *femme moderne*, rather than the woman of distinction she will become later, under Lydecker's social tutelage. Describing her diminutively as "the girl who walked into my life in the Algonquin Hotel five years before," Lydecker's narration compels us to read Tierney's gestures and movements as lacking confidence: she gets up, looks offscreen hesitatingly, and then proceeds to slip through a crowded café, elongating her body and clutching her illustrations closely to her person. In a two-shot, Tierney approaches Webb with short steps rather than an assured stride, first positioning herself across from Lydecker and then moving closer to him, next to his table, as if quite unsure which position will grant him the most flattering look at her. Tierney nervously rubs her left thumb over one of her sketchbook's corners as she begins to ask Lydecker for her endorsement in a hushed, mousy voice. As Lydecker admonishes her character for interrupting his lunch, Preminger cuts to a close-up of Tierney's nervous, reserved expression, establishing the emotional power his words hold over her. As Laura discovers the humane journalist she admires is in fact a self-absorbed snob, Tierney expresses her character's reserve and disappointment in tightly bound gestures and movements: she clutches her illustrations closer to her body, stands immobile, slightly raises the inflection of her voice, and lets slip a delicate frown, visibly offended at Webb's catty words but too quietly composed to assertively challenge him.

The Laura manifest on the screen in these moments, a Laura performed by Tierney but possessed, at least for a time, in memory and desire, by Lydecker, is, however, one of reserved and muted strength. Even in these scenes, ostensibly under the narrative authority of Lydecker, the framing, the music, and the positioning of Tierney in the shot suggest something of a free spirit, an image of a woman wresting herself free from the fantasy of a man even as she exists palpably within, is created *by*, it. As Lydecker's narration of his relationship with Laura continues, Tierney assumes a number of poses, illustrations of the way she is remembered, in stasis, in Lydecker's imagination: she stands up to demonstrate an important point at a business meeting; she helps Lydecker make dinner; she listens quietly while he plays his records and reads his articles to her. But listen to the music that wraps itself around Tierney in these shots—the record playing is the theme to *Laura*, composed by David Raksin, and established earlier in the story as one of Laura's favorites, a piece surely too much of the easy listening variety for Lydecker to tolerate without his beloved in the room. Something of Laura seems to always be slipping away from the diegetic narrator in these shots, an autonomous woman with, possibly among other things, her own choices in music. Something of this inner life that slips away from Lydecker's possession is conveyed by the way Tierney gazes, glacially, out of frame, while he prattles on about his education of this young woman. Is he educating her—or is she envisioning something else?

In the next sequence in the flashback, Lydecker takes her to a fashionable party. A painter, Shelby Carpenter, approaches Laura. Already we are positioned by Webb's voiceover narration to haughtily regard Shelby as one of the typically "nondescript characters corralled from every strip of society" invited to these kinds of parties. And, initially, Laura receives Shelby with a dismissive attitude, indicative of how much her vision of the world has been shaped by Lydecker. But Tierney's gaze lingers on Price: she sizes him up, her glance full of a desire that certainly escapes Lydecker's own possession, if only for a heartbeat. Later in the scene, Tierney will go into the kitchen to grab a glass of milk for Lydecker, a prop expressive not only of the nature of Lydecker's relationship to Laura (which is more maternal and dependent than amorous or sexual), but also of Laura's own willingness to serve his demands. Yet in the kitchen scene, Tierney positions herself openly toward Vincent Price, as if to convey her character's inclination to accept another suitor. Later in the party sequence, Tierney and Price share a cigarette on the patio, puffing in rhyme. The characterization Tierney crafts in this scene with Price is consistent with the scenes she has shared with Webb: at first challenging the male in the dialogue (Laura presses the painter on his unemployment, asking him what measures he has taken to find "real" work), Tierney is also submissive to his charm, an infectious smile slipping across her face as he tells a joke about his failed attempts to find work. At the end of the sequence, Laura offers Shelby a job, a sign of her relative power over Price's character. But this occurs after Clifton Webb has stepped through the curtain separating the patio from the interior, Lydecker's presence effectively interrupting their smoke and reminding us of his sustained power over Laura, who defers to his presence by ending the conversation with Shelby.

So while all the work Tierney does here is in large part to create a Laura as imagined and conjured by Webb's Lydecker, her performance, in conjunction with camera and soundtrack, hints at an inner life, and a power, that cracks the glass of Lydecker's fantasy. Tierney thus suggests the spark of an inner life in her performance; and it is to this that Dana Andrews responds, ultimately. His various roles in their films together (I am not including here Ford's *Tobacco Road*, in which they play characters who never meet one another) ultimately do not involve the Andrews character possessing or positioning Tierney, as other men in the films might. Instead, the Andrews character always *thinks* about Tierney, and what she says, and acknowledges her agency over the impact on his course of action these thoughts and words will have. In William A. Wellman's Cold War drama *The Iron Curtain* (1948), Andrews's Soviet spy, Igor Gouzenko, must arrive at a moment in which the Tierney character, his wife, inhabits his waking dreams; it is her plea for a democratic future that motivates Igor's decision to turn over what he knows of the Communist operations in Canada to the other side. And in Preminger's later *Where the Sidewalk Ends* (1950), it is the Tierney character's love for her father, her belief that he is innocent of the crime of which he is accused, that inspires Andrews, who successfully conveys the torment of his guilt throughout the performance, to admit that he, and not the father, is responsible. In these films Tierney plays characters whose devotion to ideals (democracy and truth) inspires the Andrews character to a renewed commitment and course of action. But in those films this "thinking" is presented rather conventionally, as something read into Andrews's stoic appearance. And the characters played by Andrews there are the primary social actors. Tierney plays the helpmate, who provides inspiration to the male figure, to get him going.

In *Laura*, by contrast, we *see* Tierney possess Andrews, slip almost imperceptibly into his dreams, in the film's most memorable scene, the scene in which Andrews falls asleep in front of a painting of Laura, a scene in which, improbably, a man courts a painting and a painting gazes back at him before taking on life, as Tierney, in a waking dream. McPherson has returned in frustration to Laura Hunt's apartment to stand watch for the evening. Preminger's staging of Andrews's movement emphasizes his connection to a series of key objects: first, a brandy glass, placed in the foreground of the shot when Andrews walks into the apartment, a prefiguration of the intoxication which will, after a moment, initiate his sleep; a mirror, on the wall of the background behind Andrews, the first of several mirrors we will see in the scene, and indicative of the slow breakdown of McPherson's calmly assured subjectivity; and, finally, the portrait of Laura Hunt herself, still hanging above the fireplace. As Andrews stops and gazes at the portrait, Preminger's tracking camera stopping with him, David Raksin's score repeats, in a slower, subdued variation, as if accompanying McPherson in a slow drift into fantasy. Later in the sequence Lydecker will reveal that McPherson has put in a bid to own this painting—like other men, he would like to possess her too. Yet Preminger's framing of Andrews's gaze at the painting emphasizes, instead, the way it gazes, in stillness, back at him—what he seeks to possess has beaten him to the punch. Andrews, for a moment, resists the lure of the portrait, and turns around and takes off his jacket in a medium shot, a cigarette still nonchalantly dangling from his lips and the brim of his hat shadowing his eyes as he makes a concerted effort to gaze away from the painting.

Taking off the hat, loosening his tie, and grimacing with each of these gestures, Andrews next moves over to Laura's desk to sort through some letters. Andrews puffs on his cigarette, smoking his way through rote detective duties. Yet something is still bothering McPherson; nothing about this discovery of a potential new clue has satisfied him. The high pitch of the violins in Raksin's score complements the grimace on Andrews's face, the impatient tapping of the letters against his palm, and the sudden, forceful extinguishing of the cigarette. Just as quickly, McPherson resumes his detective work, striding into Laura's bedroom and rifling through her belongings for other possible clues. Yet as Andrews steps out of darkness and into the high-key lighting of the bedroom, it is also possible to wonder if he is really looking for any clues at all, to wonder if he is not, in fact, prying into the private life of a possibly dead woman out of some erotic desire, initiated by the painting looming above the fireplace, a painting that has already begun to woo him. Andrews's rather rough handling of objects in the bedroom—the way he brusquely tosses the letters onto Laura's nightstand; his casual disarranging of Laura's belongings as he rifles through one of the nightstand's drawers; his quick sniff of the perfume in a glass vial; suggest a certain disgust for the violation of privacy he finds himself performing. McPherson will have to reckon with all this—that is, with himself—on his way out the bedroom, when, after opening one of Laura's closets to take a quick look inside, he will spy himself in the mirror, briefly contemplating the visage of a man whose calm, stoical, impersonal attitude towards detective work is starting to break down.

So he does what any noir tough guy might do in this situation—he drinks. Pouring a glass of brandy, and with Raksin's score once again cued on the soundtrack, Andrews walks over to Laura's portrait, and gazes at it briefly, before turning away from it and placing his drink down. The dream will not happen just yet. First, his character must call the precinct to check in, perhaps to reestablish some outwardly professional grasp on what he is doing here, in the apartment of this woman. Lydecker, who has unexpectedly returned to Laura's apartment, interrupts him, arriving to take back some of the possessions he previously gifted her. But Lydecker's unwanted presence does not break the hold Laura's portrait has over the detective; McPherson has already tried, and failed, to break that spell with the professional call back to the precinct. Far from breaking the spell, Lydecker diagnoses it, hinting in the dialogue that he knows exactly what has attracted Andrews back to the apartment—the portrait. But what Andrews reveals through position and concentration as Webb goes on speaking is more important. While Lydecker looms behind him, McPherson sits down on a couch, and pulls out his pocket baseball game. The film has highlighted this object before, in the earlier scene in Lydecker's dressing room, another moment during which the detective calmly listens to the words of a writer who desires to control the direction and meaning of talk. But here, his calm demeanor cracks; once Lydecker baits McPherson further, with his suggestion that the detective dreams of a woman beyond his station, who might accompany him to policemen's balls and listen to his tales of heroism, Andrews slams down the game in frustration, gets up off the couch, and demands Lydecker leave. An object formerly expressive of McPherson's cool control now connotes his breakdown, and the condition seems permanent—the pocket baseball game won't be seen again. As Lydecker leaves, the camera tracks in to a close-up of Andrews, who takes another quick drink as Laura's portrait looms. But where, before, McPherson struggled to keep some semblance of control over himself, and his reality, he now gives in to the dream.

A dissolve from the close-up. Lydecker has left; McPherson takes another swig of brandy. He is facing screen right, near the liquor cabinet on the side of the room opposite the portrait, but soon turns to face it, and walk toward it, brandy flask in one hand, a glass in the other. He sits down in the chair near the fireplace, beneath the portrait, the space between the painting and McPherson now forming a diagonal compositional line that cuts across the shot (figure 4.7). Andrews pours a bit more brandy, and places the flask on a book resting on an end-table near the chair. Without contemplating, he raises the glass to his lips and drinks (still facing away from the painting). Raksin's theme has returned on the soundtrack. Andrews cradles the glass in his right hand, bringing his left hand over its opening. He appears to be glancing at something out of frame—but the movement of his eyes suggests he is not really looking at anything, but rather trying to occupy his look so that Laura, still looming above him, cannot come to possess him. But after a couple of heartbeats, he gives in, and meets the diagonal line formed by his position and the placement of the painting with his own gaze (figure 4.8). He looks at the painting. Then, he turns his head back forward, still holding the glass. His eyes, however, have not quite escaped the possession of the painting's gaze; its vision now lies in a far more dangerous place—his dream.

We now come to something of an interpretive crux in *Laura*. As noted earlier, it is impossible to establish if what happens, from this point forward, is a vision of what McPherson is dreaming, or a return to reality, wherein Laura Hunt is still alive. Preminger's camera and its movements, as well as the framing and lighting of the scene, generate this ambivalence. As Andrews nods off into sleep, his brandy glass in his left hand, the camera tracks in toward his face, bringing Andrews into close-up and relegating the painting, now the stuff of his dreams, to offscreen space. Then, it tracks backward again—another example of the film's tendency to pass to-and-fro across and through the same spaces repeatedly—once again situating the painting of Laura in a diagonally arranged composition. Throughout the movement, we see that it is raining outside the window, indicating no significant passage of time—if McPherson is sleeping before Laura Hunt wakes him upon her pending return to her apartment, it is only for a few quick minutes. Yet something has changed

Figures 4.7 and 4.8. Dana Andrews falls in love with a painting in *Laura*.

across this tracking shot. When the camera tracks back out from its close-up of his character, Andrews is no longer holding the brandy glass in his left hand. If the shot had otherwise indicated some passage of time—a dissolve, say, on the close-up of Andrews, to indicate that the detective might have been asleep for some hours—it would be entirely possible to believe that, at some point, the glass merely slipped out of Andrews's hand, or that he got up at some point to place it somewhere else, and then fell asleep again. But no time has passed: the downpour of rain outside the window behind Andrews, on the right side of the close-up, is one steady, continuous stream. The only aspect of Andrews's position and placement in the scene that has changed in this tracking movement is his holding of the glass. The most obvious explanation is that he simply dropped it, but the sound of glass breaking is not heard, and once Preminger returns to a long shot of the space later in the scene, no glass, broken or otherwise, can be glimpsed.

There seem two reasonable explanations. The first is a continuity error, in which the glass suddenly went missing. And this error shouldn't bother us; the return of Laura Hunt is amazing enough, after all, to hold our complete attention. But the more creative explanation for this, I think, is that McPherson no longer possesses his means of intoxication. It is Laura who does—her presence, now, as a living figure, in his dreams, ensures that brandy will no longer be necessary. The very vision of Tierney is enough to intoxicate.

Upon the release of *Laura*, one reviewer complained that the title character's return to the film, the revelation that she was not really dead, was not startling or vivid enough (Pryor). Indeed, as filmed by Preminger, it is an understated moment. When she returns, it is in an evenly lit long shot, dressed in a raincoat, and carrying a suitcase. In other words, the effect is of a simple, even everyday event—a woman returning to her apartment, rather than from a journey to death. Instead of relying on expressionistic stylistics or music to convey the shock of Laura's return, the film calls upon Andrews to fully convey the woozy confusion prompted by it—the impact of Laura Hunt's arrival is happening inside Andrews's character, forcing him to grapple with emotions his hitherto concrete detective behavior has not required. More, the evolving movements and positioning of Andrews in the scene—in relation to both Laura and the painting of Laura looming above them—suggest that he is now moving beyond any interest in a fetishistic possession of the painting, desiring to make contact with the flesh and blood woman standing before him. When he wakes up, sleeping on the right side of the frame, he is greeted by a vision of Laura, positioned on the left side of the frame. The portrait figures in-between them, creating a triangular composition.

Andrews gets up, slightly dazed—he cannot believe his eyes. He walks closer, nearly to the edge of the portrait, partially obscuring it (Laura's painted visage still remains visible, momentarily, on the upper right side of the frame). Instead of immediately cutting to a close-up of Andrews, though, the film cuts to a close shot of Tierney, who insists she will call the police if McPherson, whom she takes as an intruder, refuses to leave. By cutting to a close shot of Tierney first, her character is established as the figure to which McPherson must now respond: his fantasy relationship with a painting, it would seem, is over. Cut to a close shot of Andrews: "You are Laura Hunt, aren't you?" No response. He takes a step forward, now to the edge of the painting, a few strides away from the "real" Laura. "Aren't you?" She threatens to call the cops again, interrupting his woozy line of inquiry, and it is not unimportant that she never answers this question. Andrews pulls out his badge, preventing her from calling the cops by informing her he is one. At this point, McPherson shifts into detective mode, interrogating her about her whereabouts on the night of the murder. Yet he betrays, throughout the rest of the film, a desire to court Laura—his questions, ostensibly about the case, frequently run up against his desire to know whether or not Laura intends to marry Shelby, who is now less a suspect in a murder and more a threat to McPherson's still unarticulated desire to have Laura for himself.

All of this is revealed in the film's most brilliant and mind-bogglingly complex scene, in which McPherson brings Laura in for interrogation at the police precinct. In the previous sequence, he has arranged a party with all the suspects present, the sort of situation familiar from detective films (like *The Thin Man*) in which all of the players are rounded up before the identity of the murderer is declared by the investigator. *Laura*'s variation on this formula, though, is ironic—McPherson does not know yet who is guilty of the murder. At the end of the sequence, he declares that he will bring in someone to police headquarters for questioning. He hopes the guilty party will step up and admit culpability once McPherson declares that it is Laura he intends to take in to question. But no one does. The eventual interrogation is not a complete farce—as he later reveals, he is only "99%" sure that she is innocent, so she still is a legitimate, if highly unlikely, suspect in the murder. (Her only possible motivation for killing Diane is jealousy of her friend's love for Shelby—but it has already been established that she is no longer interested in the painter.) So what McPherson is ultimately interrogating is not his guilt, but desire, or desire's future. What he wants to know is not quite if he is in love with Laura, or she in love with him, but rather if love might be possible, in the future time toward which the love in this film seems always to gesture.

The interrogation scene is a master class in performance, staging, framing, cutting, and lighting—and it is one of the most evasively complex, and perhaps one of the more subtly perverse, presentations of love's discovery in the history of movies. (No noir film would match the tone and texture of this interrogation scene until *In a Lonely Place* [1950], Nicholas Ray's anguished story of a screenwriter, played by Humphrey Bogart, who watches while the woman he will come to love, played by Gloria Grahame, is grilled by a cop.) Andrews and Tierney walk into the interrogation room, and the detective orders Laura to sit down. As he does so, he creates a diegetic parallel for Hollywood's familiar three-point lighting setup, flipping the switch to the room's corner light, which will serve as the scene's backlight, before shining two bright lights, a key and a fill, onto Laura's face after she sits down. As Andrews does all this, Preminger's tracking camera moves toward the interrogation desk, in a close two-shot (figure 4.9), in which we see McPherson, perched on the edge of the desk, on the left side of the frame, and Laura, sitting in a chair, on the right. The high-angle would seem to situate Laura in a position of powerlessness, although the camera looks down on McPherson, too—the power he wields as a detective, as a figure of an institution, is not really what interests him, as we will discover. Laura is looking down—McPherson orders her to look up. She does, after Preminger cuts to a close-up of Tierney with Andrews's face still visible in the shadows on the left side of the frame, with a cutting, reproachful glance (figure 4.10). "What are you trying to do, force a confession out of me?" she asks. After this pointed question, nearly every line of dialogue Andrews will deliver will seek to evade her query, even as what he says retains the superficially hard-boiled, on-the-nose surface quality that helps him keep the outward appearance of a cop merely doing his job. But Laura, not McPherson, controls the emotional trajectory of the sequence. She claims aloud that he has already decided she is guilty—and, raising her hands to her head in pain, asks him to turn off the harsh lights. He does—the high-key interrogation now has a few more shadows. Laura's cue to change the lighting prompts McPherson to change positions. After she states again her innocence, Andrews stands up, and begins to walk around to Tierney's side of the desk, bumping into the chair next to the front of the desk (conveying McPherson's own fragile grasp on the situation). He positions himself next to Laura, looming above her but now in an eye-level shot—he is shifting authoritatively into the rhythm of the interrogation (figure 4.11). His questions mean to clear up the holes in her story: Why did she claim her radio was broken while she was away, and thus avoid hearing of her reported death (McPherson had found, in his investigation, that it was working)? The local handyman fixed it, she claims. How did he get in? She left a key under the flowerpot. These are conventional, even clichéd detective questions—the kinds of questions that mean to discover holes in her story, questions given the kinds of responses that mean to fill those holes in.

But these are not the questions that ultimately interest McPherson. Andrews circles behind Tierney, positioning himself behind her as she continues to sit in the chair. The interrogation light continues to loom on the left side of the frame—threateningly, as if he might turn it on again at any moment. It is at this point that the line of questioning takes a subtly personal turn:

> MARK: The main thing I want to know is why you pulled that switch on me about Carpenter. You told me last night you decided not to marry him.
>
> LAURA: Yes, I guess I did.
>
> MARK: But today it was on again. Why?
>
> LAURA: Well, I—I changed my mind.

This answer prompts a frustrated grimace from Andrews. He leans forward, taking his hat off and placing it forcefully, but with a modicum of gentleness, on the desk. Mark sits on the side of the desk, immediately to Laura's left. The distance between them is intimate. Andrews's positioning darkens Tierney's face. If we were not in the middle of an interrogation scene at police headquarters, we might think he meant to kiss her. Tierney gazes offscreen, blankly, as Andrews leads up to his next question:

> MARK: This is no time for secrets. Now, did you really decide to call it off . . . or did you just tell me that because you knew I wanted to hear it?

Figures 4.9, 4.10, and 4.11. Dana Andrews interrogates Gene Tierney in *Laura* (Twentieth Century-Fox, 1944).

After the words, "because you knew I wanted to hear it," Tierney's gaze offscreen is suddenly broken. Something in these words has stirred her. She brings her eyes up, and meets his gaze. Her eyes move up and down, searching his. He has been asking the question, but now her look is asking him a silent one, searching for the motivation behind this mysterious last question. Again, if this frame (figure. 4.12) were in some other film, it might be the beginning of a kiss.

The viewer searches Andrews for motivation just as Tierney's eyes do. What has led his character to ask this particular question, and to phrase it in this particular way? The bizarreness of the question, before she brings her eyes up to meet his, is easy to miss, because the staging of the scene situates us to read the Andrews character as a tough detective in charge of an interrogation. But what he is betraying, in the way he phrases his asking of this question, is a personal stake in the outcome of the case. Did Laura tell McPherson that she was no longer with Shelby, earlier in the film, because that is what McPherson wanted to hear? But why would McPherson, or any detective, *want* to hear that she was no longer with Shelby? Certainly, this is something he might *need* to know,

Figure 4.12. Dana Andrews and Gene Tierney—it might be the beginning of a kiss—in *Laura* (Twentieth Century-Fox, 1944).

to polish off the case and connect the dots—but personal desire should not have anything to do with detective work. This code seems now to have suddenly popped itself back into McPherson's head. McPherson claims, as he continues to interrogate Laura, moving away from his intimate position next to her (perhaps unconsciously aware of the internal desire he has betrayed here, and seeking to distance himself from it), and circling around the desk once again, that Shelby has convinced Laura to keep up the semblance of their engagement so that people would not suspect him of murder. But why would McPherson *want* to hear this? Certainly it would lead him off the scent of Shelby as a suspect, but it is not clear even from this that McPherson should have any particular desire for one outcome or the other. Finally, after a few more police-like words, McPherson cuts to the quick. Andrews, leaning rigidly against the side of the desk, now closer to Laura but not as intimate as before, asks the key question. As he does so, he breathes quickly—the surface of Andrews's suit jacket rising with nervous palpitation:

MARK: Are you still in love with him?

After Laura answers, in close-up, that she does not know how she ever could have been, Preminger cuts back to a medium two-shot. This is a crucial shot in the scene, for it does not simply betray the detective's love for Laura but makes it palpable, and present, in the form of breath and body. Andrews relaxes his character's rigidity. He lowers his shoulders. He exhales in relief, almost in pleasure. If this were not the end of an interrogation, it might be the beginning of an orgasm. No, she is not in love with Shelby. She is his.

But this is no kind of possession. He tells her she can go home—he is satisfied with her explanations. As she gets up, to confront him about what has been happening in this interrogation room—she knows that nothing she has said should have cleared her in the case—she asks if he has been merely playing with her, turning this detective work into some kind of game (perhaps like the baseball game he keeps in his pocket). He tells her he did have a bit of doubt about her, that nagging one percent. But then he reveals his true reason for bringing her to the interrogation room, the reason that has been bubbling up in Andrews's performance throughout the sequence:

MARK: I'd . . . reached a point where I needed official surroundings.

For anyone attuned to the kinkiness of this scene—to the idea that we have been witnessing, for a few minutes, an ostensibly by-the-books police detective use the vehicle of an interrogation room as a means to discover if he might have a future with a woman he deeply desires—Laura's response only ups the ante. Rather than have her character get more upset, Tierney smiles as Andrews speaks these words. Preminger cuts to a close-up as a doe-eyed look of love descends upon Tierney's face:

LAURA: Then it was worth it, Mark.

The first few times I watched this film, I heard the line as a question: "Then it was worth it, Mark?" The breathy inflection at the end of Tierney's delivery of the line, I would contend, makes it possible to legitimately receive the line that way, even though the DVD's closed-captioning would seem to want to persuade us that it is a statement, not a question. If it is a question, then Laura is asking if the liberties McPherson has taken with his profession have been worth it—that is, if her possible love for him is worth losing the credibility he has in fulfilling his social role as a cop. If it is a statement, however, it means that the several tough minutes they have experienced together in these "official surroundings" have indeed been worth it, for they have discovered love, and perhaps even a future together complete with a kind of intimate kinkiness. But that, of course, is a future they share offscreen, beyond the frame of the narrative.

Laura seems to recognize, in Mark's rather perversely achieved status as a true gentleman in a film full of deceitful men, a possible mate. We might be left wondering how twisted Laura herself is for reading qualities of courtliness in a man who interrogates her for murder, who can only confirm his love for her by effectively chaining her to a desk and shining harsh light in her eyes. I leave *Laura*, and Tierney's performance, no longer knowing if the line above is a statement or a question, but I do not think it finally matters. The fact that Tierney's delivery makes both readings possible is a sign that her character is, still, at the end of this film, quite like the painting she was at the beginning—an object, a still image, onto which we project our own answers to a question we are not even sure she is asking.

Ostensibly, the narrative of *Laura* resolves these ambiguities by confirming the successful courting of Laura by McPherson: in the film's penultimate scene, before leaving her for the evening (and before Lydecker returns to try to murder her, having overheard the couple's discussion of the recovered shotgun), Andrews leans forward to kiss her across the door frame to her apartment (figure 4.13). This is the very same door she will lock and that Andrews will be unable to force open when he hears Lydecker attack her as he goes to leave (Andrews will have to burst in through a side entrance)—another possible gesture toward the

Figure 4.13. Dana Andrews, Gene Tierney, and a kiss across a door in *Laura* (Twentieth Century-Fox, 1944).

sort of physical relationship the couple will enjoy once the narrative is over, and away from our eyes. But all of this is conjecture. We are, throughout, kept on the surface of Laura by Tierney's positioning and poses, which hint at subjective depth in a woman who inhabits a world in which women are treated as objects. Indeed, given the way he handles his courtship of Laura, I am not quite so sure that McPherson won't go on treating Laura as the others have treated her. (Perhaps, if he is ever tempted to hurt her, he will pull out his baseball game, and regain his calm.) In *Laura*, performance paves the way for love. But love remains unperformed—in the film's noir world, a world in which love is found only in dream and in memory, it is unperformable.

5

Wooing Bogie, Courting Bacall

Humphrey Bogart and Lauren Bacall in *To Have and Have Not, The Big Sleep, Dark Passage,* and *Key Largo*

HUMPHREY BOGART AND Lauren Bacall restore noir's ties to screwball, with their emphasis on the rhythm, movement, and good talk two lovers might share together. They first discover a shared rhythm in *To Have and Have Not* (1944); perform a few indelibly lusty moments in *The Big Sleep* (1946, release version); confirm the durability of their relationship in *Dark Passage* (1947); and end, somewhat uncharacteristically, with *Key Largo* (1948), forming a makeshift family, a formation confirming ongoing belief in American ideals shaken by a decade of war. These films, too, tell the story of the discovery of a performer—Lauren Bacall—who, one uncharacteristic flop besides (*Confidential Agent*, opposite Charles Boyer, in 1945, in-between *To Have and Have Not* and *The Big Sleep*) would discover her own ways of moving, onscreen and off, with Bogart in the forties, before moving on to a variety of films opposite different leading men in the fifties and sixties (see this book's discussion of *The Cobweb*, and her work opposite Richard Widmark, in the next chapter, and *Written on the Wind*, opposite Rock Hudson and Robert Stack, in chapter 7).

Bogart's story precedes both Bacall and noir, of course. He began in the theater, playing butlers, juveniles, and second-bananas during the Depression (Sperber and Lax 17); around the same time, he earned low

Figure 5.1. Humphrey Bogart and Lauren Bacall, keeping an eye out, in *To Have and Have Not* (Warner Bros., 1944).

billings in supporting roles in Hollywood films, such as *Big City Blues* (1932) and *Three on a Match* (1932). In these films, Bogart strikes a screen presence different from the legendary one established in John Huston's *The Maltese Falcon* (1941) and Michael Curtiz's *Casablanca* (1942). If Brooks Atkinson once remarked of Bogart's performance in a stage play (*Chrysalis*, 1933) that he "plays the wastrel in his usual style" (quoted in Sperber and Lax 43), it was this sort of rather wooden wastrel (spiritual, physical, or otherwise) that he was usually called upon to play in his early films, a far cry from the gestural range and quiet dignity found in his later performances as Rick Blaine, Sam Spade, Harry Morgan, and Philip Marlowe. *Three on a Match*, the first film in which he plays a tough guy, offers a representative example of Bogart's performances during his early career. Bogart plays Ace, a tough involved in the kidnapping of a child belonging to Vivian (Ann Dvorak), the wife of a racketeer (Lyle Talbot). As Ace, Bogart speaks in a voice that, compared to the smoky baritone of his later work, is relatively high-pitched, with a nasal delivery of the typical early-thirties gangster. Bogart's work in *Three on a Match* is, further, unsubtle: to convey to his cronies that the Dvorak character is hooked on drugs, Bogart gestures as if to wipe cocaine from under his nose, an act unthinkable after the enforcement of the Production Code two years later. That moment, and the moment a beat later, when he violently pushes Dvorak into another room when she begins arguing with him, strikes a discordant chord for today's audiences, familiar with the more sympathetic and romantic aura of Bogart characters after *Casablanca*.

According to actress Louise Brooks, who knew Bogart during their early years in Hollywood, Bogart's way of moving, speaking, and gesturing onscreen began to change with *The Petrified Forest* (1936) opposite Bette Davis and Leslie Howard. Brooks writes that Bogart's training in the theater "exposed more showing off than acting, more of a flight than a play. Every actor's aim was to kill the other actor's lines—especially if the lines provoked laughter" (61). Brooks claims Bogart learned a more cinematic manner of film acting from Howard, on the set of *The Petrified Forest*:

> After thirteen years of conditioning by this kind of 'stage' acting, when Bogart got a job in Robert Sherwood's *The Petrified Forest* . . . nothing but searching ambition could have enabled him to see in Leslie Howard's quiet, natural acting technique a style he could adapt to his own personality, a style that would prepare him for *The African Queen* [1951]. In that film he developed a character with his voice alone. Nothing but inflexible willpower could have enabled him to tear down his ingrained acting habits in order to submit all over again to the self-conscious agony of learning to act. Working with Leslie gave him command of the Duke Mantee part in the play and, later, in the film. (61–62)

It is questionable how much this evolution in Bogart's acting style is due to the influence of Leslie Howard; as Brooks admits later in this passage, "the films of the following five years reveal the terrible struggle for supremacy between the new Bogey technique and the old theatrical habits of Humphrey" (62). As Virginia Wright Wexman notes, Bogart's performance in *The Petrified Forest* continues to incorporate some of the "broad, overdrawn effects that he had carried over from the stage" (26), and that we find visible in films like *Three on a Match*. Nevertheless, a quieter, more inwardly drawn Bogart is visible during certain moments of *The Petrified Forest*. For example, after his character, Duke Mantee, takes hold of a highway gas station with a gun, Bogart spends most of his screen time sitting down, quietly assessing the situation, shoulders straight back against the chair and arms hanging down, like a marionette, between his seated legs. This relatively immobile position throws into relief quieter expressions, such as the shifty movement of his eyes, the quivering of his right cheek, and, as Brooks describes in her piece, the expressive use of his voice, closer to the baritone familiar to later audiences (and all the more distinguished in *The Petrified Forest* through its contrast to the relatively higher pitch of Leslie Howard's delivery). Narratively, too, Duke Mantee in *The Petrified Forest* is more complexly positioned than Bogart's earlier tough guys: although his hold-up of the gas station necessarily exhibits a tough-edged masculinity, he also exudes an intellectual contemplativeness as he listens to the Leslie Howard character share his philosophy of life, which includes a love of women—an appreciation the Bogart character seems genuinely to share.

By the time of *The Maltese Falcon* the performative transformation begun in *The Petrified Forest* was largely complete. Wexman points out that Bogart had developed, in his role as the neurotic and self-defensive Sam Spade in Huston's film, a range of expressive mannerisms that would be lost, in their finer-grained details, on the theatrical stage: smoking constantly; projecting watery eyes and moist lips; pulling stressfully on his lip; "stroking his jaw, rubbing his nose, or pulling at his lower lip" (29). Sam Spade's rough attitudes toward Mary Astor's Brigid O'Shaughnessy in *The Maltese Falcon*, however, are hardly the stuff of swooning romance. As Rick Worland notes, it would be *High Sierra* (1941), and its "poignant or romantic scenes . . . or similarly relaxed moments with [Ida] Lupino" in which viewers began to see "the mannerisms we know from his most famous roles—the comfortable slouch punctuated by reflexive lifts of his shoulders, the teeth-baring grin, and dry laugh" (76). By the time of *Casablanca*, Bogart's performative transition was more or less complete, and Warner Bros. was beginning to market him as a romantic figure, emphasizing a romantic aura in advertisements for the Michael Curtiz film as they had a year earlier with *High Sierra*, in which Bogart is sold as a man with skills in "tough but tender love-making" (qtd. in Worland 78).

Lauren Bacall would meet Bogart less than two years later, brought by Howard Hawks to Hollywood, after Hawks's wife, Nancy "Slim" Hawks, spotted Bacall, then a seventeen-year-old Betty Perske, on a *Vogue* cover. Famously, they were later married, but Bacall, in her biography *By Myself*, suggests that Bogart's screen persona, in the years before she met him, was not initially appealing:

> One Saturday morning in 1942, Mother and [Aunt] Rosalie took me to the Capitol Theatre to see a movie called *Casablanca*. We all loved it, and Rosalie was mad about Humphrey Bogart.

I thought he was good in it, but mad about him? Not at all. She thought he was sexy. I thought she was crazy . . . Bogart didn't vaguely resemble Leslie Howard. Not in any way. So much for my judgment at the time. (70–71)

Physical differences between Bogart and Leslie Howard notwithstanding, what Bacall was perhaps missing at the Capitol Theatre in 1942 was not only the extent to which Bogart had been influenced by Howard's own playing style just six years earlier, but also the extent to which his persona and performances were shaped by the cultural figure of the dandy, a type that Howard himself also inhabits in a number of pictures (and perhaps most emblematically in his role as Sir Percy Blakeney in *The Scarlet Pimpernel* [1934]). In his "The Painter of Modern Life," Charles Baudelaire writes that "[t]he distinguishing characteristic of the dandy's beauty consists above all in an air of coldness which comes from an unshakeable determination not to be moved; you might call it a latent fire which hints at itself, and which could, but chooses not to burst into flame" (29). Perhaps surprisingly for modern audiences who tend to associate Bogart only with toughness and a romantic self-sufficiency—the sort of cultural image Jean-Paul Belmondo would try to imitate as he gazes at a photo of "Bogie" in a shop window in Jean-Luc Godard's *Breathless* (1960)—Bogart's screen image exudes many of the dandy's traits as outlined by Baudelaire, including stoicism, elegant attire, and maintenance of one's self and self-philosophy beyond the laws imposed by one's society. As Jim Hansen points out, earlier inhabitations of the dandy type, such as "the martini-sipping dandy played by [William] Powell" were "being superseded by the tailored, world-weary, hard-drinking film noir protagonist played most memorably by . . . Bogart" (153). Although many of Bogart's criminal characters in his early films are well-dressed and coiffed in a manner recalling the superficial aspects of the dandy image, it is only in Bogart's screen persona after *The Maltese Falcon*, and especially in the first film with Bacall, that he begins to transpose aspects of Baudelaire's figure into the world of noir.

In his performance of courtship alongside Bacall in their first two films together, Bogart also evokes aspects of the dandy's attitude toward love, as defined by Baudelaire:

> If I speak of love in connection with dandyism, this is because love is the natural occupation of the idle. The dandy does not, however, regard love as a special target to be aimed at . . . [The dandy's passion] is first and foremost the burning need to create for oneself a personal originality, bounded

only by the limits of the properties. It is a kind of cult of the self which can nevertheless survive the pursuit of a happiness to be found in someone else—in woman, for example; which can survive all that goes by in the name of illusions. It is the joy of astonishing others, and the proud satisfaction of never oneself being astonished. (27–28)

Bogart is not quite "idle" in his films with Bacall—in *To Have and Have Not* and *The Big Sleep*, his character is at least intermittently employed (first, as a seaman, then, as a detective). But in these films, he does project, as Robin Wood has written, the image of "a man who exists exclusively from his own center, his actions stemming from the immediate perceptions and impulses of his consciousness" (21). If Wood's conception favors a more traditional image of the hero, it nevertheless offers a fair picture of how Bogart's tough guys share the dandy's attitudes about love. In the first two films, and especially *To Have and Have Not*, Bogart's regard for Bacall is never one of salient, melodramatic astonishment. If she astonishes him, and him her—as they, of course, do—it is a quiet, inwardly drawn astonishment, performed with fine-grained gestures, movements, and expressions. Additionally, in neither of these films is the Bogart figure felt to *need* Bacall (as the Cary Grant character in *Bringing Up Baby* needs Katharine Hepburn in order to learn how to have a good time). However, his "pursuit of a happiness" can very much be stretched to accommodate her (and vice versa), and he can, in quiet ways, learn from her, and she him. They create a vision of shared self-sufficiency not surpassed in this book.

In publicity surrounding the release of *To Have and Have Not* in 1944, Warner Bros. christened Lauren Bacall "the look" (see Morris, "Lauren Bacall"). This phrase refers to her way of looking at Bogart—chin lowered, eyes gazing up, face framed by twin curtains of blonde hair. That the marketing materials should guide us to Bacall's eyes—the way she looks at a man—rather than the way she looks to him, suggests Bacall herself can be regarded, at least in *To Have and Have Not* and *The Big Sleep*, as something of a female dandy, the androgynously feminine counterpart to Bogart's hero. She is a woman who does not need him but rather desires him for reasons fully her own. The first meeting between Bogart and Bacall in *To Have and Have Not*, indeed, showcases "the look." But it already moves beyond it, suggesting there is more to Bacall's performance than her eyes.

Bogart's character, Harry Morgan, captain of a fishing boat, returns from an expedition. The proprietor of the Martinique Hotel, Frenchy (Marcel Dalio) encounters Harry at the bar downstairs, and asks if he might loan his boat to some "friends of friends of mine"—code for French Resistance smugglers. Harry declines; Frenchy persists, continuing the conversation upstairs. It is in the hallway outside Harry's room, walking to his quarters on the right side while Frenchy follows, where Bacall first spies Bogart. Bogart swings his jacket over his shoulder while removing his key; Bacall gently closes the door to her own quarters on the left side of the frame. Right before the cut to a medium-shot of Morgan walking into his room, Bacall glances sideways—she has seen Morgan in the corner of her eye. The effect here is to place emphasis not on the figure she is looking at but rather the way she is looking at him. After we hear Bacall ask "Anyone got a match?" offscreen, cut to a shot of her, on the left side of the frame with Bogart closer to us, on the right—her right hand cupping the tip of the cigarette as she looks up at Bogart, from under brows and parted hair, chin lowered only slightly and only for a beat, before she raises her glance to a more level eyeline. This is "the look." She is scoping him out (figure 5.2).

Figure 5.2. Lauren Bacall scoping out Humphrey Bogart in *To Have and Have Not* (Warner Bros., 1944).

But she does more than just look at him. Bogart, in the same shot, throws a pack of matches to Bacall, which she catches, without changing position, with an outstretched right arm: she does not yet need to move to match his rhythm. In fact, she is far ahead of him. Cut, briefly, to a medium-shot of Morgan, wary. Then cut to a closer shot of Bacall, framed in a medium distance rhyming with the preceding shot of Bogart. But she doesn't adjust her posture—in this shot she is a beat ahead of Morgan, ready for whatever he might have to offer, and positioned perfectly to begin to remove a match from the box Bogart has thrown. She is commanding the rhythm here, setting the pace. In the middle of her gesture of opening the match box, cut to a closer medium-shot of Bogart, now not so wary, his eyes moving up and down in an appreciative glance as Bacall's offscreen play with the matches dances before his eyes. Then, one more "look": cut to a closer shot of Bacall, lit match raised in her right hand, illuminating the contours of her hair and the side of her face, her eyes glancing, again, sidelong at Morgan—conscious of, but not entirely concerned with, the fact that she is being watched and appreciated (figure 5.3). Bacall discards the match over her shoulder (figure 5.4), without looking, into the hallway—and, then, after thanking Morgan, casually tosses the matchbox back to him. It is not that the match has not meant anything to her. It is only that she continues to stand independently, with her own rhythm, which uses but is not dependent on others. After Bacall leaves, cut back to a shot of Bogart; he has caught the matches she has thrown to him. Perhaps he can join this rhythm.

The central importance of these subtle expressive gestures—the caress of the cigarette tip, the lighting of the match, the casual discarding of objects—goes some way to establish Bacall's character, Marie

Figures 5.3 and 5.4. Lauren Bacall, dancing with a match, in *To Have and Have Not* (Warner Bros., 1944).

Browning, as a dandy, distinctive and aloof. She is thereby the perfect match for the Bogart persona as it had developed up to 1944. Her first appearance onscreen in *To Have and Have Not* also suggests how far Bacall, in her first film, transcends the studio definition of her image as one centered wholly on the way she holds her chin and eyes. Her way of looking is important, of course, but it is only one technique Bacall uses in the creation of a distinctive performative presence and tempo. If Bogart's character, quietly and appreciatively watching the way Marie gestures and moves in their first encounter, recognizes that the independence and uniqueness of her particular rhythm is tied to the way she handles things and moves about, some writers on Bacall know this, too. James Agee, in a review of *To Have and Have Not*, writes that Bacall exudes "a javelin-like vitality, a born dancer's eloquence in movement" (340), while journalist Mary Morris, writing for *Variety* in 1944, began her interview with Bacall with the following words:

> Lauren Bacall is the girl who moves in big, slow, curvy glides through that sex-charged film, *To Have and Have Not*. When the camera comes into closeup, she ducks her chin and looks up from under her brows while her long hair does a measured sweep across the frame . . . She delivers her lines in a sort of female growl. Her first one, "Anybody got a match?" is followed by silence. Then Humphrey Bogart hurls a matchbox the width of the room. It cracks against her hands as she makes the catch. (7)

Morris dutifully describes "the look"—but her paragraph also usefully describes this expression alongside other performative techniques that Bacall displays in the moment, including her voice, the sound of the matchbox cracking against Bacall's hand, and the way she moves across the screen. Indeed, as Joe McElhaney has written, there is much more to this actress than her "look"—her "literal way of moving through the spaces of the film has its own implications" (2014). And so it should be in a Hawks film—in which, as we have seen earlier in this book (in *Twentieth Century* and *Bringing Up Baby*) a performer defines her character's presence in the world through the way she moves, and the way others orbit her. From her first moment onscreen, Bacall proves herself worthy of inheriting this Hawksian tradition, and begins to develop a performative rhythm that, indeed, throws down a gauntlet: can Bogart match it?

To Have and Have Not asks an even more interesting question, though: Does she (Bacall the actor, and Marie the character) *possess* this rhythm? Certainly the screwball comedies of the thirties implied that characters possess rhythm: the command over movement exuded when John Barrymore's Oscar Jaffe directs a scene; or the way William Powell circles a room while serving a tray of martinis to party guests; or how Katharine Hepburn sweeps up Cary Grant in her whirlwind—these figures all exude a performative distinction and rhythm that far outpace others in their worlds. *To Have and Have Not*, though, depicts something rather different: a public space in which collectivity and togetherness is a glimpsed possibility, a world in which rhythm, even the most distinctive rhythms created between two lovers, might be socially shared, rather than only individually possessed. Later in the film, Bogart is enjoying a coffee and a cigarette at a table. He lights his cigarette, looks up, and squints, spying Marie across the room. In the corresponding long-shot (established somewhat ambiguously as Morgan's point-of-view), she sits with a man, Johnson (Walter Sande), who owes Morgan money, on the left side of the frame, while Hoagy Carmichael, playing the piano player Cricket, taps out a tune ("Am I Blue?") on the right. Cut to a closer two-shot of Marie and Johnson. Bacall looks up, with a hint of suspicion, at Johnson. Cricket begins his song, just offscreen, as Bacall looks up and sees Bogart looking at her, in a long-shot. Cricket keeps on singing, as, now, Marie, who has perhaps been lingering in her own headspace, seems to notice Cricket for the first time, turning her head to the right as the camera pans to follow her gaze to the piano. After Carmichael sings a little more, he takes a toothpick out of his mouth, places it on the piano, and matches Marie's glance with his own, in her direction, offscreen. It is an implicit invitation to join him at the piano. She does—after a few more moments. First, Hawks cuts to a shot of Cricket's percussionist, a man reading a newspaper; he puts the paper down to support Cricket's singing, and the rhythm of the entire scene, with the gentle, percussive caress of a pair of feather drumsticks. The cut to this drummer reminds us, as Cricket's inviting glance to Marie also does, that rhythm is something that spreads, that invites others to join in. Some others aren't invited, though—when Hawks cuts back to a medium-shot of Marie, we see her rebuke Johnson's own caress of her shoulder, an annoyance that prompts her to answer Cricket's call to join him at the piano. She gets up, quietly saunters over to the piano, and rests her right elbow against it, glancing offscreen left (at Bogart, no doubt) before joining in the song (figure 5.5). "Take over," Cricket tells her—but the whole point of the scene is that no one is going to "take over" this song. It involves everyone—even Bogart, who, while still seated at this table, is enjoying the performance, as a cutaway shot confirms (figure 5.6).

So here is a world where rhythm is collective, an almost infectious property spreading between people. This would be seem to be true

Figures 5.5 and 5.6. A shared world of performance in *To Have and Have Not* (Warner Bros., 1944).

whether one is an actor, Lauren Bacall, working for Howard Hawks, a director who makes films "largely articulated through the physicality and rhythm of the actors" (McElhaney, "Howard Hawks" 33), or whether one is a character, Marie Browning, who sings a tune alongside a pianist in a bar in Martinique, before moving across that same space with an inimitably unique, but still socially situated, physicality. This is what distinguishes the film from *Casablanca*; where the Michael Curtiz film has the Bogart character give up love for a greater cause, in *To Have and Have Not* Bogart accommodates the cause only when it moves to the rhythm of the love he has discovered in this little French club.

But although rhythm is a shared, collective property in *To Have and Have Not*, not every figure onscreen exudes the same qualities of physicality and movement. The way Bacall glides across the screen, after singing the song, in the scene's next moment, demonstrates her peerless command of space and movement. Joe McElhaney has described the moment beautifully:

> She moves in a zigzag pattern through the crowd, shoulders turning left/right, left/right, eyes straight ahead, aside from a glance down at Bogart as she is about to pass his table . . . As she walks, Cricket and his band play an up-tempo version of "Limehouse Blues." Bacall's walk here is so fast as to be . . . almost imperceptible in its mechanics. With her legs out of the frame, the effect is more of a glide than a walk, something stealthy and expressing a desire to be unseen even as it is fully visible and aware that it is being watched. The Look is, above all, a woman who looks back, defiantly, and then moves on. At the same time, this fast glide past the

bar betrays no visible strain of hurrying, no overt signs of desperation. (2014)

And the walk continues—right up the steps, Bacall's strain-free walk expressing the assertion of a woman who knows exactly where she wants to go, and is moving there. Bogart is intrigued by all this, and catching her walk past him in a sidelong glance, he gets up to follow her—she is still leading this courtship, shaping its rhythm.

Cut to the top of the steps, and to Marie, who digs in her purse for her room key while walking quickly (a little quicker now that she is out of public view) to her room. "Limehouse Blues," drifting up the steps, continues offscreen. It is soon joined, offscreen for a moment, by the sound of Bogart's footsteps. Bacall turns around. Bogart knows she's up to something—he grabs her by the elbow and guides her into his room, and locks the door, shutting out the sound of Cricket's song and the applause downstairs. Here the film makes its first fascinating transition from the public space of the bar downstairs to the intimate, private space in the room above, where the Bogart-Bacall romance will be clinched. The mood has suddenly changed: the jovial rhythms of the music on the lower level now blocked out after Bogart locks the door, Harry Morgan is bidding to control the movements of the scene in a more overt display of tough authority. But Bogart has noticed, and appreciates, how she moves, and aptly christens her with a moniker that means to describe her way of slinking through the world: "Slim." She immediately resists this label: "I'd rather you wouldn't call me Slim; I'm a little too skinny to take it kindly." Bogart moves closer to her—now at a breath's length. "You know, Steve, I wouldn't put it past you—"—the *it* here tantalizingly ambiguous, as ambiguous as the moniker "Steve," which she bestows upon him. After saying this, Bacall reaches into the breast pocket of her jacket and nonchalantly hands the wallet to him, stepping away, the light of the lamp on the room's desk illuminating her downcast face. This light is something like the glow of the match in the earlier scene, except now the illumination guides her movement, to a desk chair, upon which she sits while Bogart rummages through the wallet. Bogart, eyes still fixed, mostly, on the wallet, moves closer to her, finding the cash Johnson owes him and a plane ticket indicating he was planning to skip out of town before paying. "After all, I am entitled to something—don't you think so, Slim?" Then cut to a shot, from over Bogart's shoulder, of Bacall giving him a slightly contemptuous glance. She does not like this nickname, but she accepts a cigarette from Bogart. He leans in to light it.

This scene plays out somewhat differently in a revised treatment by Whitman Chambers, dated January 1944, which itself revises an earlier treatment written by Jules Furthman, one of the film's two credited screenwriters. In this treatment, Marie ends up in Harry's room because she has stumbled, feigning drunk, to the wrong door. Morgan notices her:

MORGAN: That's the wrong door, Slim.

MARIE: For me it's the right door. I'm ducking, account of being a little gone at the knees—

MORGAN: You're not so drunk, Slim.

MARIE: All right, I'm ducking because I want to duck. And nobody ever calls me Slim, because I'm too skinny to take it kindly.

MORGAN: All right, Skinny. Go ahead and duck—but first (he holds out his hand, palm up)—give!

MARIE: Sure.

[She comes to him and gives him a swift, hard kiss. She backs away, smiling.]

(Chambers, revised treatment).

On film, though, Marie is never drunk. The film also avoids the easy, rather witless humor of the Bogart character switching to "Skinny" upon Marie's protestation of the nickname "Slim." But what is perhaps most surprising about this earlier version of the script, in light of the eventual characterizations achieved on film by Bogart and Bacall, is that it has Marie plant a "hard kiss" on Morgan's lips to distract him from the question of the wallet. Bacall's Marie would never do this—her first kiss with Morgan is hardly casual and not at all a throwaway moment. Indeed, it is the culmination of the courtship's initial phase, a carefully orchestrated event (over which Bacall has sober control) fundamentally changing the relationship between the two characters. The eventual kiss is the event during which Bogart catches up to Bacall's rhythms, rhythms they will share, and share with others, as the film reaches its conclusion.

This famous kiss—two kisses, actually—happens a little later in the film, the kiss that ends with Bacall telling Bogart that it's better if he helps, the sparkling moment everyone who has seen the film remembers. But the performative moments preceding, surrounding, and following these first kisses are crucial—they indicate what, precisely, has been won for Marie and Morgan in their newfound intimacy. At another hotel, Marie tricks a bottle of wine out of a fellow, and brings it back to Harry's hotel room in the next scene at the Martinique. Marie hands the bottle to Morgan, he pours two drinks, and Bacall moves over to a mirror and checks her hair—all the while teasing "Steve" about his being upset she has stolen the wine. She moves over to a mirror, briefly stopping in front of it to tidy her hair. In a film that is otherwise about social camaraderie and rhythm—about the way one moves, in time with others—this is the only time a character stands still to contemplate herself with the help of a reflective surface. It's a dandyish moment, but where Baudelaire's dandy preens, the moment when Bacall stands in front of the mirror is only ostensibly about physical appearance; after all, Bacall doesn't need much tidying—she is already beautiful. Instead, the mirror, as it often does in cinema, implies here that she has something quite complex on her mind. What makes this moment preceding the famous kiss remarkable, then, is how much it focuses on Marie's interiority—and the imagination which has produced a mysterious figure, "Steve," bestowed upon Harry Morgan as a nickname. Unlike his name for her, "Slim"—which refers to her slenderness, a visible physical trait—"Steve" seems to refer not to Morgan himself (whom Marie barely knows), nor to any physical trait he bears, but rather to some fictional figure that Marie is conjuring, a figure that she takes pleasure in projecting onto Morgan, to his, and our, puzzlement.

That something quite complex is happening inside Marie's mind in this scene is indicated not only by Bacall's positioning—after she is done in front of the mirror, she moves back over to the desk, and then the couch, contemplating her tendency to steal from men with gently downcast eyes—but in the rhythmic patterns of the dialogue. She seems to be responding to some invisible figure in the room:

MARIE: Would you rather I wouldn't?

MORGAN: Wouldn't what?

MARIE: Do things like that.

MORGAN: Why ask me?

MARIE: I'd like to know.

MORGAN: Of all the screwy—

MARIE: All right, all right. I won't do it anymore.

MORGAN: Look, I didn't ask—

MARIE: I know you didn't. Don't worry. I'm not giving up anything I care about.

Marie, here, is not simply talking to a man; she is trying to shape one in the image of her replies (as he has perhaps shaped her, in his mind's eye, as "Slim"). There is a slightly kinky, sadomasochistic shade to this dialogue, exuding as it does Marie's desire that the "Steve" she wants Morgan to become should punish her for her transgression. The dialogue, as delivered onscreen, takes on a jagged rhythm complementing this kinky content, a "languid, liquid, stately largo" (Mast 259), with each line effortlessly breaking into the next.

Who is this "Steve," this mysterious figure Marie is imagining Harry Morgan to be, this figure she seems to call into existence in her replies to questions Bogart has not asked—this Steve who would punish her for using her wits to scavenge and survive? Finishing pouring the drinks, Bogart moves over to the couch, where Bacall now sits. "How long have you been away from home?" he asks. This question initiates a series of close-ups, as Morgan begins to resist the role he has been cast into by Marie; he refuses to become the companion who does not want her to steal, who wants to punish her. Instead, he insists he already knows precisely what kind of person she is—one who can take a slap, having already taken several—and by doing so, he somewhat callously reduces the mystery she has worked to project throughout the first half of the movie. (Perhaps this brief cutting-down-to-size is his version of the punishment she has imagined.) Bogart looks down at Bacall, here, but Bacall answers his ostensible position of power with a strong gaze and a defiant rise to her feet when she refuses to answer these questions. She slams the door on the way out, causing Bogart to jump—just a bit, but enough, perhaps, to shake him out of his reductive assessment of her.

Morgan, after a moment, goes to her room with the wine, while Bacall moves over to her suitcase and begins rummaging through a few of her things as she talks (she's disappointed at how quickly and thoughtlessly he has sized her up). He walks up next to her, holding the bottle up to the side of the table with the tips of his fingers. "I brought that bottle up here to make you feel cheap," she admits. Cut to a closer two-shot as Bacall begins to walk toward the camera, with the camera tracking back to keep her in the center of the frame as she leans on the table. Bacall, facing away from Bogart, wrings her hands and wipes wet from her eyes—a nervous, sentimental display her character has up to now not revealed—and then implores him to leave. As she says this, Bogart, standing behind, lets slip a slight, sympathetic grin, and begins rummaging through her suitcase, too, finding a vial of perfume that he considers with both hands. Bacall turns around to face him. He raises the perfume up and smells. "Remind you of somebody, Steve?" So she is still calling him Steve—but now, the meaning of it has changed. No longer is she projecting an image onto him; she is asking a question about his past, wondering about the women he has possibly known, about who he really is. His answer—"This is brand new to me—I like it"—confirms his Slim *is* totally new to him, too, despite his earlier efforts to pin her down to a type. Bacall is quivering; this is the apology she has wanted. Yet she doesn't make a move. It takes Bogart to do this, in a cut into a close two-shot—as he gently pinches her chin with a thumb and a forefinger, guiding her face toward his, preparing to kiss her (figure 5.7). But he doesn't. Her eyes, illuminated by a shaft of light bordered by shadows created by Bogart's closeness, betray a youthful vulnerability hitherto masked. It is a romantic moment, but now Morgan knows the

Figure 5.7. Prelude to a kiss: Humphrey Bogart and Lauren Bacall in *To Have and Have Not* (Warner Bros., 1944).

woman he thought was streetwise is in fact somewhat less experienced. Cut back to a longer shot, as Bogart places the perfume in her hands. "Quit worrying, kid; you'll be all right," he says before he leaves.

After Morgan leaves, a dissolve brings us to his room, as he tightens a screw on a fishing rod. Bacall enters his room, again with the bottle, the prop linking all three of the scenes leading up to the first kiss. Some banter establishes that Marie doesn't want Morgan to help Frenchy's Resistance friends—she even offers to pay him to stay—while Bogart lights a cigarette which dangles out of the right side of his mouth. The camera tracks backward to keep Bacall in frame as she approaches Bogart, seated with his cigarette. The words she speaks establish that, to her, he is still "Steve"; but now her Steve is no longer an imaginary figure she is projecting out of her imagination. It is the man she is about to kiss:

> MARIE: You know, Steve, you're not very hard to figure. Only at times. Sometimes I know exactly what you're going to say. Most of the time. The other times . . .

Bacall sits on Bogart's lap as the camera pans down to follow her movement.

> MARIE: The other times you're just a stinker.

She kisses him.

> MORGAN: What'd you do that for?

> MARIE: I'd been wondering whether I'd like it.

> MORGAN: What's the decision?

> MARIE: I don't know yet.

They do it again. This time, we are in a closer two-shot, and the kiss lasts twice as long. Now Bogart leans forward, fully a participant. As she draws away from him and gets up to move to the door, she purrs: "It's even better when you help" (figure 5.8).

Bacall has brought this kiss, and the stunning film moment surrounding it, into being. But the scene ends with Bogart, finally, matching her in rhythm and movement, becoming a participant in rather than being engulfed by the kiss. This kiss has happened after Morgan has questioned Marie's strength, her honesty, and her experience—but the

Figure 5.8. Lauren Bacall, with some help from Humphrey Bogart, in *To Have and Have Not* (1944).

fullness of the moment is proof that she is not the "Slim" he has imagined. And when he leans forward, enthusiastically helping a bit with the second kiss, he proves he is not quite the punitive Steve she had earlier projected onto him. For a stretch of film, which began with the Bacall character nearly begging for punishment, this kiss is perhaps less kinky than we expect. Shot in a soft close-up that is not entirely characteristic of Hawks, and lasting long enough to temporarily blot out of mind whatever political pressures will impinge on Harry Morgan as the film proceeds, the kiss, in this otherwise most social of films, has drawn us into the most intimate center of this most intimately drawn of spaces.

The rest of the film will function as if it were one long tracking shot pulling back from this kiss—not in order to lose sight of the passion, but rather to continue to inscribe privately felt rhythms of love in a larger social context. As a moment of courtship, the kiss presents the couple discovering love not only through confirming their trust in one another, but in discovering a shared rhythm: Bacall has proven her fortitude to Bogart with this kiss, and Bogart has, finally, after following her throughout the first half of the movie, caught up with the way she moves, and the way she moves into a kiss. The rest of the film will draw on this rhythm as Bogart and Bacall commit to a cause without losing any of their individual distinction.

❦

Rather than establishing only another heterosexual couple, Bogart and Bacall shimmy out of *To Have and Have Not* with Bogart's pal, Walter Brennan's faithful Eddie, by their side. They form, effectively, a threesome, one that does not sacrifice, for the sake of a collective, the individually distinctive quality of the way each moves: Bogart, with a confident stride; Bacall, with a hip-shaking shimmy and a gleeful grin at Bogart; and Walter Brennan, with percussive bounce as he carries their suitcases out of Martinique to the boat that awaits to take them to the next adventure. But where *To Have and Have Not* proceeds from the long shot of social rhythms, to the intimate two-shot of a tender kiss, and then back out again, the courtship between Bogart's Philip Marlowe and Bacall's Vivian Rutledge in *The Big Sleep* has an altogether staccato structure, their intimate moments shielded from the prying eyes of others and never quite reintegrated into a healthy, collective social world. Indeed, as the silhouettes of the couple cast on a screen behind the film's opening title sequence imply, Bogart and Bacall had already become archetypes in this second film, the very established and "known" figures that Marie Browning so strongly resists being reduced to in *To Have and Have Not*. So, to add some mystery to the mix, and some competition for Bacall, *The Big Sleep* throws a seemingly endless supply of young actresses at Bogart—the very number of which might horrify the Bacall of *To Have and Have Not*, who becomes playfully jealous when she spies Bogart talking with another woman. *The Big Sleep* is about a murder plot, yes (one that has been analyzed in terms of narrative form; see Bordwell, *Narration in the Fiction Film* 64–70), but it is more tantalizingly about the way in which Bacall must throw herself into relief against Martha Vickers (playing Vivian's sister, Carmen Sternwood), Dorothy Malone (as the Acme Book Shop clerk), Sonia Darrin (Agnes, the "clerk" of a bookstore that is the front for a pornography ring), and Joy Barlow (playing a taxi driver). Martha Vickers, Raymond Chandler famously felt, won this competition: according to the author of the source novel, "she shattered Miss Bacall completely" (McCarthy 385). If *To Have and Have Not* is about the establishment of a common rhythm, *The Big Sleep* is, metaphorically at least, and in terms of the cultural image established by the Bogart-Bacall star pairing, about fidelity. This makes the film something of a bedfellow with the screwball comedies discussed in the first part of this book; at the beginning of the film, we "know" Bogart and Bacall are the couple brought together in silhouette, but the film's various challenges to Bacall's sexual sovereignty over Bogart serve, intriguingly, to create a thematic of commitment in *The Big Sleep* that is an interesting, noir-ish variation on the "comedies of remarriage" form that Stanley Cavell has discussed in *The Pursuit of Happiness*.

The first to compete with Bacall in *The Big Sleep* is Martha Vickers, who saunters up to Bogart's Marlowe, when he arrives at the Sternwood Mansion to hear the details of the case he is to take on. She strides down the staircase and walks to a glass vase perched on a table, giving Bogart a clean view of her. And her of him—"You're not very tall, are you?" she remarks. She slowly moves forward, twirls her hair and brings it to her mouth, chewing on the end of it, teasing him, before moving forward and then falling backward into his arms, looking up at him in a pose that recalls some of the production photos snapped of Bogart and Bacall for the marketing of the film. The next woman Marlowe will meet, besides Bacall, is a bookstore proprietress named Agnes (Sonia Darrin). The bookstore is a front for a crime ring controlled by Geiger, whom Marlowe has pegged as a possible suspect; the proprietress, Mona Mars (Peggy Knudsen), doesn't have the knowledge of antique books to see through Marlowe's phony questions, and, unlike Vickers, who flops onto him, Knudsen stands stiffly and upright—statuesque, and uninterested in Marlowe. She is no competition. But the next woman Marlowe encounters, across the street, in another bookstore, as he waits to spy on Geiger, *is*—and although the character is not named, she is played by Dorothy Malone, and is unforgettable. Her performance is a collection of carefully patterned, sexually suggestive gestures and expressions: the caress of a pencil, as Bogart walks in to ask about Geiger's store across the street; the folding of her arms, which produces the effect of raising the pencil upwards, erect; the suspicious glance, up and down Bogart, with an open mouth; the nuzzling up next to Bogart, as he "begins to interest" her, "vaguely"; the way Bogart leans into her, slightly, as she leans there, explaining that he is a "private dick on a case"; the way Malone appreciates Bogart as "medium height," as she looks him over in an ostensible effort to describe Geiger; the way she teasingly bites her tongue between her teeth when Marlowe, upon this exact description of Geiger, complements her detective skills; the way she lightly strokes the tip of the pencil as Bogart stands at the window, contemplating whether or not he should brave the rain (which is now pouring down outside); and the way she takes off her glasses and undoes her hair in front of a mirror, and then circles her mouth with her tongue—all of this before one of the more suggestive dissolves in cinema history, complemented by the clap of thunder outside, a sonic punctuation mark to all this sensuous, flirty quivering.

By the time, in the subsequent sequence, Marlowe meets a taxi cab driver (Joy Barlow) who offers her his services day or night, the viewer might be left wondering if these patterns of possible sexual encounters between the character and a motley of available women are a regular event, an everyday occurrence, one that Bogart's dandyish Marlowe greets with something only slightly more than a bemused shrug. And if they are—and the movie gives us no reason to believe they aren't—what of Bacall, in this film, attracts Bogart in particular, and more than these others?

In an article on the kinesics and proxemics of performance, Warren Buckland uses Bogart's encounters with four of the women Marlowe encounters (Vivian, Carmen, Malone's bookstore proprietress, and Agnes), to study the way "actors in a classical Hollywood film construct their characters by reproducing and exaggerating a small number of significant postures, gestures, and stances that signify courtship readiness in Western society, a system of rituals that maintains and reinforces normative heterosexual behavior" ("Bodies in Filmic Space"). He ably shows how each encounter functions as something of a courtship ritual. But beyond stating that the interactions between Bogart and Bacall amount to a test of "each other before initiating a serious relationship," he does not say *why* Bogart should want to pursue a serious relationship with Bacall's Vivian and not the others. Perhaps it is obvious enough in the cases of Carmen (who may be, the film implies, seriously ill and in more immediate need of something other than romance) and Agnes (who is a front for a pornographic book ring), but it is less so in the case of Malone's unnamed bookstore clerk, who plausibly has sex with Marlowe while he waits for the rain to abate and in any case gives the substantial impression of being an intelligent, independent, and adventurous companion who might well match Bacall in her movements, if given the time. Some thinkers have pointed to a resolution to this question by noting that Marlowe's other encounters with women amount to little more than a distraction from *The Big Sleep*'s "real" plot—as when Gerald Mast suggests that the film is not about its detective plot but really about "Marlowe's and Vivian's discovery of one another" (276), specifically their discovery of the ability to trust one another. Without contesting Mast's point that their romance is substantial to the narrative trajectory of the film, I think the discovery is not so much one of trust in *The Big Sleep* but rather of sexual and sensuous compatibility: since Bogart-as-Marlowe already has quite a few other available female options, there must be something in particular about Bacall-as-Vivian that attracts him, that makes him, in other words, want to need to trust her—after all, like

Carmen Sternwood, or the bookstore proprietress, or the taxi driver, he could just move on after closing the case. Something beyond plot and trust makes him linger on her, and her on him.

The Bogart and Bacall courtship in *The Big Sleep* begins in the Sternwood mansion. Bogart has just spoken to General Sternwood in the sweltering greenhouse after enduring the encounter with flirty Carmen. Bacall's performance in the scene, and Bogart's responsiveness to it, begins to establish what makes Vivian a distinctive presence in contrast to Carmen. When Marlowe first enters Vivian's sitting room, Bacall is pouring water into a glass from a bottle; she glances sideways, suspiciously, at Bogart before returning her attention to the glass. She slides away from the tray and walks toward Bogart, hooking her right thumb in the pocket of her pants as she remarks upon Marlowe's disheveled appearance (the greenhouse has left him sweaty). After a cut to a close two-shot, Bogart responds to Bacall's first insolent volley with an awkward snort; "I'm not very tall, either," he remarks, a reference to Carmen's earlier critique of his stature. Yet Vivian carves out a presence quite different than that of her sister. The blocking positions Bacall between Bogart and the tray of drinks; Marlowe interrupts Vivian's line of questioning about the case—she wants to know what her father has spoken to Marlowe about—by asking for a drink. Vivian refuses to get it for him—after telling him to "get it yourself," she moves to the right side of the frame, passing Marlowe and opening a path for him to proceed to the drink tray. Bacall looks down for a moment, contemplating her next move, cradling her drink with both hands, while wondering why Bogart hasn't gotten himself that drink—and by his own insolent response it's clear that what he desired, playfully, was for her to get it for him, for her to become subservient. But he doesn't, really; he is, to a point, enjoying this insolence. The scene has already gone on longer than his first encounter with Carmen (who, in her flopping into Bogart's arms, darted straight to copulation), and Vivian has already established a tougher, more angular presence in counterpoint to Carmen's soft flirtation. Bogart watches as Bacall, her character continuing to press Marlowe about the case, moves over to the window and leans against it, raising her right knee at a sharp angle against its light. He gets impatient, though, with her questioning; hooking both thumbs on his belt, he takes a deep breath and straightens his posture. No nervous ear-tugging now; Bogart has reestablished, for a moment, his private detective's professional authority. Or perhaps he has learned that the only way to match Vivian is not through talk—she circles words around him in this scene—but through moving, or getting ready to move. With both thumbs hooked on the belt, Bogart, near the end of this scene, standing behind Bacall as she walks past him, looks nothing less than a Western gunslinger about to mount a horse—a pose that prepares the way for the film's infamous double-entendre dialogue in a later nightclub scene, in which both characters compare each other to thoroughbreds that one needs to observe carefully before riding.

So Bacall's Vivian moves better than Vickers's Carmen; where Carmen, in the words of McElhaney, "is defined by her difficulty in being able to simply maintain a vertical position for long" ("Lauren Bacall: The Walk"), Bacall's tough, fully horizontal position is a challenging turn-on for Marlowe. But what does she offer that Malone's bookseller can't? Unlike Carmen, Malone remains perfectly upright, and like Bacall, exudes a sharp intelligence (in part through her wearing of glasses, and the film's association of her with a knowledge of antique books). This is, perhaps, where the murder plot actually does become important—not in its details, but in the opportunity it provides Marlowe more time to see Vivian again. Time, by contrast, is precisely what he lacks with Malone, given that their sexy scene is foreshortened by an ellipsis and by Marlowe's own requirement that he get back to trailing his suspect. Thus, it becomes crucial to the Bogart-Bacall courtship that several of their subsequent scenes together will in fact have the time to amplify performative tropes and stylistic touches already seen in Malone's bookshop scene. For example, the thunderclap: it is heard, on the soundtrack, when the flirtation between Marlowe and the bookseller reaches a climax. And thunder rumbles again during Bogart's second meeting with Bacall, when Marlowe returns Carmen's drugged-up body (which he has discovered at Geiger's apartment, one of the film's central crime scenes) to the Sternwood mansion. Bogart and Bacall are positioned together, in a tight two-shot. Bacall has just revealed, unwittingly, that she knows Carmen may be implicated in the case Marlowe is investigating—at which point Bogart clenches both of Bacall's arms tightly, drawing her closer to him. "Take it easy," he says; "I don't slap so good around this time of the evening." At this, outside, a thunderclap—and a flash of lightning, through the Venetian blinds behind them. And the flash seems to initiate some change in Bacall's expression; after a cut to a close two-shot, a slight smirk passes across her face, as if she were taking a degree of pleasure in the sudden degree of roughness Bogart is exhibiting in his attempt to take some control over the case. The moment recalls the kinkiness glimpsed in some of the dialogue in *To Have and Have Not*—and in the earlier film's references to ropes "tying down" Harry Morgan as his relationship to Marie Browning takes its first steps. "You go too far, Marlowe," Vivian tells him; to which he responds, "those are harsh words to throw at a man—especially when he's walking out of your bedroom." But in *The Big Sleep*, the fulfillment promised in this moment the thunderclap has initiated is deferred to a future time. Unlike his time with Malone, which will be foreshortened (or perhaps fulfilled too quickly), his encounters with Bacall promise a kinky future, an ongoing flirtation.

While the thunderclap offers an example of a stylistic touch in the scene with Malone that is repeated in a scene involving Bogart and Bacall, the central couple also performs a variation upon a specific performative trope first glimpsed in the earlier Malone scene. In the bookstore scene, as mentioned earlier, Malone, after removing her glasses and untying her hair in front of a small mirror, walks back toward Bogart as he prepares two drinks—and as she does, she circles the inside of her mouth lustfully, a performative detail that we see but that Bogart, eyes still cast downward at drink, doesn't. This play between a sexually charged expression and a glance that does not quite meet it is repeated in the scene between Bogart and Bacall in Marlowe's office. Vivian has returned there to tell Marlowe about some letters she has received about Carmen's involvement with certain suspects, letters that threaten blackmail. But the scene is concerned less with this detail than in the dance between gesture and glance. Wearing a French beret and a checkered suit that recall the fashions of Marie Browning in *To Have and Have Not*, Vivian walks into the office with an aura of confidence, dropping a Marcel Proust reference that she takes to be over Marlowe's head. Bogart points for her to sit in a chair next to him—but instead, Bacall perches herself on the edge of Marlowe's desk, removing the blackmail letters and handing them to the detective. As he looks through them, Bacall grasps the edges of the desk with her hands and reaches out a single leg to pull the chair closer to her—she wants it for a footrest. Bogart glances up at Bacall, but does not look at her leg, now pulling back to draw the chair, which she has had a moment's struggle in corralling, back toward her. As Marlowe and Vivian begin talking about the photographs (nude pictures of Carmen that are the subject of the blackmail), Bacall begins fidgeting with her gloves (a nervous gesture that to some degree parallels Bogart's repeated ear-tug throughout the film, and which will be repeated in the later nightclub sequence), all the while keeping her legs dangling in front of Marlowe, her checkered skirt just covering them above the knee. He keeps his glance on her eyes. She begins fidgeting, now, with her left knee, scratching it through the fabric of the skirt. Bogart, by now, cannot help himself—he is looking downward, for the only time in the scene, at her leg, her efforts to scratch. And she does—discreetly lifting the left side of her skirt; and, now, at this, Bogart, equally discreetly, returns his gaze to her eyes (figure 5.9). It is not that Marlowe is perhaps too much of a gentleman to look at her. It is, instead, a playful effort to extend the flirtation—the longer Bogart goes without a full view of Bacall, the

Figure 5.9. Humphrey Bogart, Lauren Bacall, and the dance between gesture and glance in *The Big Sleep* (1946).

more reason he has to see her again, and then again. This is what gives the relationship durability, and mystery, beyond the apparently quickly consummated tryst with Malone's bookshop owner, even as the scene plays upon relationships between gesture and glance that have already been initiated in the film by Malone and Bogart in the earlier scene.

And it is what ensures that we will want to see further scenes between Bogart and Bacall, too, as the film goes on; if the murder plot's function, in this regard, is to keep providing reasons for Marlowe and Vivian to get together (as they will do, in the nightclub scene full of double entendre; and later, as they ride to Geiger's house in a car, a car that is the site of their first kiss), the actual gestural content of the moments they share together continues to defer the consummation of their relationship in ways designed to guarantee the Bogart-Bacall coupling retains freshness in its repetitions.

However, these specific variations upon the Malone bookshop scene point to a contrast between *To Have and Have Not* and *The Big Sleep*. In the earlier film, social context is something into which the couple is integrated, for a larger communal and political purpose that makes no undue sacrifice upon individual distinction. In *The Big Sleep*, however, social others are put into less flattering contrast with Bogart and Bacall: Bogart is positioned as superior to the other men in the film through his indifference to suspects, beyond their function in the case he is trying to solve; and Bacall is positioned as attractive not only for her inherent qualities, but for the ways in which her qualities of movement and gesture compare favorably to the other female characters. *The Big Sleep* even stages moments that stand in contrast to earlier encounters between the couple in *To Have and Have Not*. When Marlowe, later in the film, visits Eddie Mars's casino, he spies Vivian singing a song to piano accompaniment. Vivian, in turn, looks Marlowe up and down as he interacts with a flirty cigarette girl—and she's looking the girl up and down, too. The moment parallels not only Marie Browning's singing in the earlier film but also her tendency to size up her female competition. But where Marie's jealousy in *To Have and Have Not* is largely feigned (her references to her opposition's weight are made in playfully self-deprecating reference to her own "skinny" stature), Bacall's glance at the cigarette girl in *The Big Sleep* strikes a note of genuine suspicion—as if someone were honing in on a figure firmly established as "her man." This makes for a film that ends much more conventionally than *To Have and Have Not*, with a close two-shot of the pair, the dark world of noir kept at arm's length, for a time, without a third participant (like Eddie) to complicate coupledom. As the variations and comparisons between Bacall and the other characters have shown, the other figures in the movie simply do not measure up (by the end, even Dorothy Malone is a distant memory). Where love was a rhythm shared, collectively, in *To Have and Have Not*, in *The Big Sleep* it is a quality possessed, finally, by only two.

The Howard Hawks films starring Bogart and Bacall give the stars room and time to roam, to walk, and to check one another out as they move and gesture. By contrast, *Dark Passage* and *Key Largo* condense the relationship between the couple to a handful of intense moments that play out in close shots emphasizing not full body motion and positioning but rather eyes, mouths, brows, and facial quivering. Perhaps this is why Manny Farber, an admirer of Hawks, did not much like Daves or Huston: Delmer Daves is caustically referred to by Farber as a director "who intelligently half-prettifies adolescents and backwoods primitives" (497); and Farber reserves the strongest opprobrium for Huston: "The Eisenstein of the Bogart thriller, [Huston] rigidly delimits the subject matter that goes into a frame, by chiaroscuro or by grouping his figures within the square of the screen so that there is hardly room for an actor to move an arm: given a small group in close quarters, around a bar, bonfire, table, he will hang on to the event for dear life and show peculiarities of posture, expression, and anatomy that only the actor's doctor should know" (*Negative Space* 34). We need not share Farber's negative assessment of Daves or Huston as filmmakers in order to find usefulness in the stylistic comparison he makes between Hawks and the directors of Bogart and Bacall's final two films together. Indeed, *Dark Passage*, in its handling of moments between Bogart and Bacall, is very nearly as claustrophobic as *Key Largo*, which is set almost entirely in a hotel off the coast of the Florida Keys. Neither film offers an opportunity for us to appreciate, for long stretches of time, how the performers move through space. Instead, these films function primarily as studies of faces and hands.

Dark Passage, in its first act, experiments with the stylistically radical idea that the camera can manifest character perspective through camera perspective, a notion that complicates any study of performance on the screen. In the film, a man named Vincent Parry escapes from prison and then tries to track down the murderer of his wife (Perry had been wrongly incarcerated for her murder). In the second act, Parry will undergo risky plastic surgery to remodel his face to look like something other than the man depicted in newspapers reporting on the escape—and someone more like Humphrey Bogart, who will play Parry in the second half of the film after the surgery is complete. In the first act, however, *Dark Passage* eschews showing us Parry's image; instead, the camera, at certain junctures, assumes his point-of-view in an approximately first-person perspective. This results in Bogart's gravelly voice (the one bodily constant between the two Parrys, before and after plastic surgery) emanating from offscreen, while we see his hands occasionally jut below the frame of the shot in order to situate the camera in a point in space that is, roughly speaking, "his face." Another film of the same year, Robert Montgomery's take on the Philip Marlowe character, *Lady in the Lake* (1947), experimented more thoroughly with a similar stylistic device, committing itself almost completely to the claim that, in Vivian Sobchack's words, "Marlowe's body is *identical in material* and *isomorphic in situation* with its body" (238). But as Sobchack observes, *Lady in the Lake*'s attempt to join camera perspective with character perspective is problematic because, as the film goes on, "the disparity between the nature of the film's lived-body and the nature of the human lived-body emerges . . . as . . . inauthentic" (238). That is, the film's attempt to make camera and character coincide eventually gives way to the fact that camera and human, inevitably, see differently; humans do not process the visual field in ways that directly parallel the engagement of reality by the camera lens. By contrast, *Dark Passage* admits, from the start, that camera and character cannot possibly coincide: in the film's first shots the camera is located outside of the main character's visual perspective, and even if a subsequent shot will present the camera assuming the ostensible position of Parry, inside the barrel, as he rolls himself off the truck and down a nearby hill, we see, at the end of this action, Parry leave the barrel and run off in the distance in the same shot while the camera remains inside.

The camera's gestures, then, are not finally to be conflated with Bogart's own, even in shots ostensibly conveying Parry's perspective. Beyond the inherent distinction between human perspective and camera perspective in all films, it is also true that Bogart, after all, was very likely not present on set during many of these shots, and the hands occasionally jutting into the bottom of the frame are not likely his own. This means that when Parry, still stumbling alongside a rural road after escaping from prison and fleeing from his oil barrel in the first part of the movie, encounters a woman played by Lauren Bacall, what we see when we see Bacall gaze into the camera as if she were gazing into a set of human eyes is a woman who is not gazing at a face at all, but rather at a lens, a lens that she, as a performer, must imagine is human. As a performer, Bacall never sees, in the flesh, Vincent Parry as he is depicted in the newspaper article about the prison escape that the camera-as-Parry will glimpse after he is brought to her apartment. But if she literally sees a camera, we can only believably manifest in our minds the figure who will become her lover by reading the expressions that pass across her face and the gestures and movements with which she regards this figure she conjures in her mind's eye. It is appropriate, then, that her character, Irene Jansen, is a painter, for Bacall paints Bogart with her eyes—the Bogart we have yet to see, a Bogart she paints for us with the way she moves and the way she looks and gestures at his invisible specter. Until Bogart is unmasked roughly halfway through the movie, it is this imagined figure Bacall's character finds love in, a love that presses beyond the ostensible psychological motivation provided by the script (her father was similarly falsely accused of murder, and she has taken an interest in Parry by reading of his case in the newspapers), a love that glides elegantly, by film's end, into a more private *mise-en-scène*.

The first meeting in the film between Bacall and this Bogart, a Bogart assumed by the camera and soon to be conjured by Bacall, occurs after Parry has stolen a pair of shoes from a suspicious motorist from whom Parry had hitched a ride. As Parry hears the car arrive, the camera looks up, and he sees Bacall, who approaches him cautiously, stopped near the side of the highway, not yet walking further toward him. She is guarded—justifiably wary. She has an ideal to save men wrongly imprisoned like Parry, but she does not yet know what kind of man Parry particularly is. Irene drives him to her apartment, narrowly avoiding discovery at two roadblocks. She will next gaze into the camera lens, conjuring him, as she guides him up the elevator to her residence—itself a job of furtiveness, with the camera-as-Parry following a few paces behind so the two are not seen together. When the elevator door shuts—the film's most intimately claustrophobic space—Bacall gazes directly into the lens, her right eye cast in darkness, her hair pulled back tight, her brows furrowed, even more guarded than before. Bacall then turns her gaze away, glancing up and down at the elevator door nervously and fidgeting with her purse, before darting her eyes back to the camera, instructing Parry to hang behind a few steps before following her to the apartment. Then, a strange moment of intimacy: Bacall walks out of the elevator, and the camera follows her, coming close to, very nearly touching, the back of her head, the surface of her hair. This Bogart specter, it seems, is drawn to the Bacall we see—he now begins to sees something of himself, perhaps, in the figure of him she is conjuring out of the camera lens with her eyes. Bacall walks forward a few paces to make sure the coast is clear, motioning for the Bogart-camera to follow. Inside the apartment, her posture relaxes: no longer on guard, she invites the Bogart-camera to put on a record and begins to explain to him her motivation for saving him on the road.

But the real content of the scene, played out in an intimate space, is not to explain this element of the plot, but for Bacall to dress Bogart up to her heart's desire. She notes that the police will spot him in his ratty clothes, and offers to run out and grab him some new ones. Jotting down his measurements, she takes one more long look at him, this time motivated by something slightly in excess of the plot's demand that Parry be able to avoid cops. Lowering her brow and glancing up at the camera lens—in the closest expression to "the look" that this rather atypical Bacall performance achieves—she notes that he needs a shave and a shower. Later, after Parry has had his plastic surgery and can be revealed, finally, onscreen, he removes his bandages, after which point Bacall will tell him, again, that he needs a shave, not this time to avoid any cops, but to more suitably adhere to how she desires him.

In something of an inversion of *Laura*, in which an imagined vision of Gene Tierney was possessed by the various male characters, the Bogart unseen in the first hour of *Dark Passage* (first under cloak of camera perspective, then under mask of bandages) is Bacall's performative possession, an object shaped in the eye of her desire: first kept at arm's length cautiously, then embraced as a figure she might dress up, shave, even perhaps save. For the first hour of *Dark Passage*, Bogart is seen only in her eyes. Extra-textually, of course, audiences in 1947, as today, would know that the figure she was imagining was Bogart, so substantially was his persona, and the publicity of their offscreen romance and marriage, part of the audience's awareness. This fact is what lends the beginning of their courtship in *Dark Passage* a credence that it might otherwise lack with a different pair of actors, in the same situation of having to act toward, or be substituted by, a camera. Love must, eventually, be performed onscreen; the camera can only participate directly in these gestures for a time. It is only the fact that we can imagine, alongside Bacall's Irene, her figure of desire—the Bogart persona and performer as it had developed up to 1947—that allows *Dark Passage* to get away with the device for longer than most films might be able to, and to create lovely moments out of it. One such moment, in the next sequence, finds the pair on something of a date, with Bacall's character sitting by the other side of her patio table, coffee cup and candlelight positioned between her and the lens. Two hands extend out from under the frame of the shot to light her cigarette, a gesture that is believable not because we believe in any real sense that the camera is a valid substitute for Bogart (it isn't) but because Bacall's face betrays palpable pleasure in the cigarette lit by these glimpsed hands, cracking the first substantial smile in her performance (figures 5.10 and 5.11). (The moment is like a mannerist variation on the cigarette lightings in *To Have and Have Not*.) Here, still, this Bogart lighting the cigarette is wholly her imaginative possession, a possession to gaze at in her mind's eye, and take pleasure in. This is a unique moment in the history of screen courtship, for while love-filled gazes at the camera (temporarily assuming the look of a lover, in shot-reaction shots, for example) are *not* unique, for a lover to take sole possession of the other lover's image for a long stretch of time—long enough to let a cigarette burn slowly—*is*.

"What about faces?" Parry will later ask of a taxi driver. His question reverberates throughout the film. Parry's exposed face, and Bacall's face in response to his revelation, changes everything about their relationship in *Dark Passage*. Bogart, once un-bandaged, is no longer the sole, desired possession of Bacall's mind's eye. This necessarily changes Bacall's performance: no longer needing to directly gaze into a camera, a gaze from out of which she was able to conjure, for a time, an imaginary man, she will have to make do with the one that really exists. Irene notes, too, in the dialogue, that the revelation of a new face will be the beginning of a new life. The moment during which Vincent Parry is "unveiled" as Humphrey Bogart is presented, appropriately, as a moment of shared

Figures 5.10 and 5.11. Lauren Bacall and a slow burn in *Dark Passage* (Warner Bros., 1947).

intimacy, a key moment in their courtship: it begins in Irene's bedroom, with a bandaged Bogart perched on the side of her bed as she begins to clip off the masking, a process that is preceded by a close-up of Bacall's own quivering, tremulous face, as if to suggest this onscreen revelation of a figure that may or may not conform to Irene's imagining is as life-changing for her as it is for Parry. Indeed, throughout the sequence, we cut back to reaction shots of Bacall, contemplating the visage that is slowly revealed, forehead-down, as Bogart. Only after four close shots of Bacall's face have been presented does the film cut to a close shot of the unveiled Parry. If there was any doubt up to this point that the interest of *Dark Passage* tends toward Bacall's gaze at Bogart rather than the revelation of his face, when the bandages are finally pulled off, the camera remains fixed, in a two-shot taken from behind Bogart's back, on Bacall's reaction as the unveiling happens. It is a surprisingly ambiguous expression she betrays (one that perhaps reminds us of Bacall's own account of her initial, real-life meeting with Bogart on the set of *To Have and Have Not*, in which there was no "clap of thunder"). Does Irene desire him—or, more accurately, does he match the desire she has already envisioned in her gaze at the camera?

After the face is revealed, Bacall clutches the side of her collar, pulling back from Parry, her expression a blank. Bogart moves over to the mirror. "I sure look older," he says as he looks at himself in the mirror, prodding and rubbing his new facial contours. The source of Bacall's possible displeasure here is possibly revealed: "Can you shave?" she asks. It's the stubble that bothers her—this isn't quite what she has imagined. She wants him to clean up, so he may make a fresh impression—and when she tells him this, she expresses a flirty smile, one that promises this particular manifestation of the Bogart-Bacall courtship, despite Irene's initial reservations about the face, will proceed as the others. So Bogart does shave, and when he returns to the living room of the apartment in the next scene, he looks more like the dapper figure she has perhaps imagined in her mind's eye earlier in the film.

Bacall's performance in *Dark Passage* suggests both the possibilities and the limits of imaginative female desire in Classical Hollywood coupledom: in the first half of the movie, we can collaborate with Bacall's performance to freely imagine, as she gazes into the camera lens, the sort of male figure that might suit her; but the one that finally does, inevitably, is Humphrey Bogart, a figure whose presence we have been conditioned to expect and whose visage, eventually, both excites and limits the free range of Irene's imagination.

Bacall's request that Bogart shave, and the nicknaming that occurs once Vincent Parry realizes he needs a moniker to survive on the city streets still full of cops looking for him, recall similar passages of dialogue in *To Have and Have Not*, effectively condensing the earlier, film-length flirtation between Bogart and Bacall into a few economic minutes. The final pairing of Bogart and Bacall, John Huston's *Key Largo*, a film derived, without great fidelity, from a 1939 stage play by Maxwell Anderson, mostly lacks these repetitions, and its presentation of the Bogart-Bacall courting is even more sparse. But it does share with *Dark Passage* an even more intensified claustrophobia. Apart from a handful of exterior scenes (occurring, first, on a bus, which transports Bogart's character, ex-Army Major Frank McCloud, to the Florida Keys, and, then, near a pier which will serve as the departure point for the film's climax at sea), *Key Largo* takes place entirely indoors, in the space of the Largo Hotel, owned and operated by James Temple (Lionel Barrymore) and his daughter-in-law Nora (Bacall). Nora's deceased husband, and Temple's son, George, was under McCloud's supervision during the war, and Bogart has arrived at the hotel to tell them of George's final resting place and to deliver a narrative about his final, heroic moments. Of the four feature Bogart-Bacall films, *Key Largo* is the one least concerned with the performance of romance: the bulk of the narrative involves a showdown between Bogart and Edward G. Robinson, who plays an aging gangster holing up in the Keys. While Bogart's characterization grapples with the same questions of social commitment that faced his Rick Blaine (in *Casablanca*) and Harry Morgan, Robinson's recalls an aged version of his criminal figures in *Little Caesar* (1931) and *The Hatchet Man* (1932). But McCloud wants nothing to do with Rocco: if in 1948 America still allows this gangster figure to exist, he surmises, then his effort in World War II was for naught, and he will not become embroiled in any further commitments that put his personal well-being at risk. It is the Bacall figure who, as the film goes on, implores Bogart to take action: her gaze at McCloud is less one of desire and flirtation, as it is in the earlier films, and one of ideological demand that conjures a vision of postwar masculinity to which Bogart must conform. If Bogart is to be her man, he must be a good American patriot, one who ensures that the fighting of the previous decade was not in vain.

As much as the film's expressionistic, claustrophobic style, it is this ideological focus that sharply distinguishes *Key Largo* from the earlier Bogart-Bacall pictures directed by Howard Hawks, and from *Dark Passage*. In the earlier films, performed gestures and expressions still belonged, with individual distinction, to the characters played by Bogart and Bacall: even as they became entangled in the French Resistance in *To Have and Have Not*, their embodiment conveyed an individual way of inhabiting rhythm that, while socially contextualized, was still uniquely theirs. But in *Key Largo*, performance no longer expresses individuality, and generates no socially shared rhythm; instead, it gestures toward symbolic, ideological norms to which the Bogart and Bacall characters now must conform. The trajectory of their relationship's development in the film begins with their first meeting on the hotel pier. Bogart walks out of the hotel toward Temple, who sits in a wheelchair on the right side of the frame; Bacall, on the left side of the frame, in the distance of the shot's deep staging, can be seen on the edge of the pier, working. Once it dawns on Temple who McCloud is, he calls for Nora, and we see, in long shot, Bacall run toward the pair, across the depth of the frame. Her way of moving here is already distinctively different than the earlier performances: rather than the languorous, sensual movement of an independent woman she projected in *To Have and Have Not* and *The Big Sleep*, this run in *Key Largo* is one of daughterly commitment, an answer to a call, bound up with the work she does to maintain this hotel and its pier (she is clutching the rag she has been using to wipe down the pier glimpsed in the distance). As Bogart glances around the landscape, and as his character makes small talk with Barrymore, the film cuts to a closer shot of Bacall, taken from over Bogart's shoulder. Her eyes dart back and forth across Bogart's face, eager in anticipation for information this man might know about how her husband died; she circles the rag in her hands nervously. Bacall's characterization is of a woman who *wants* something from Bogart: confirmation that her husband was a hero; confirmation that the war effort (to which she also contributed, as a USO volunteer) was worth something.

The confirmation that Bacall and Bogart belong together in *Key Largo*, that a shared patriotism and consciousness for the sacredness of American history unites them in their affections, is expressed in a handful of symbolic gestures early in the film. After introducing himself, McCloud moves inside with Nora and Temple, telling them of George's heroism and his burial site in Italy. The music on the soundtrack is lightly patriotic—triumphant trumpets and strings—but the wind begins to rattle the window blinds, a prefiguring of the threat to this patriotism that both natural (the impending hurricane) and human (the gangster Rocco) forces will shortly bring. Nora gets up to shut the windows. Then, she and Bogart walk outside, the music reaching a crescendo, the camera following them toward the edge of the pier. As Bogart looks up at the sky, Bacall looks at him sidelong, asking him what he did before the war. They arrive at the edge of the pier. In a close shot of their hands, the two unhook ropes that hang on hooks on one of the pier's planks (figure 5.12); the rope forms a circular image evocative, in this context, of a marriage ring, as if their eventual personal commitment to one another will be bound up in the meaning of this sequence. The two approach the

Figure 5.12. Bogart's gift of a metaphorical ring to Bacall in *Key Largo* (Warner Bros., 1948).

end of the pier: Bacall walks to the edge, the wind blowing in her hair, while Bogart stops, briefly, to exchange pleasantries with two of the men who will be revealed, later as Robinson's partners in crime. Bogart then moves to the edge of the pier with Bacall, helping her pull in a boat with another rope. The skill McCloud and Nora share in tying the boat to the pier cements their eventual love as one grounded in work, duty, and historical consciousness. In the next moment they greet the arrival of several Native Americans on the pier, including an aged woman whose lived-in face inflects the couple's courtship as one which is intended to protect the ideals (mythical though they may be) of American history. That the most important moment of contact between Bogart and Bacall in the first part of the film occurs in a close-up of their hands, untying a boat, suggests the extent to which *Key Largo* eschews the focus on movement in the earlier Hawks pictures, linking the formation of this couple instead to family and duty, an idea confirmed in the narrative's trajectory, which places Bogart and Bacall together in a threesome that includes Barrymore's Temple. This makeshift family, far different from the adventurous, rhythmic trio formed by Morgan, Marie, and Eddie at the end of *To Have and Have Not*, prefigures the more conventional formation of family that we will see in the family melodramas in the fifties, complete with two patriarchs and a dutiful, loving woman.

Key Largo is a film that demonstrates Bogart and Bacall's adaptability to a range of material and directorial styles. But for fans of Bogart and Bacall as lovers pitching woo, it can register as a slight disappointment: the sultriness, the suggestiveness, and the aura of their earlier coupled characterizations is, in Huston's film, mostly absent. It presents a rather stolid maturation of, rather than a flirtation between, the couple that links growth and maturity with adherence of one's movement and gestures to larger, pre-articulated symbols and ideas that, finally, have nothing to do with desire individually defined. I would like to end this chapter by suggesting that the Bogart and Bacall that *Key Largo* presents (whatever the film's many virtues) is not the Bogart and Bacall we really want to remember. That couple, free from the normative ideals endorsed by *Key Largo*, is instead much more palpable at the end of *Dark Passage*. There, Bogart's Parry has eluded the authorities and is planning to make his way to Mexico. He is waylaid at a bus station. He spies a woman with two kids and a man, both complaining of heat and exhaustion. He gets up and moves over to a jukebox. He puts on a record. It's a vaguely romantic tune, and as the cutting together of two close-ups suggests, it serves to bring this anonymous woman and this anonymous man together. (Their kids, looking down at their books, are less interested.) As a shot of the new foursome boarding the bus ahead of Bogart confirms,

Figures 5.13 and 5.14. Bogart, Bacall, and an open future in *Dark Passage* (Warner Bros., 1947).

Bogart's playing of the jukebox record has assisted in the formation of an old-fashioned American family, not unlike the family that appears to be promised as the product of McCloud and Nora's future together at the end of *Key Largo*, and perhaps not unlike some of the families we will glimpse falling apart at the seams in the family melodramas in the next two chapters. But Bogart, the Bogart of *Dark Passage*, is not a part of this family. He travels instead out of the United States, to Mexico. When we last see him, it is in a nightclub, waiting for his beloved to appear (figure 5.13). He looks as cool here as he does in *To Have and Have Not*. Bacall, after a moment, shimmies in (figure 5.14). Under the soft light of the club, she is as radiant as in her first moments in *To Have and Have Not*. Their courtship begins, again, here, a "fresh impression," sending us back to our memory of their first encounter in the earlier film—"anyone got a match?"—as if in a loop. The future is open.

Part III

Love and Melodrama

6

Lipstick on a Teacup

Performance in Vincente Minnelli's *The Cobweb* and *Tea and Sympathy*

Vincente Minnelli's *The Cobweb* (1955), a drama about patients and doctors at a psychiatric hospital, involves an argument over which drapes are to be hung in the institution's library. Victoria Inch (Lillian Gish), the administrative assistant to the hospital's director, Dr. Douglas Devanal (Charles Boyer), desires the most economical route, sensibly inexpensive chintz. Karen McIver (Gloria Grahame), the wife of the clinic's chief psychiatrist Dr. Stewart McIver (Richard Widmark), has her own plan to hang more expensive, decorative drapes. Meg Rinehart (Lauren Bacall), one of McIver's assistants, wants to turn over control of the aesthetic design of the drapes to the patients themselves, selecting Stevie (John Kerr), as the head designer. Prior to taking her job in the hospital (shortly before the start of the film's plot), Meg has herself undergone psychoanalytic therapy to cope with the trauma of the death of her husband and son in an automobile accident. So she understands that the design of the drapes offers an opportunity for the patients to contribute to their own therapy by designing a *mise-en-scène* suitably expressive of the sort of world they would like to live in, or at least reflective of the one in which they currently do. Minnelli uses this triangular conflict over interior decoration as an illustration of the human "cobweb" the hospital comes to form when personal desire becomes tangled with institutional politics.

Throughout this book we have encountered actors who intervene in the *mise-en-scène* around them, characters who channel desire into a

Figure 6.1. John Kerr and Lauren Bacall in *The Cobweb* (MGM, 1955).

relationship with objects, furniture, light, and people in the frame—characters who work to make the frame a suitable context for the event of their own appearance, and the event of their loving movement toward others. In this shaping and reshaping of *mise-en-scène*, gestures have changed the space to accord with our lovers' desires. Of course, the desire to change the space—or, in the case of *The Cobweb*, the desire to redesign it—is felt more acutely nowhere else than in the family melodrama. This desire to refigure social form through the expression of desire, or to at least find some moment of reconciliation between public and private, drives the melodramas of Vincente Minnelli, who might be regarded as Classical Hollywood's most sophisticated poet of décor's relationship to performance. James Naremore, in his enduring and canonical study of Minnelli, calls him an "engaging blend of the aesthete and the modern entertainer, working not in words but in clothing and decor" (*Vincente Minnelli* 17). *The Cobweb* is emblematic of Minnelli's sensibility in this regard.

Miss Inch and Karen aim to design the library drapes as expressions of key aspects of their individual personalities: Inch, economical and practical; and Karen, appreciative of finer things, and needing an expressive outlet she does not find in her marriage to Dr. McIver. Stevie's drawings for the drapes, glimpsed throughout the film, are, by contrast, somewhat more complicated. Where Miss Inch and Victoria express themselves through the sort of floral patterns one might expect of drapes (that is, masking their expressive subconscious through the feign of abstraction), Stevie designs recognizable figural representations of the hospital and its inhabitants, reconfiguring people and things he sees in the film's social *mise-en-scène* in light of his own expressive vision (here I invoke the distinction between social and expressive *mise-en-scène* as Adrian Martin discusses it in his work; see Martin, *Mise-en-Scène and Film Style*, especially 21–42 and 127–154). Each of Stevie's paintings recall, condense, refigure, and anticipate moments of performance elsewhere in the film. The gestures performed in the film are thus echoed in and celebrated by Stevie's loving, if tortured, work as a visual artist. The first illustration, of Dr. McIver, might well be taken from one of Stevie's therapy sessions, as Richard Widmark reclines thoughtfully as he listens to Stevie work through his problems. The second image, depicting Dr. Devanal and Miss Inch conferencing in the director's office, echoes the confrontations between the Boyer and Gish characters over control of the hospital's administration. And the third image is of Sue Brett (Susan Strasberg), the young girl who takes a liking to Stevie and who will accompany him to the movies in an effort to overcome her agoraphobia later in the film.

Stevie's paintings, however, take expressive liberties in their depictions. Stevie does not so much recognize through his art the distinctive quality of time each of his painted figures offer within a social *mise-en-scène*, as Miriam Hopkins does when (as we saw in the introduction to this book) she draws Gary Cooper and Fredric March in *Design for Living*, but instead filters each of the represented characters through the temperament of his own artistic personality, each of them refigured in the rather insular expressivity of the *mise-en-scène* of his paintings. Further, Stevie *freezes* moments of fluid performance in the depth of Minnelli's staging into still tableaux, effectively sieving the gestures and expressions we have seen in the film through the relatively narrow field of fantasy projection taking shape in his mind. In the painting of Mr. McIver, for example, Stevie eliminates certain details of Widmark's performance in the earlier, corresponding scene, such as the actor's slouch in his therapist's chair (in the painting, McIver appears to be sitting thoughtfully upright) and the cigarette (Widmark smokes two of these in the earlier scene). And where the window behind Widmark in the earlier scene offered a glimpse of the hospital lawn, in the window of his painting Stevie imagines the figure of a woman, eyes downcast. Perhaps most crucially, Stevie has removed himself from the performed moment (figures 6.2, 6.3).

Perhaps it is Karen he is imagining the doctor imagine, for Karen herself is a topic of discussion during their session (Stevie hitches a ride to the hospital from the doctor's wife, and guiltily admits his attraction to Karen during the therapy session). Stevie's rendering of Miss Inch and Dr. Devanal, meanwhile, is also a fantasy projection (he has not been present for the meetings between the two, and thus can only imagine their encounter), but he refigures details of the scene his painting anticipates. In his drawing, Gish's Miss Inch, although sitting down, is a much more commanding figure than Devanal, who looms in the background of Stevie's drawing much as he looms in the background of Stevie's life (in

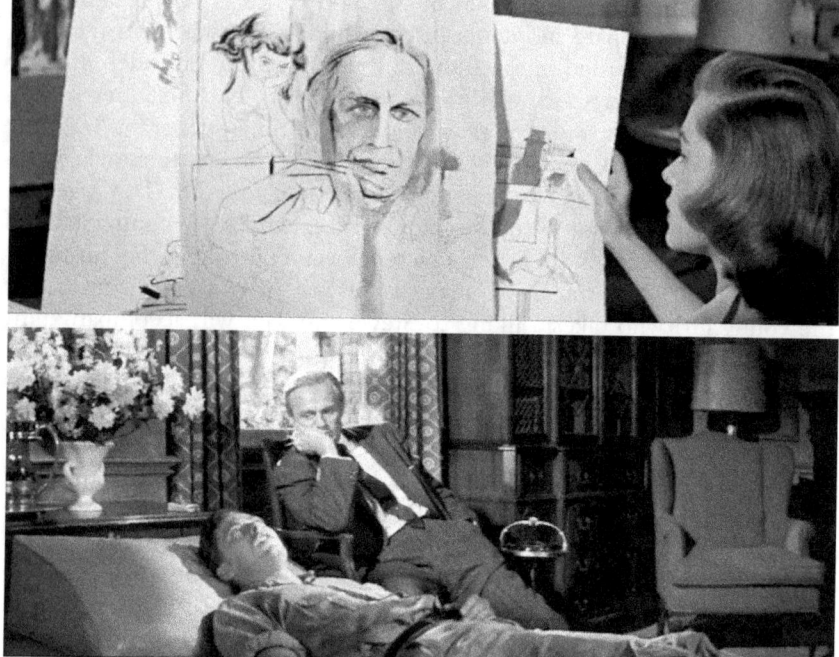

Figures 6.2 and 6.3. Stevie's paintings, freezing moments of Richard Widmark's performance in still tableaux, in *The Cobweb* (1955).

the film, we never see Devanal treat a patient; and he spends as much time with Mr. McIver's wife as he does in the hospital). Later in the film, when we see Gish and Boyer perform together, Gish is standing up, and Devanal is sitting down. But it is Gish who still hovers powerfully in the frame, standing over Boyer and ordering his secretary out of the office (figures 6.4 and 6.5).

If Stevie has glimpsed something of the institutional power conflict between these two administrators in his painting, his depiction of Sue—no less imaginative in the liberties it takes in his expression—is more personal. Prior to the presentation of Stevie's drawing, Sue is seen only fleetingly. In the patient committee meeting in the library, she is a demure, petite brunette, dressed in a dark green skirt and a white shirt, surrounded by the other patients in the clinic in the library. In Stevie's drawing, however, she is seated alone, against an expanse of white space. Rift from any recognizable social context, her dress and hair are both reimagined as a vibrant red. Remarkably, however, after seeing Stevie's drawings in a later scene, Sue recasts herself in the mold of his vision,

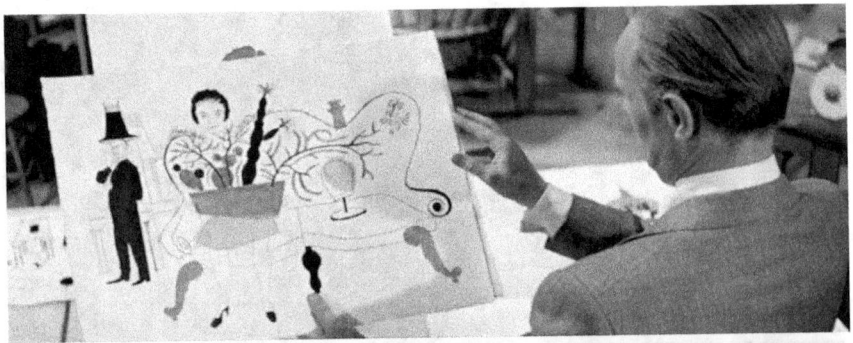

Figures 6.4 and 6.5. Charles Boyer and Lillian Gish, refigured in Stevie's paintings in *The Cobweb* (MGM, 1955).

decorating herself in a red dress similar to the one in his painting (figures 6.6, 6.7, and 6.8).

Stevie's drawings are not direct transcriptions of moments of performance surrounding him. Indeed, in the case of at least one of these, he has not even seen the moment. Instead, they are personal interventions into the story world's social space and the flow of the film's own visual design. These drawings are, in fact, a redesign, the beginning of a plan that aims to substitute the tired old library curtains with a tapestry representing, in concrete fashion, its space and the people who inhabit it. Stevie, most vividly and visibly in his role in prompting Susie to change her way of dressing and moving, changes the space of Minnelli's film at one thoughtful remove: in the design of pictures that are not the *mise-en-scène* of the film as a whole but rather a crucial part within it, and a fantasy of what it might become. By reimagining the world of the clinic around him from this gentle, safe distance, he is also creating a design with the intent of allowing those fantasies and desires to flow more freely and fluidly, as freely and fluidly as wind blowing through

Figures 6.6., 6.7, and 6.8. Sue (Susan Strasberg) painted in red in *The Cobweb* (MGM, 1955).

curtain drapes. Thus, it is not a tapestry of solitary desire as much as it is a design that would allow others in the institution to recognize their own desires in his visions, and to live more healthily as a result. The fact that Sue refashions herself in the image created in Stevie's mind's eye is not so much an indication that she is suiting her figure to the mold of his desire, but rather a sign that she recognizes something of her own desire in his (this recognition marks the beginning of their tender courtship in the film). Stevie's designs are like a clearing in a subconscious fog: by making desire legible in his paintings, he aims to create, from out of his private, expressive visions, a spatial and social tapestry, in response to other performances in Minnelli's *mise-en-scène*, which might house healthier relationships among the citizens of the hospital.

By interjecting Stevie's visions into the flow of the film's narrative, Minnelli is striking a major key through a minor character, reflecting, through Stevie, on the way each of us, as viewers, project desire onto images of figures onscreen as film performance unspools. Such a notion is important to think about for many films and performances, but it is especially important in the mode of fifties family melodrama, the subject of these final two chapters, in which the image's kindling of the viewer's deepest and perhaps hitherto unrealized sensations serves as something of an analogue to the characters' own struggles to make manifest in their social world (the images we are watching) their innermost desire for connection and meaning. In doing so, Stevie and Minnelli have reminded us again that our descriptions of performance are always something of a recontextualization and fictionalization, fictionalizations that allow us to move forward in our criticism, driven by a certain desire, even as those fictions remain tenderly connected to the performed actions on the screen. And by putting this painted fictionalization of performance into the hands of one of his supporting characters, Minnelli has to some extent allegorized the way in which performance, as an accumulation of moments of acted reality, intermingles with a certain way of seeing, a certain way of moving forward meaningfully in the form of criticism, as written on the page. More specifically, and in regard to our relationship to performance in fifties melodrama, Stevie's desire to control the unspooling of cinematic, figural movement in the still, painted frame, itself an effort to heal the disjunction between his psyche and the external figures of his life comprising his reality, might also parallel Minnelli's own attempt to stage the confrontation between the smooth flow of classicism and the disjunction of modernism in *The Cobweb* and the other melodramas discussed in this chapter. As Joe McElhaney has discussed in *The Death of Classical Cinema*, Minnelli's late work (which *The Cobweb* anticipates) stages a confrontation between the continuity system of narrative cinema in Classical Hollywood and the burgeoning art cinemas and modernisms of the late fifties and sixties. "Classical cinema," McElhaney writes, "creates a world in which our primary desire is always to know more and see more, not simply as part of the inevitable process of a cause-and-effect narrative unfolding, but also in terms of the organization of the images themselves" (20). The late works of certain Hollywood directors (for McElhaney, Minnelli is one of the most important among them) anticipate the film modernisms of what were then, in the fifties, the burgeoning art cinemas, through staging confrontations with edges or boundaries that are no longer the smooth, continuous passages from image to image staged in classical cinema, but now, rather, edges that function as "objects of desire [that] increasingly become the source of a new kind of search, a new kind of secret, a new kind of image" (24).

The performances in the family melodramas (by Minnelli and by Sirk) that I examine in these final two chapters stage gestures that enact "this new kind of search," gestures that displace something of the kinesis of the screwball heroine's bounding across the screen, or the noir figure's tantalizing kiss, onto shimmering spaces and homes decorated by color and doors, windows, and edges at once trapping characters while also offering the liminal site through which they might pass onto a new form of living. That something of the vibrancy of performance is displaced onto décor, and objects, and color, in these vivid family melodramas, is not to suggest that the actors I will study in this chapter and the next do not possess the same inherent interest as the actors of the previous chapters. It is to suggest, however, two fundamental shifts fifties melodrama introduces in this story of love's performance in Classical Hollywood. First, although this has so far been a book about the way performative figures come to form couples—rather than a book about the fact of the star couple as an already existing entity—it is nevertheless true that certain star tandems that occupy a central place in mainstream film appreciation (Loy and Powell, Bogart and Bacall) have dotted the pages of this study. One can, indeed, approach *The Big Sleep* in complete forgetfulness about the fact that one is watching a film in which the Bogart and Bacall characters must woo one another; so cemented are their public personas as figures of achieved romance that the gestural, future-looking content of their performances sometimes gets lost. The figures in the family melodramas taken as the subject of the next two chapters, though, do not possess the same iconic status (at least beyond cinephile circles) as the couples appearing earlier in this book: John Kerr and Deborah Kerr, in Minnelli's *Tea and Sympathy* (1956), for example, occupy a distinctly different cinematic and cultural position than the stars discussed in earlier pages. This shift, indeed, is part of the story I want to tell: although fifties Hollywood cinema does not lack for couples with "chemistry" (Rock Hudson and Doris Day, for example, in their comedies, or the ongoing pairing of Katharine Hepburn and Spencer Tracy, in their battles of the sexes), the fifties melodrama, as a form, tends to draw back from the confidence projected in the star couple in screwball and noir, and takes as its subject a much more complicated and, as we have already begun to see in *The Cobweb*, institutionally inflected and troubled courtship. If *Key Largo*, as we have seen in the previous chapter, offers the first vision in this book of a romance taking place against or under the pressure of an external world of ideological demand rather than using the performance of love to change that world, a similar conception forms the proscenium of the family melodrama, precisely because the homes and institutions on display in these films are no longer harmonious ground for the starry-eyed star courtships of previous Hollywood years. Indeed, the search for a "beyond," or as McElhaney puts it, "a new secret, a new image," suggests that the figures, to find their love, must move beyond the space of the film presently on the screen. This fact, then, changes the performer's relationship to object and space; no longer are decorations (such as chintz library drapes) or objects (the glossy handbag Bacall is given in *Written on the Wind*) merely or only expressive of individual character psychology and agency in the family melodrama. As these complex performances will suggest, these objects and decorations begin to take on their own vibrancy—they, in a sense, begin "performing" independently of the actors who wield them, taking on meaning that at times extends beyond the individual.

Performance in *The Cobweb*, then, and the other Minnelli melodrama discussed in this chapter, *Tea and Sympathy*, becomes concerned not only with how and why characters move forward but with their difficulty in doing so, and in their expressive articulation (and, at times, frustrated lack of articulation) of objects of desire that they themselves do not always quite know how to name. Stevie in *The Cobweb* can name these objects only by painting them (when he tries to articulate them in his therapy sessions with Dr. McIver, he is like a caged animal, pacing back and forth between the walls of the office); the drapes he means to design are not simply or only décor but rather provide an expressive backdrop for an object of desire that might provide Stevie with a new reason to move through the world. In the flow of the classical continuity system, character movement, and the smooth flow of performance, was vividly invented by vibrant performative social agents. In Lubitsch's films, as we saw earlier in the book, movements are smooth, graceful, elegant; even though *Trouble in Paradise* asks us to question, contrast, and contemplate the differing value of time spent with particular actors, the film never really questions the fundamental armature of continuity through which this performed time is expressed. In the screwball comedies of the thirties, the flow of performance is possessed by fast-talking and smart-moving characters, emblemized by Hepburn and Grant in their quartet of films together; the continuity armature there, too, is never questioned, and indeed its presence is confirmed through editing's very effort to keep up with the quicksilver movements of the figures on the screen. In noir, characters are sometimes reduced to stillness so as to be possessed—as in *Laura*—but the genre quickly recoups its emphasis on continuity in the films of Bacall and Bogart. But in Minnelli's proto-modernist melodramas, the very movement in and out of the frame is tortured: in *The Cobweb*, each of the patients struggles with moving forward (a struggle that itself is shared by the doctors and administrators in their personal lives) and the plot pivots around conflicts between differing ideas in how the space of their living will be designed. Performances in the family melodrama—especially in Minnelli and Sirk—fundamentally question the very space of their occurrence. Further, performance in this genre makes its effort to create a site of a livable future in ways that are as displaced as Stevie's paintings are. Aesthetic, costumed, and decorative design (of which even performative gesture becomes a part in some moments in the films) become, collectively, a metaphor for what the characters cannot directly achieve in the existing social worlds in which they are presently figured.

Of course, in some moments in these films, the most sensible solution for the characters is not to refigure one's setting, but to extricate oneself from it. Families and institutions in Minnelli and Sirk often seem designed to be left behind for good, rather than merely "reformed." (This, in fact, is why the genre of melodrama, at least when performed in frames composed by Minnelli and Sirk, is perhaps the most meaningfully radical of all Hollywood objects, one in which the desire for simple reform is left behind in favor of the gesture for a more radical dismantling, expressed in the form of the films through their gestures toward modernism and in the performances within the films through an expressed lack of ease with the surrounding world or any effort to remake it.) The goal of the psychiatric hospital in *The Cobweb*, as an institution, after all, is to have patients eventually leave. In fact, it should be a great boon to everyone in the film if it ceased to exist. The "reforming" going on is a mere way station to achieved health and eventual departure (only the doctors, who must stay to continue to cure, remain present and sick). But in his very attempt to make the environment of the hospital more conducive to healthy relationships, Stevie's design for the drapes threatens to arrest these same relationships in an eternal present. This is the repeated tragedy witnessed throughout the performance of love in melodrama: the gesture of love, transposed and displaced onto objects of design, rather than creating a new world, threatens merely to decorate an intolerable one, a world felt everywhere in these films as ultimately something that must finally be left rather than merely reshaped.

Critical literature on Vincente Minnelli has often noted the relationship between actor and décor, and between character and environment—or, more broadly, between the gesture of performance and gestures of design felt elsewhere in the film. Thomas Elsaesser draws a parallel between Minnelli's artistic protagonists and Minnelli as auteur, writing that, in Minnelli's musicals, we are introduced to "a liberated universe, where the total freedom of expression (of the character's creative impulse) serves to give body and meaning to the artist's vitality in the director, both being united by their roles as metteurs en scene of the self" (*Vincente Minnelli* 86). Elsaesser, further, sees Minnelli's melodramas as films that "aspire to the condition of the musical," their characters (artistic and sensitive, regardless of their professional occupation) themselves yearning to express something of their sensibility, becoming "highly sophisticated and cunning daydreamers . . . confusing—for good or ill—what is part of their imagination and what is real, and trying to obliterate the difference between what is freedom and what is necessity." Or, as Elsaesser goes on to write in the same passage, "When Gene Kelly begins to dance, or plays with the first words of a song, say in *Brigadoon* (1954), the world melts away and reality becomes a stage"; but in Minnelli's non-musical films, this reshaping of the world of the character becomes an expressive struggle, a clash of social worlds and expressive styles, "the confrontation of an inner, dynamic reality and an outward, static one" (85). These comments have much import for writing on performance in Minnelli's films; the amount of psychological expressivity the performances may be seen to bear at any given moment must be put into a dialectical connection with the performer's relationship to surrounding and socially articulated *mise-en-scène* (particularly décor), and with the performer's own efforts, through this relationship, to convey something of the character's efforts (which may or may not be fully conscious) to reshape his environment in the vision of his aesthetic sensibilities. This often becomes manifest in Minnelli's universe through the way actors, as Joe McElhaney has written, become "hidden within the décor only to suddenly, surprisingly emerge out of it ("Vincente Minnelli and *Some Came Running*" 332), or how the color of surrounding environment or costume is sometimes made to carry symbolic meaning that the characters, and the performers, themselves do not otherwise articulate, as in the function of the color blue (used to convey John Kerr's innocence and protracted boyhood) in *Tea and Sympathy*. As David A. Gerstner has pointed out (see "The Production and Display of the Closet," especially 286–291), this symbolic use of color is exemplary of Minnelli's tendency to "aestheticize the text," that is, take nominally conservative narrative structures and imbue them with signs of desire that otherwise go unarticulated.

Receiving less comment in this critical literature are the relationships, or the attempts at relationship, between characters, as crafted by the performances themselves, and the way in which performers create characterizations in which characters may be felt to convey erotic desire or intention toward one another (even if the social world in which they live figures the final fulfillment of the courtship as ultimately impossible). McElhaney, in one of the few pieces that explores in depth performance and gesture in Minnelli's cinema, describes eloquently the "duel and duet" (331) that unfolds between Frank Sinatra and Dean Martin in an early scene in Smitty's Bar in *Some Came Running* (1958), and Elsaesser notes how Minnelli explores conflicts and connections in human relationships "as a clash of settings, an imbalance of stylistic elements, such as a contrast of movements or a disharmony of colors or objects" (91). James Naremore, in his book on Minnelli, suggests how Minnelli's actors rely upon "a formalized, somewhat pantomimic style that resembles a dance" and that tends to reject, in its favoring of relationship with external environment over tortured expressions of interiority, the trends of Method acting popular in the 1950s (40). Yet few other writers explore the effort at connection between performers/characters in Minnelli's melodramas—the effort to form a couple (or to go beyond this form with some alternative formation) through expressive gestures and expressions. This lack of comment on the performative and social formation (and frustration) of love in Minnelli is related to a larger problem facing writers who take Minnelli's performers as their subject: psychological significance, that outcome of performance for many writers, is not always easily read into Minnelli's figures. As the writings of the various authors cited above have taught us, the Minnelli character (in the melodramas, at least, if not the musicals) is defined by the very tendency to lack liberation, to be unable to express an inner life with the psychological and intentional agency of a screwball heroine or a noir tough guy. Of course, we have seen a certain restraint of expressivity before, in this book, in the chapter on *Laura*; and yet the problem in Minnelli's melodramas is not the same. Where Gene Tierney and Dana Andrews reduce their ostensive range in the Preminger film, in Minnelli's films the actor is often quite busy with a range of gesture, movement, and expression; she is never quite still in her attempt to reshape environment in the mind's eye of her vision. Performance in Minnelli's melodramas is geared toward the external conveyance of an expressive struggle, a struggle that, for the figure in Minnelli who finds herself attracted to another, often fails to attain the final figuration of coupledom achieved in the screwball comedies and noir films discussed earlier in this book. Where the Sirk lover will often find herself locked in a tangle of desire that goes beyond even the couple (the quartet of Bacall, Stack, Malone, and Hudson in *Written on the Wind*, explored in the next chapter, is emblematic of this idea), the Minnelli lover, by contrast, is quite often alone, and left there.

And this is a loneliness that, perhaps, points to a lack of direct representation or inscription of identity and sexuality in the performances we find in Minnelli's fifties work. An attendant issue in writing on performance in Minnelli, and the way in which performers convey the desires of characters for others, is the limits of 1950s Hollywood cinema in conveying character desire explicitly, to the point that sometimes it cannot be read at all. This concern is at the very heart of the performances in *Tea and Sympathy*, Minnelli's 1956 adaptation of a 1953 Robert Anderson play about a male college student who is suspected, by his peers, of being a homosexual. Minnelli's film version makes no overt reference to homosexuality, and instead tells a story of Tom (John Kerr), a senior at Chilton Prep School, who develops a relationship with Laura (Deborah Kerr), the wife of a faculty member, while dealing with the social pressure put upon him by other male students who taunt him for not sharing their interests in macho activities (football, bonfires, girls). David A. Gerstner has closely studied the way in which the PCA and the Catholic Legion of Decency pressured MGM and Minnelli to craft a film that "would clearly punish the sexual transgressions of the married woman, and that . . . would not overtly or covertly make any reference to homosexuality" (275). Minnelli's film version gets around possible implications of homosexuality by adding a narrative frame in which the adult Tom (complete with wedding ring on his left hand) returns to Chilton as a successful author of his experiences (he has published a book about his relationship with Laura and the other boys at the college), prompting a flashback to the film's own recounting of those earlier plot events. Gerstner has convincingly argued that Minnelli, unable to tell a story of homosexuality in narratively explicit terms, instead "practices a process of aestheticization on the mise-en-scène in order to make visible and hyperbolize the cultural anxiety of masculinity," visible in Minnelli's use of symbolic color in order to suggest emotional meanings that the characters themselves cannot (287). Gerstner's description of Minnelli's aestheticization practices is certainly important, but in placing special emphasis on the expressive agency of the director's use of symbolic color, a focus on what is communicated by the performances themselves tends to recede. If color is the primary agent of expressive meaning in *Tea and Sympathy* (and if the homosexual as a character is effectively rendered "invisible," as Gerstner suggests, in typical narrative or performative terms), it is difficult to see what John Kerr (or indeed Deborah Kerr) add to the film themselves, in their performances, in relation to but also, at times, beyond décor. If the homosexual cannot be represented in *Tea and Sympathy* (if, as a figure, the homosexual is invisible in performance in fifties melodrama, as in much cinema before and after), then this opens up the question of what, precisely, John Kerr and Deborah Kerr are doing through their gestures, movements, and expressions (a problematic of representation, social identity, and performance that is applicable to all melodramas but is especially and acutely felt in this one), and what relationships their characters have (consciously or unconsciously) to whatever metaphorical meaning is suggested through their performances. To ask this question, further, is to open up the related inquiry into how any connection, or courtship, between these two characters is performed: certainly we are conscious of Minnelli's aestheticization (of the way the color blue, for example, comes to represent Tom's clinging to boyhood), but the characters themselves seem cognitively distant from such symbolic concerns (unlike Stevie in *The Cobweb*, who expresses some control over symbols through his paintings), even as their gestures and movements on the screen elsewhere convey some desire to break out of the social norms indicated by them. As realized on the screen and in terms of performance, I suggest, *Tea and Sympathy* is less an explicit narrative about a homosexual persecuted by his classmates for his different desire than it is about the feminine desire for a feminine, perhaps even boyish, man (who may or may not be a homosexual; his identity, still in the process of formation at the end of the film—despite its ostensible narrative form as a flashback—remains an open, shifting question); and the desire of a feminine man for a woman who welcomes, indeed finds attractive, the free expression of his femininity.

    John Kerr and Deborah Kerr convey their shared desire—their connection—through their positioning in space, and their performances suggest the problem they face in continuously moving forward into different social spheres (coded, in this film, as alternately masculine or feminine). In *Tea and Sympathy*, these social spheres involve interior spaces (such as the domestic home managed by Laura, and coded as feminine); exterior spaces (sites of masculine activity and, with some exceptions, coded as male); and certain unseen spaces (such as the sites of Tom's committee work for the school's musical theater, coded as feminine but unrepresented on the screen and never shown as space into which Tom, who is prevented from performing in the school play by the macho football coach, may ably move). In the first scene of the film's flashback (which appears after we have seen the older, married Tom, perched next to the window of the room that was his during his time at the school, begin to reminiscence about his past), a dissolve takes us from the barren, weed-ridden landscape of the backyard Tom presently sees to the colorful garden tended by Laura, the garden of his past. Framed from above, the camera looking through the bedroom window at the garden below, Laura is arranging and planting flowers while Tom sits perched next to the window, singing a song of love—a Minnellian troubadour (figure 6.9). Cut to a medium-shot of Laura, digging dirt to plant a flower—momentarily held in stillness by the sound of Tom's song drifting from the window above. After that moment, she shakes her head—just a silly song, not worth contemplating. Deborah Kerr, foregrounded here, is saliently thrown into relief against the green of the grass and the pink and blue flowers behind her, although her orange dress, yellow-orange hat and orange-red hair tend to render her figural presence relatively monochromatic. Tom looks down and sees Laura lifting her planter's box of flowers. Bringing his song to an abrupt end (if his intended audience is leaving, he has no more reason to sing it), he bounds out of the window, jumping down on the grass and stepping quickly down the small hill to help her, a display of physicality that is nevertheless not quite the equivalent of a classical movement of continuity that might serve to connect different social spheres together in the guise of a goal: we have instead been introduced to Tom in a feminine sphere (in his bedroom, strumming a love song on a guitar, an activity coded, in the social world of the film's diegesis, as feminine) and his movement is to another feminine sphere, the outside world of the garden, hemmed in and separated from the outside masculine world of duty and athletics by a brick wall and fence that surrounds the home. Tom begins telling Laura of his past (his parents are divorced, his father did not like him gardening) as he shares advice about where to place which flowers (certain kinds of flowers, Tom tells her, will wilt in the bright sun). As Tom goes on to tell Laura that he has not seen his mother since he was five years old, Deborah Kerr removes her orange-yellow hat and places it on the table, running her fingers, for a moment, through her red hair. It is a gesture that pulls in two directions at once: as an object of sensitive and possibly erotic attention for Tom, it associates Laura, her pale skin now exposed to the sun with the removal of the hat, with the flowers Tom has tended to, placing them in shade for protection; but it is also a gesture that appears after Tom has mentioned his absent mother, linking whatever erotic desire Laura may feel for this boy to a complementary set of maternal feelings. Laura and Tom move back inside (again demonstrating the fluid connection between these equally feminine spaces), Tom carrying a vase of flowers behind her. (Deborah Kerr is no longer salient in this space, as she was in the garden a minute before; her orange dress is a perfect match for the orange-yellow curtains through which the wind blows into her kitchen.) Yet a beat later, Laura mentions that she thought Tom was to be at a varsity athletic club meeting—where, according to the strictures of this film's social world, he is supposed to be, rather than singing songs of woo to a faculty wife—again reminding us of the difficulty Tom will face in moving from a feminine space to a masculine one later in the film.

As the scene progresses, the performances continue to suggest the theme of the difficulty one faces in moving through and across spaces, the difficulty of connecting interior rooms that shelter feminine desire with exterior ones that display the activities of the masculine. And this difficulty in moving through spaces is felt in more than just movement, but now in every aspect of performance, from spatial relationship to décor to line delivery. Tom notices that the front door to the living room is still open, the door which leads out onto a corridor and a staircase connected to the various rooms Laura and her husband, the faculty member, housemaster, and Coach Bill Reynolds (Leif Erickson) share with a handful of students. "Do you want the door open, or shut?" Tom asks, stammering slightly, after which Laura answers that it does not make any difference. Tom moves over to close it, light from the front window streaming in. A beat later, Laura changes her mind, telling him to keep it open in case her students return early from the varsity club

Figure 6.9. John Kerr, the troubadour, in *Tea and Sympathy* (MGM, 1956).

meeting. Kerr moves over to the door, and re-opens it, but now leaves it only slightly ajar, with, now, most of the exterior light shut out by the door frame—a gesture that ostensibly leaves the door somewhat open (a social necessity, since other, more masculine boys may still pass through it) while still warding off those outside influences.

As Tom moves to and from the door, Deborah Kerr moves in and out of the kitchen, her routine and domesticated movements in counterpoint to John Kerr's somewhat clipped steps through the home. His shrugging and slouching of shoulders, his twiddling of fingers, and occasional, slight stuttering, further, all suggest a lack of certainty in movement. Indeed, this scene, which for Tom would seem to have been set up as a scene of ongoing flirtation with the faculty wife to whom he sang a song of woo in the earlier part of the film (he is ostensibly here to ask Laura to be his date for a school dance), is instead marked by John Kerr's staccato line delivery, in which certain fragments of sentences come inflectively undone from the clauses and contents coming before them. This is audible in the dialogue Kerr delivers while nervously suggesting Laura accompany him, member of the school's music committee, to the dance, informing her that her husband will be out of town that weekend, so she may as well:

TOM: As a member of the com—mittee, I am taking you.

. . .

TOM: Well, he's not . . . gonna . . . be in town. The mountain climbing club has its, uh, final outing . . . that weekend.

It is worth noting that, in contrast to this nervous stuttering, Tom has no difficulty at all with, but indeed rather a passionate interest in, tea and teacups: Kerr leans forward with interest and holds his teacup carefully and daintily, projecting a strong gaze at Laura now that he is sharing with her another activity, like the gardening, that he knows and enjoys. And he has no difficulty, either, a beat later, trying on the blue dress Laura is letting him borrow for a theatrical production—a theatrical production never glimpsed onscreen and that Tom, barred from participating by his anxious father (who fears, perhaps, that he is becoming queer), will never perform in. This is why he has kept the door mostly closed, precisely to inscribe a space in which he may enjoy these activities, with a woman who appears to take delight in his interest in enjoying them. Tom only becomes uncomfortable, and anxious, when Laura asks him to practice a dance: awkwardly raising his hands to take her in his arms, Tom waits for Laura to embrace him rather than taking the active role. "We look kind of silly, both of us in skirts," he says. Self-consciousness, slipping in like the shaft of light in the door that Kerr had shut, keeps Tom from pushing this scene past propriety and into desire.

Laura, later in the first act, at the beach, will sew and gossip with two other faculty wives. Framed by Minnelli in a laterally composed widescreen image (with Deborah Kerr on the right side of the frame, farthest away from the camera), they are chatting about the male students and their ignorance of women. "This is the age Romeo should be played," one of them says—and then Minnelli cuts to this film's Romeo, John Kerr, as he slips into the view of the image from behind a set of rocks serving to separate the feminine side of the beach (where activities like sewing and gossiping go on) from its ostensibly masculine side (where one roughhouses, throws a football, takes fan magazine surveys about masculinity). Where Kerr is coming from, we cannot see—has he been previously with other male students, having left them? Has he tired of pretending to enjoy throwing a football or has he avoided it altogether? The question points to the film's repeated insistence on Tom's inability to connect different social spheres through the fact of his movement, and the film's own mirroring of this struggle through its own reluctance to connect these spaces through *découpage*. Instead, he moves into this exterior space populated by the faculty wives, a space—like every other space in which we have seen him so far (garden, kitchen)—that lacks a proscenium for pronounced and foregrounded masculine activity.

After Kerr approaches, he sits down next to the wives, framed on the left side of the image (opposite Deborah Kerr on the right), with the two other faculty wives seated between them. John Kerr's positioning—knees bent, hands hugging legs—keeps him still and reserved, his arms preventing any display of flesh from making an ocular impression on these women. He observes that one of Laura's friends isn't sewing as efficiently as she might—he knows a lot about sewing, he reveals, having learned from the maid who raised him in absence of a mother. Somewhat cattily, this friend throws the sewing at him and invites him to take a shot at it—which he does, an acceptance greeted by the other friend as a sign that Tom will "make some girl a good wife." Laura bristles at this suggestion, quickly remarking that her current husband, an ostensible picture of acceptable and comfortably socialized masculinity, learned how to sew buttons in the army. She will, further, impel Tom to go join the other boys when a pair of them spots him sewing after an errant football goes flying over the rocks. He does, but the boys won't throw the ball to him—he is not recognized as a competent social performer of this sport. And at this, John Kerr disappears from the scene. Expelled from the feminine sphere of sewing by Deborah Kerr's worried, motherly gesture, and rejected as a performer of athletics by the other boys, we never see, in this scene, where he goes next. Tom is rendered literally and metaphorically invisible here, neither connecting nor existing within either of the scene's masculine and feminized spaces. This is, nevertheless, an invisibility made palpable and heartbreaking through John Kerr's performance in the scenes, such as this one at the beach, which bracket his disappearance; if *Tea and Sympathy* renders the homosexual invisible, it is Kerr who figures for us the heartbeat of the one who this social world removes from our vision, a social world full of those who would say what his heart wants is invalid.

Tea and Sympathy, given this theme of invisibility, does not spend much time in the one social sphere in which Tom would seem to be accepted—that is, visible: the school's musical theater. Tom is a member of the music committee on campus; his teacher responds with great disappointment when Tom informs him (over the phone) that he will not be able to perform the cross-dressing role required of him during the next theatrical production. This teacher is never glimpsed in the film, although we do see Tom, once, in the school's music rehearsal space. But rather than existing as a sphere in which Tom may confidently perform his own sensitive, feminine inhabitation of a certain kind of masculinity, it instead becomes a space in which he is instructed, self-consciously and cruelly, with everything that is wrong about the way he moves. Indeed, in this scene, the character is taught the very movements and expressions that will render what is visible about the femininity Tom desires to inhabit invisible, unseen and cloaked under the gestures of normative manhood in which he is here tutored. His friend Al (Darryl Hickman), worried that his friendship with Tom will damage his chances at becoming the captain of the football team, arrives in this space to have a talk with him. Piano is heard in the background, but Tom is not playing; he is listening to a phonograph record, sitting facing away from Al by the window, lost in thought. Al, approaching, leaves the door open—perhaps to keep the larger social world within reach, to reduce the intimacy of the scene—and walks toward Tom. "Come up here to listen to records?" Tom asks, to which Al nervously responds "no"—but perhaps he has in the past, the first sign in the film that perhaps another male in Tom's social circle has tried to traverse the masculine world of athletics and the feminine world of music. Tom paces back and forth, with nervous anger, telling Al he (Tom) is no longer a member of the dance committee—and without that, he seems a caged animal, with nowhere to go or to be. "The terrible thing," Tom says, of this bullying he has endured, "is that I find myself self-conscious about things I've been doing for years." At this, Al—sitting next to the bust of Bach that rests on a desk, his arm around the figure as if the composer were a chum he were sharing drinks with at the local bar—makes an effort to inscribe Tom into "the way people look at things," as he puts it. He will teach him how to walk manly, how to look and to talk, drafting him into a masculine code of behavior just as helpless Bach has, with one gesture, become the unwitting buddy of next year's football captain. After a brief argument about the impossibility of changing one's behavior and appearance, Tom finally settles on the idea that Al might have something to teach him, and so he asks him to show him how to walk. At this, Al asks Tom to demonstrate his way of moving through space, so that he may observe where the deviance lies. John Kerr leans forward as if his character were about to tiptoe onto a high-wire—and almost tips over onto the floor. He then walks, elevated on tiptoes, in a circle, around the room—a self-conscious gait that, importantly, is completely unlike any way in which John Kerr has actually walked up to this point in the film (even for the viewer who has not consciously noticed Kerr's manner of walking prior to this moment, his demonstration of walking to Darryl Hickman will come across as mannered and stilted). Al can't articulate what makes the walk funny—he can only gesture up and down in air with an extended palm, as if to imply an unacceptable queerness about Tom's way of moving. When Tom asks for Al to demonstrate the oddness of the walk, Al protests: he can't do it! Instead, he performs a demonstration of the masculine gait that Tom should adopt, the result being every bit as gingerly awkward as John Kerr's earlier movement—the only significant difference being the fact that Al walks in straight lines where Tom walked around in circles. Tom tries to copy the walk, but the result is nothing: just frustrated interiority, an inability to move. The only pedagogy Al can now offer, in the face of this failure, is to suggest Tom take out Ellie Martin (Norma Crane), a local waitress perceived by others as "trashy." (This advice does not work out, either.)

 The film's final sequences end in loneliness and separation, a failure to find in romance an opportunity to either reform or move beyond one's present social sphere. In the first of these sequences, Tom is about to run downstairs, after struggling to work up the confidence to go to the dance. He spots the ajar door belonging to Laura Reynolds, an open invitation inside. He initially resists it, but is lured in by the sound of Laura's voice. Laura walks over to a table on which she has arranged a bouquet of yellow roses she has received from Tom, a gesture he had intended as part of their date to the dance, a dance to which Tom now does not want to go. She moves over to him, and invites him to share a cup of tea, handing him a cup and saucer, the same dainty glassware he pleasurably sipped from before. Yet there is a difference with the cup, now: this was Laura's tea, before Tom's arrival, and although she has "only had a sip," her lipstick marks the side of the cup Tom brings to his lips (we cannot see the red on the edge of the glass, but he does, and stops from sipping). Such is the importance of object and décor in Minnelli's cinema; even lipstick on a teacup is enough to constitute a gesture of passion. Tom twists the cup around, awkwardly, to drink from the other side, in order to conform to social decorum.

Laura matches this modesty by moving to the other side of the frame, the yellow flowers once again visible in view between them. She is a good hostess, and wants him to stay, so compels him to remove his overcoat—an act she helps him with, but one that stops her short when she realizes he is dressed for the dance he claims he no longer wants to take her to. It is this vision of Tom, dapper, young, and confident, at least in this feminine interior space, with his particular form of sensitive, feminized masculinity that sparks in Laura the desire to share her memories of her deceased first husband, who was killed during World War II in an act of foolish bravery. This is a tale that projects onto John Kerr the image of Laura's deceased husband (and thus articulates, for the first time in the film, one subjective source of her potential desire for this young boy) but it is also clear that she means it as a moral lesson—that is, to be himself, to act confidently with the kind of feminized masculinity that she finds both desirable and admirable. After sharing this reminiscence, she invites Tom to sit with her, again offering him the teacup with one outstretched arm. After a beat, though, she remembers the lipstick traces on its brim, and, with a raised eyebrow and slight smile indicating amused caution, pulls the teacup back and turns it around, offering it to him again. "He was kind, and gentle, and lonely," Laura says of her deceased husband, while Tom sips from the cup. "We knew it wouldn't last, we sensed it; but he always said why must the test of everything be its durability?" Her words suggest that while love is no more durable than the fragile teacup Tom presently holds, it is possibly and nevertheless as sweet as tea; and as she speaks of this sweetness transcending durability and time spent, we have perhaps noticed John Kerr on the other side of the frame, now sipping from a teacup that he has turned back around, now sipping from the side with the lipstick.

The words Deborah Kerr speaks here, of course, not only capture something of her earlier marriage to the deceased John, but also rebound onto Tom's own fragile and precocious courtship with her, a romance so brief that its second kiss also marks its finality. In their final encounter in the flashback, Laura finds Tom alone, lying down in a forest, after a failed effort at making love with Ellie Martin has led to a suicide attempt. Where earlier scenes in the film have been framed by tension and boundaries between different social spaces, here, in the space of the forest, Tom and Laura are cordoned off from society, in a "natural" space. But in Minnelli's hands, it is no less aesthetic: the diffused lighting and deeply textured array of color (the forest, although lit low-key, is awash in various tonalities of green flora) position what is performed within it as an ongoing creative construction between two social agents struggling to realize themselves, rather than a site for some revelation of naturally existing personality. Laura, on the left side of Minnelli's wide frame, with a large tree trunk and extending branches compositionally separating her from Tom, begins this construction in a maternal key, kneeling down to Tom, pleading for him to realize that his actions with Ellie meant nothing. John Kerr, on the right side of the frame, is cast in low-key light, his facial expressions kept ambiguous. He is here, something like the flowers he has guarded from sunlight earlier in the film, unwilling to recognize in Laura any figure that might help him out of the darkness his failed courtship with Ellie Martin has led him to. He rejects Laura's help and lies back down on the cold forest floor, as she gets up and begins to walk away up a small hill leading out of the forest. Laura stops, though, and turns back around, looking down at Tom (now curled up, like the small boy to whom he would perhaps like to regress) from a position that inverts the staging of the two characters in their first shared scene in the film (where Tom had been looking down at Laura in her garden from the view of an upstairs window). Laura, pressing her fingers against her Adam's apple, walks back over to Tom. There is a brief cut back to Tom, to show he is aware of her returned presence, before another cut back to Laura, who lets her hand fall from her throat as she slowly gestures her palm outward, to help Tom stand up. In an equally gradual gesture, he takes her hand and is lifted up. Cut to a closer two-shot, as Deborah Kerr takes the sides of his face in her hands, a gesture positioned ambiguously between the erotic and the maternal, the sexual and the cautious (figure 6.10).

"Years from now," she says, "when you talk about this—and you will—be kind." She leans in gently while guiding him toward her lips. Now, no teacup mediates the moment. They kiss.

This kiss is quite unlike any other in this book. It is not like a kiss in a remarriage comedy, such as *The Philadelphia Story*, which would confirm a certain kind of "known" beyond, the promise of future marriage. It is also quite unlike the first kiss between Bogart and Bacall in *To Have and Have Not*, in which the latter engulfs the former in a cascade of hair. This kiss in *Tea and Sympathy* is cautious, dream-like—whatever erotic charge it possesses is balanced by Minnelli's aestheticization of the natural set-

Figure 6.10. Deborah Kerr and John Kerr, in the moment he will kindly talk about years from now, in *Tea and Sympathy* (MGM, 1956).

ting, detaching the moment from any social reality that might be transformed, where desire might be fulfilled. The kiss, instead, as moments like this in Minnelli often do, opens up another world—but only for a moment, before inevitably slipping away from the figures on the screen. Tom tries to prolong the memory of the kiss, tries to make it last a little longer, guiding his lips down to Laura's palms and kissing them, and then burying his head in her shoulder. Laura, earlier, has remarked upon the undue emphasis placed on durability and time in matters of love; love, for her, is valid in a single moment, perhaps more valid by virtue of the fact that it does not and cannot last in a society so inimical to what is discovered in that moment. Deborah Kerr conveys, throughout the film, passion tempered by wisdom and maturity; she knows both of them will have to return to a social sphere in which moments like this are impossible. She tells him only, in the years to come (the years whose durability and ongoingness will outstrip that of the kiss) to be kind. He will be—the author of a book that perhaps tries to teach kindness. But he will also be, in the absence of this woman who understood and responded to his femininity and despite the wedding ring we see on his finger, alone, as Minnelli's final image of a tearful John Kerr sitting in the once again barren garden of the Reynolds home, more than implies.

7

Hudson, Bacall, Stack, Malone

Love and Gesture in Douglas Sirk's *Written on the Wind*

As Jean-Luc Godard reminds us, in his piece "Montage, My Fine Care," the orchestration of love in cinema involves the casting of a look (which Godard allies with direction, and *mise-en-scène*), and the beating of a heart (which Godard relates to *découpage* and cutting, and which involves a dance with desires across the rhythms of time). But elsewhere, in a different piece of criticism, Godard also writes: "To look around oneself is to live free. So the cinema, which reproduces life, must film characters who look around them" (*Godard on Godard* 51). Can the loving moment of union, the performative realization of *découpage*, occur between characters who do not live free, who are too riveted in place to look around and meet the eyes of another?

The opening sequence of *Written on the Wind* (1956) introduces the viewer to Kyle Hadley (Robert Stack). He is the son of an oil baron, and his surname is emblazoned on the oversized "H" symbols dotting the landscape of this Texas town. In this first scene, he is racing his flashy car—Peter William Evans confirms that it is a "1953 Allard J2X hot rod" (7)—across a twilight landscape. The car's bright headlamps and garish yellow exterior imprint largesse on a town that shares Kyle's name but little of his wealth. In one close shot, an image created through rear projection, Stack faces screen right as his car zooms ahead, clutching a bottle of cheap, bootleg corn in his right hand. Biting off the bottle cap with his teeth, he spits it out the right side of the car and takes a

Figure 7.1. Douglas Sirk, directing Rock Hudson, Lauren Bacall, and Robert Stack on the set of *Written on the Wind* (Universal, 1956).

swig before cradling the open bottle under his left arm as he focuses forward on the road (figure 7.2). The image is not quite an emblematic moment of performance—Stack creates a wide enough variety of gestures, movements, and expressions in this film to dissuade us from the idea that anything of what he does might be routinely summarized in a single image—but it, and the sequence within which it is placed, already deliriously complicate Godard's theorem. To look is liberation, to freely arrange oneself in a social *mise-en-scène*: yet Stack only looks straight ahead, on this road conjured through studio rear-projection, possessed by invisible demons. To move is to feel rhythm, to realize one's desires in and across time, moving toward one you love: yet Stack's Kyle is being driven more than he is doing the driving, toward no lover, pursued instead by those invisible demons—his family, perhaps, whose successful oil business is in part responsible for the smooth driving that takes place every day on this road.

Does Kyle Hadley live free? Stack's first gestures in the film remind us, despite Godard's insistence on the link between cinema and freedom, that cinema often presents characters who don't know how to look, or whose instrumental, or dulled, or repressed forms of looking blind them. These opening shots of Stack racing across the highway are sumptuous in their twilight greens, whites, and twinkling yellows, this fictional town of Hadley a colorful Technicolor paradise for any lover of opulent Hollywood melodrama. But although the viewer is given quite a bit to look at and indulge in, Stack himself doesn't look around very much. It would be easy enough to suggest that he has already seen too much of this town. He has always been wealthy; he has always had time to look; and all of this is *his*—he already owns it, his name is indeed inscribed

Figure 7.2. Robert Stack, pursued by invisible demons, in *Written on the Wind* (Universal, 1956).

on it—so why look at it? But he has also been an alcoholic for all of his adult life, and a good part of his adolescent one; he will tell his wife, Lucy Moore, played by Lauren Bacall, that he took his first drink at the age of fourteen. (We are a long way, here, from the pleasurable imbibing of *The Thin Man*.) Perhaps what he has seen has been blurred; perhaps, drunken, he has not had control of his body—perhaps he has let other forces take control. Ostensibly moving forward in his hot rod, just as he will later in the film when he (at an earlier moment in diegetic story time) jets across the United States in his private plane (to New York City, to his favorite bar), Stack is truly stuck in his place.

And Bacall, playing Kyle's wife; and Rock Hudson, playing his childhood friend and adult antagonist Mitch; and Dorothy Malone, playing Kyle's desirous sister, Marylee—are they free, any less "stuck"? In subsequent images after Kyle pulls up to the Hadley manor in his yellow car, Hudson, Bacall, and Malone are filmed through what John Mercer and Martin Shingler (54–55) describe as one of the key signature tropes of Sirk's cinema: the internal frame, which is here a set of windows through which we glimpse, first, a prostrate Bacall (sick, we will later learn), on the bottom half of the frame, set apart from Hudson by a window panel. Hudson's face is bathed partially in the moving shadows of the offscreen tree blowing in the wind, on the right side of the frame, as he looks down at the driveway to the house with melancholy and perhaps already a twinge of regret right before Kyle's hot rod pulls up. And then, a few moments later, the introduction of Malone, whose Marylee, hearing the smash of the bottle Kyle has thrown against the exterior wall of the servant's quarters, approaches her window; we are a little closer to her, physically, than we were to Hudson, as she moves to the camera, but she is still figured through the sheer and gently rustling curtains on either side, and her glance, bracketed by vertical shadows obscuring her forehead and her chin, is full of portent. The actors in this sequence are, of course, moving, hitting their blocks, fulfilling the aims of Sirk's *découpage*. The low-key lighting, the rich blues, oranges, greens, pinks, yellows, and blacks, and the precise framing are all arranged as introductions to the characters. Yet the sequence is also introducing us to, or reminding us of, someone else: Douglas Sirk, the orchestrator, the ultimate conductor, of all this emotional life figured in the frame.

Certainly most of the critical commentary on Sirk's cinema, in all the various phases (auteurist, psychoanalytic, genre-based) through which it has passed, takes Sirk as a central or key figure in the creation of his films, sometimes obscuring or deprioritizing—or, more pointedly, and in a word that creeps up often in Sirk criticism, *distancing* us from—our intimate connection to performance in his films. Sometimes the actor, and the character she plays, is dismissed almost entirely in Sirk criticism. Paul Willemen, author of magisterial articles on Sirk exploring the European émigré's importation of Brechtian distanciation to Hollywood cinema, goes so far as to opine, in an interview, that he finds "the acting in Sirk's films, for the most part, boring, and the characters completely uninteresting. One of the reasons I like Sirk's films, one of the reasons they talk to me, is because the characters become supremely irrelevant. Characters are totally flattened out, are simply strings of clichés put together" (244–45). If Willemen takes the distanciation from the actor in Sirk to its extreme, other commentators have found a place for the performer in Sirk's cinema, but without quite bringing an affection for the actor to the forefront. Thomas Elsaesser's canonical article "Observations on the Family Melodrama" shows how Sirk's stylistic strategies work to project ideas about character psychology and emotions that the characters themselves cannot articulate, or which are repressed, onto elements of *mise-en-scène*, "a sublimation of dramatic conflict into décor, colour, gesture and composition of the frame, which in the best melodramas is perfectly thematised in terms of the characters' emotional and psychological predicaments" (52). The word "gesture" would here seem to signal a priority of place for the actor in Elsaesser's conception of melodramatic style, but his sentence subtly divorces gesture from character, intriguingly positing that the performative gesture might itself be yet another tool of stylistic distanciation that provides the viewer with a significance the character herself cannot quite articulate. John Gibbs, in his reading of Elsaesser's piece within the context of a study of *mise-en-scène*, remarks that "in the melodrama the physical and social sphere in which the characters live means that they cannot openly express themselves or resolve concerns through dance"—as in the musical—"or decisive action"—as in the Western (71). Indeed, it is telling that when Elsaesser comments appreciatively on performance in "Observations," often it is on a trait of the performer that is "quite consciously employed" by the director rather than a direct contribution by an actor; Elsaesser's example from *Written on the Wind* is "the psychoanalytic significance of Robert Stack's voice . . . sounding as if every word had to be painfully pumped up from the bottom of one of his oil-wells" (51–52).

If performative gesture or vocal inflection function as a sign of a psychological content of which the character, and perhaps even the actor, herself knows nothing, Sirk's complex visual style, as the Elsaesser article suggests, makes direct emotional access to the performer tricky, and, if we are to agree with Willemen's hard-line Brechtian approach to Sirk's cinema, impossible, or at least uninteresting. James Harvey, likewise, has noted how, in *Written on the Wind*, objects take on a presence that sometimes obscures, or deflects attention away from, the actor.

> The inanimate objects in this movie are . . . intensely *present*. Like that yellow roadster, or those ceaselessly nodding oil pumps (like grazing pterodactyl heads) that often turn up at the sides of the screen in exterior shots. The *things* in the movie get your attention even when they don't seem to be calling for it—even when they're not foregrounded or otherwise highlighted. Not because they seem "so real"—we don't normally, for example, see colors at such intensity as they have here, in Russell Metty's Technicolor photography—but because they seem so powerfully sensuous, so intractably material. And they are everywhere. . . ." (346)

And being everywhere, the tactility, the *presence* of these objects turn the actors themselves, for Harvey, into abstractions.

> It's a sort of shock, then, when this effect first happens to a person—when a human figure is objectified in the same way: when Bacall—who is now married to Stack and on their honeymoon—arises from their bed and moves her sleeping husband's pillow to make him more comfortable, disclosing the revolver concealed beneath it. What gives this revelation its impact is the seeming tactility of everything in the shot: Stack is on his back, sleeping deeply, his face turned to the left, his upper body exposed to the waist, the smooth-skinned, deeply tanned flesh against the blue-tinged whiteness of the pillow and sheets; and Bacall, at screen right above him, standing in shock at her discovery, holding the pistol with its blue metal barrel and pearl-white handle in the palm of her hand over the brown form below. And yet while Stack's character looks almost alarmingly *embodied* here, heavy and inert and scarily exposed, Bacall is made to look almost bodiless, chic and gaunt in her diaphanous but concealing nightgown. And throughout the movie, with its insistent materiality, she becomes an almost *abstract* sort of presence. (346)

What Harvey is writing here echoes what Sirk himself said of the reasons behind Bacall's casting in the movie—"Because she has this ambiguity in her cold face. She has almost a designing quality at times . . . She has this wavering light about her—and she is not a lover. The whole relation between her and Stack remains ambiguous then" (qtd. in Harvey 350).

Harvey's thinking on the film also emerges as an extrapolation of a notion both Fred Camper and Dave Grosz, in separate pieces, had about Sirk back in a 1972 issue of *Screen* devoted to the director's work. Camper likens the visual style of *Written on the Wind* to a medieval painting (a notion that evokes Godard's quip that Sirk's magic is located in his "delirious mixture of the middle ages and modernity" [Godard 96]), with its abstract figurations of human characters and its visual attention to odd objects and settings, writing that

> [o]n the deepest expressive level, his frames never possess anything remotely resembling three-dimensional perspective, but rather they all operate in a kind of pre-Renaissance flatness . . . The camera, in wide angle, shows a deep and apparently 'realistic' room. But simultaneous with this perception we feel that the back of the room, the background, seems to have as much force, power, or presence as the foreground. The shot often places the foreground objects to the sides of the frame, leaving large spaces at the center for the background. This background seems to impinge, come forward, make itself felt with a rare and mysterious force. Finally, we feel that all the parts of the frame are fused into a single level of depth, a single surface. (51)

Dave Grosz extends these observations into a study of how the vision and perception of the viewer is enabled by Sirk's modernistic variations on the flatness of space, remarking that to watch Sirk's tendency to "use 'backgrounds' which, for one reason or another, attract attention" prompts in the viewer an effort that is much like walking "toward a distant scene in which objects were intermingled with each other so that, as far as location is concerned, they are indistinguishable. With some movement forward, although the parts might not yet be distinct, a certain tension becomes evident, an expectation of contact is still not visible. The perception itself eventually becomes a kind of deduction from that expectation"; that is, a perception that lacks the fulfillment of intimate contact with a figure in the frame. Grosz goes on: "The impossibility of emotional fulfillment for the characters is transformed into the impossibility of perceptual 'success' . . ." (101).

This failure to intimately connect with actors in Sirk's cinema, then, becomes, in Camper's, Grosz's, and to some extent Harvey's line of reasoning, the content of the Sirk film: the ambiguous connection, or, to use a more frequently employed word in the literature on Sirk criticism, the "distance," between a viewer and her filmic beloved redoubles onto the ambiguous and frustrated intimacies of the characters on the screen. Yet, remarkably, there are signs in the critical literature on Sirk that the actor has nevertheless occasionally and powerfully intervened in writing about this auteur's films. James McCourt, writing in a 1975 issue of *Film Comment*, weaves many words around Sirk's actors, remarking in particular upon Bacall's ability to "maintain tension. Oddly enough, and gratifyingly, this actress, whose entire career was founded on smart back-talk—elegant lip, ready mouth—plays the seriously wronged wife without a trace of miscast wanness. In casting terms it was like asking a thoroughbred to just stand there and rear its head from time to time. It's a perfect balance" (20). However, no less an authority on Sirk's poetics that Rainer Werner Fassbinder finds Malone and Stack, playing the "villains," to be far more interesting than Bacall and Hudson, signaling his intimate bond as viewer with one particular actor by referring to her via the first name: "Dorothy does something bad . . . I love her as I rarely love anyone in the cinema" (23). So, taking my cue from McCourt and Fassbinder's demonstrated ability to form affective bonds with the Sirkian figure, what if these orchestrations and visual complexities on display in Sirk's lavish film style in *Written on the Wind* were not felt as impediments to our understanding or intimate attachment to character, but rather viewed as partners to performance? What if objects, décor, lighting, music, cutting, color, and all the delectable techniques on display in Sirk's film style were approached not as obstacles over which one must hurdle in order to get close to Stack, Hudson, Bacall, or Malone, but rather taken or treated as if they were emotional instruments guiding (without ever quite explicitly or vulgarly underlining) our eye and our feeling toward gestures, movements, and expressions that perhaps might not be noticed otherwise? And what if becoming intimate to gesture and performance in Sirk might itself, in turn, inflect our understanding of the filmic world within which the characters struggle to be free? Such an approach might take style in Sirk as a two-way street, in which style, as has often been noted, might serve to comment on character psychology or frustration, but in which also, moving the other way, gestures of performance might, if we let them touch us, come to inflect the way we see color, light, music.

Steven Peacock, in his study of color in cinema, moves toward just this sort of approach to Sirk; as he studies the magisterial use of Technicolor in *Written on the Wind*, he often yokes his observations about a certain shade or hue with extensive descriptions of what the Sirk actor is shown to be doing. In his study on Sirk's film, he comments upon, for example, the way in which

> Lucy and Kyle's first encounter forms in red flushes for both of them. There is the flush to mark a sudden intense feel-

ing, the beginning of an exciting period, a sudden increased number of things, and the flush that causes one to become red in the face . . . Whereas the red [tablecloth] previously added only an edge of colour, it now fills the frame in a burst of brightness . . . Here is the first flush—too much. As the camera tips into the dazzling red surface, it threatens to overwhelm. The move matches the effect of Kyle's own grandiose gestures; both over-reach. (68–69)

Peacock approaches Stack, Bacall, Hudson, and Malone mostly as soloists: in his astute chapter on the film in his book on color, he parses out his observations about performance across different sections which treat different colors, and which tend to focus on one actor at a time, as in the association above of Stack's "grandiose gestures" with the sudden "flush" of red color in the frame. Later, blue will be linked with Kyle, and pink with Marylee. This approach, indeed, makes some sense: *Written on the Wind* is very much a film about isolation. In approaching a description of performance in which the Sirk actor is coupled with, rather than seen as obscured by, elements of the director's style, I want to take my cue from Peacock's method of weaving description of gesture alongside description of camera, color, and framing. But I also want to move toward appreciating what the actors in this film (functioning, at various different points, as soloists, couples, threesomes, as quartets) accomplish together: how their gestures, movements, and expressions respond and react and are blocked and staged in relation to one another, and how they, as tandems, trios, and foursomes, convey various forms of emotionally fraught existence within a film world that is felt everywhere (as we have already seen, in Kyle Hadley's drive through a landscape he is indifferent to) to be dissatisfying and stifling. Through this approach, we will move not only toward a fuller appreciation of what Sirk accomplished with his actors in *Written on the Wind*, but also, equally, a fitting end to the story of love this book tells; and through the close study of a family melodrama that, in its complex and fraught maneuverings of style and acting, gestures toward the performance of love in modern cinema, a more recent tradition I will comment on, briefly, in the book's final pages.

℮

After the opening prologue depicting the tragic end of Kyle Hadley in November 1956, *Written on the Wind* will flash back to just over a year earlier. It is October 24, 1955, as the calendar on a desk tells us, and Lucy Moore, played by Lauren Bacall, is jotting down a note. What she writes is obscured by a pair of ceramic bookends, and her attention soon shifts to the mock-up of an advertisement placed on the left side of her desk. This workspace, and the rest of the office—which we see as Bacall gets up from the desk and walks across to the window—is meticulously ordered, fashionably modern, everything in its right place. Except, perhaps, these advertisements—five of them, drafts of a project intended to display and market the glory of the Hadley Motor Oil Corporation in a tapestry of reds, oranges, greens, and blues. Bacall walks over to the sliding-glass door, opens it, and for a moment stands looking out at the Manhattan skyline, before turning her attention back to the advertisements. Sirk's camera has traced all of this in one unbroken movement, beginning on a close high-angle shot of Bacall's hands as she writes the note, before settling on a long view of her walking across the room to the drafts on display at the other end. Enough room is provided, on the right side of the frame, for the entrance of Rock Hudson, playing Mitch Wayne; but Lucy is preoccupied with her advertisements and doesn't see him. The stands on which the ads are mounted separate Hudson from Bacall, and when he enters he can only see her legs, or more exactly her feet, and the bottom of her calf-length blue skirt. This shot, a high-angle point-of-view image of what Hudson sees, is as abstract as anything in the film: four shafts of overcast light cutting across a purple floor, with Bacall's black shoes thrown into relief (figure 7.3). Yet what does Hudson see? He has walked in the room confident, and he's handsome: he must be looking at her legs. But the shot is abstract enough to suggest that Sirk's visual

Figure 7.3. Lauren Bacall, and overcast light cutting across a purple floor.

strategies not only complicate our ways of seeing, but also Hudson's: the four mock-ups of the Hadley advertisements loom above our view of Bacall, obscuring his, and our, access to her. Yet we've already seen how she moves, and appreciated her command of her office, her attention to order, and her talent for graphic design. For Hudson, however, she is an abstraction, a set of legs, a figure he encounters not because he is confident, or handsome, but because he knows Kyle Hadley, and Kyle Hadley knows, or has the power to know, women like this.

The way Sirk orchestrates this first encounter between Hudson and Bacall, then, complicates any vision of Lucy as merely an inherently "cold" character. She is an abstraction because Mitch is positioned, cannot help but be positioned, to see her that way: as a woman he has access to not because of his (or her) own inherent charms but because of his connection to the Hadley family; and she is cold not because of any emotional frigidity, but because of a certain ironic awareness, which positions her already as a character somewhat more savvy than we might come to expect in a family melodrama. Hudson, in this first scene, is also implied as a good match for her already, not merely or only because of his good looks and not simply because the orchestral music prefiguring their meeting encourages us to think "love," but rather because he shares with her an ironic awareness and certain degree of emotional detachment from the Hadley clan. But at the beginning, she knows more, is more detached and thus more aware: where she is, initially, a pair of legs to him, he is no abstraction to her. She is aware of his reputation as "friend" of the Hadley family, and of the "dashing" Hadley son Kyle—a man whose picture she has seen in the newspaper, after every drunken exploit. The first close shot of Bacall and Hudson together is a medium two-shot with implied vertical lines—the edges of the Hadley posters, by which Lucy is standing and which mark her off from Mitch—separating them in the composition. But the deeper connection between the two of them is forged through the ironic distance each of them takes. The "dashing" Kyle Hadley is no temptation, or at least not yet, to Lucy: at the mention of his name, and his dashingness, she walks out of frame, back to the desk, its meticulous order a sign of her professional achievements and her autonomy from bachelors like Kyle. Hudson follows, remarking sardonically about his employer and carving out his own detachment through his rock-solid sturdiness in the frame.

Yet, Hudson is there to bring her to Stack—ostensibly, for a meeting about the ad campaign. In the cab ride, however, his ironic detachment, and his sturdiness, begins ever so slightly to crack, as he scornfully remarks upon the over-privileged stupidity of Kyle flying to Manhattan for a steak sandwich—Hudson flings a cigarette butt out the window to punctuate his character's revulsion. Bacall's Lucy hasn't cracked, or at least not quite yet. But she's intrigued by the put-on, leaning forward when she realizes they are on their way to meet Kyle not for a business conference but because the bachelor wants to meet her—and as she leans forward, Hudson does, too, the camera dollying in for a closer medium shot. Yet, perhaps sensing that Mitch isn't quite as detached from Kyle's lifestyle as he might like her to think, Bacall pulls away from Hudson, turning her head to look out the cab window, and readjusting her hair, preserving her self-composure and autonomy. Perhaps they're two of a kind, Mitch remarks, joined in their shared distaste for Kyle Hadley's lifestyle and behavior, more deeply by their lightly ironic detachment from the sort of irresponsible passions that drive Kyle's bachelor's life.

These scenes not only serve to introduce us to Lucy and Mitch, keying us into their attitude toward the gossipy, scandalous world of the Hadleys; they also prepare us for our proper introduction to Kyle Hadley, already glimpsed in his yellow roadster in the film's opening prologue. We dissolve from the cab ridge to the 21 Club. Mitch and Lucy haven't arrived yet, but Kyle Hadley is already there, entertaining two women, a brunette on his left and a blonde on his right. He is waiting for Mitch and Lucy, and we, perhaps, are waiting, in full expectation of seeing Stack munch the favorite steak sandwich that has ostensibly led him to Manhattan. But he's doing nothing of the sort: instead, in a medium-shot that frames Kyle and the women together at a table, he's ordering up another drink, puffing smoke from between his lips as he does, turning rightwards to the barkeep and then back left to the blonde as Sirk cuts to a closer two-shot of the two of them. He's holding court, of course, enjoying these drinks and these women. But he is doing something more than this. Just as Mitch and Lucy, in the previous scene, spoke of little more than Kyle and the famous family of which he is son, so too does Kyle, here, spend all of his words on Mitch, telling these ladies that he has what money can't buy—small-town, country-boy, working-class naturalness (a naturalness that, Stack wryly comments, qualifies Mitch as a kind of "eccentric"). Then, Stack does something quietly extraordinary. He turns away from the blonde, who is now offscreen as the camera pans in rhyme with Stack's leftward movement. He's still in a two-shot, but now framed with the brunette, looking back at the door through which Lucy and Mitch will, in just a beat, walk, into the club (figure 7.4).

This moment is quietly magical. There is no plausible reason why Kyle should expect his friends to walk in and turn his head to greet them at just that moment: Mitch and Lucy have made no audible sound to announce their arrival, and neither of the women with whom Stack sits have consciously noticed the couple walk in quite yet. Nothing "cues"

Figure 7.4. Robert Stack, in quietly magical moment, in *Written on the Wind* (Universal, 1956).

Kyle's attention to turn toward Lucy and Mitch entering other than the fact that our attention is also guided there: Kyle, as a good spectator, moves with our view. This is a moment of pure orchestration, an example of a body movement being used not to signify psychology or intention or realism but to rather gesture our gaze (and the gaze of Stack and these two women) toward another element in the frame—in this case, two additional bodies whose presence in the scene now demands Kyle's attention. The moment is like a dance, between Stack's eyelines and neck movement as he looks back toward the couple, with Bacall and Hudson, and indeed Sirk's camera, serving as his partners. Stack's important role in the choreography here is underlined by his next two gestures: his placement of his glass down on the table and the stubbing-out of his cigarette in this champagne he was just one beat earlier drinking. Both of these objects might be read as expressive of psychological meaning: the cigarette might suggest Hadley's need, perhaps, to do something useful with his hands, given his general uselessness to his father; or, perhaps the drink is the sign of his ongoing battle with alcoholism, and the stubbing of the cigarette in the drink a symbol of his vain attempt to vanquish it. But in the scene, as Sirk orchestrates it and as Stack performs it, these objects are, ultimately, more like musical instruments, marking the end of one rhythm and the beginning of another, all a part of Stack's orchestration of social space and the film's own fascination with the materiality of objects.

After Lucy and Mitch enter the club, Kyle walks over to greet them. Bacall holds out her right gloved hand to greet him, which Stack holds for a long beat while he looks at Hudson, as Hudson looks down in apprehension and as Bacall darts her glance back to Hudson. The shot encapsulates the three-way (and, once Marylee is introduced, four-way) ring of desire the film orchestrates. Yet now Kyle will make his own bid at orchestration. "Your taste is improving," Stack remarks caustically, guiding Bacall over to a table as if stealing away an object from Hudson, the camera guiding our attention downward to the red checkerboard tablecloth upon which, after a dissolve, champagne will be served. This restaurant is a social space, but it is striking how, throughout the sequence, Sirk keeps the wait staff just out of frame; our only glimpse of them is early on, when Stack orders another drink, and they are seen not at all during the dissolve on the tablecloth, as the glasses of champagne almost mysteriously appear or when he orders a phone to the table later in the scene. The total effect, again, is for Stack to emerge as the orchestrator of events in the club—as if it were merely another of his playthings bought with money, as if the source of the film's *découpage* was not love but rather the stream of capital circulating within its diegesis. (In fact, once the conversation turns to the agency employing Lucy, Kyle's immediate offer is to buy it.) But what Stack wants to orchestrate here, in the club, is an intense, even desperate, flirtation, clutching Bacall's right arm, moving closer to her in a medium two-shot as Hudson is separated, for most of their conversation, in a medium one-shot, rendering him an audience to his conversation with Lucy. His progression through these initial scenes with Lucy will be an increasing foreshortening of social space: guiding her to a cab outside the club (shaking momentarily free of Mitch) where the two of them, isolated in the vehicle and lifted just slightly out of naturalistic diegetic space through the film's rear-projection technique, can be alone; and then to the plane, where Hudson furtively re-joins them, for a quick sojourn to Miami.

"I wouldn't admit this to anyone but you," Stack says, positioned below Bacall as she stands on the steps leading up to the plane on the runway; "but I drink too much." Of course, the prologue has already established this, and Lucy, having read of Kyle's exploits in the gossip pages, already likely knows this too. The moment, like many in *Written on the Wind*, is another indication that *mise-en-scène*, unlike in other family melodramas, does not in this film connote anything the characters don't already know. In fact, Mitch and Lucy's own ironic detachment from the social spaces of the advertising office and the 21 Club suggests the extent to which the characters in *Written on the Wind*, as performed by the leading quartet of players, might be a good deal smarter—more world-weary, more knowing of the space around them—than most characters in family melodramas. As we have seen, Thomas Elsaesser, in writing of the relationship between character and *mise-en-scène* in the melodrama, notes a sublimation of "emotional and psychological predicaments" that expressively inscribes into the social space of the diegesis psychological meaning that the characters themselves repress ("Observations" 52). But what is striking about the social space in *Written on the Wind* is how often, in the case of Lucy and Mitch, a character ironically detaches herself from it (as if she knew what repressed meaning it might portend), or, in the case of Kyle and, later, Marylee, how often social space is used, manipulated, and taken on as a site for the performance of desire, in ways that suggest knowingness or conscious intention. Social space in *Written on the Wind*, far from being full of portent the characters don't understand, seems to be quite exhausted. For Kyle, at least, it is played out. A few beats later, after Kyle guides Lucy up to the cockpit (with the cockpit door screening out Mitch from their conversation), their conversation reveals backstory about Kyle's and Mitch's childhood relationship. Here, Kyle nostalgically characterizes both Mitch and Mitch's father as kinds of "Daniel Boone" figures, both embodying the sort of earthy, easygoing masculinity Kyle does not possess. "It's easy to talk like this," Kyle says, "when you're 6,000 feet above the big poker table—Maine to California," reducing the entirety of social space in the United States he is presently floating above to an elaborate card game he has already lost, despite his ostensible wealth. In the shot-reverse shots here, in the cockpit, between Bacall and Stack, Sirk plays a subtle game with light, cloaking the left side of Stack's face, placed near the camera, in warm orange as Bacall looks on, her own face brightly but coolly lit and her angular profile thrown in even sharper relief by purple-and-blue sky looming outside the window behind her. The moment is enough to confirm the director's view of his characters: Bacall, serious and cool, Stack, dark, and full of torment. But despite the fact that this will be one of the only scenes in the film not full of portentous objects coming between the camera and the characters—even in the 21 Club, the vivid red tablecloth made its presence materially known—the light here is nevertheless slightly artificial, its colors (warm for Stack, cool for Lucy) inflecting our sense of character even as the actors reduce their ostensiveness to a range of neck turns and serious expressions. In this scene without objects, Kyle effectively turns himself into an object, an immobile husk of a man whose fate, as his conversation with Lucy confirms, has already been determined by his family.

But in Miami, where the plane lands, Mitch has every intention of reclaiming some sort of identity through his purchase and play with the objects of the world—objects that, here, are all geared toward enticing Lucy to marry him. After an establishing shot of Miami—drenched in blue, with yellow and white lights twinkling on the sides of buildings and from within curtained hotel rooms—we follow Kyle and Lucy following a hotel manager inside the hotel room Kyle has prepared for her. Hudson, in turn, follows two steps behind. Once inside the room, the camera pans with Bacall as she surveys the largesse Stack has arranged for her: bouquets of purple, white, and red flowers, two bottles of champagne resting in glimmering silver ice buckets, a white-grey rug, a bowl of apples, grapes, and bananas, and another bouquet of red flowers against the far right wall. Bacall gazes upon this plenitude with ambivalence, adjusting her hair as in the earlier cab scene, a gesture that is a kind of shield from possible intrusions into her autonomy and self-sufficiency. Mitch watches proudly as Lucy makes her way through the room uneasily. Hudson continues to follow, eyes cast down and away from a sumptuous *mise-en-scène*. The various objects—flower, champagne, fruit—are all, certainly, signs betokening Kyle's wealth, but how much of this bounty is specific to his intentions (we have seen him earlier, in the Miami airport, on the phone, ordering the hotel manager to arrange these things)—and how many of these heavily material and decadently conspicuous objects might already be waiting in this hotel room, for *any* guest, with the money and power to buy them? As if in answer to this question, Stack guides Bacall into the more private recesses of the bedroom, in which she will find, in the top drawer of one of the dressers, a gold, shimmering pocketbook that has been placed there just for her. (Sirk presents it to us in a close-up, momentarily abstracting its presence from the other objects in the room.) Kyle, we now presume, is the sole author of the purchase and placement in this space of this object, as he is of the full closet of glorious dresses and the row of cosmetics placed on the other side of the bedroom. But what does it mean to "author" a purchase? Kyle is certainly as alienated from the material glory of these trinkets (he has already said as much, in the airplane, when he confesses he has already lost the poker game of capitalism, despite his ostensibly winning it). And the way Sirk frames Stack, at both the beginning and end of this first sequence in the hotel, would seem to suggest as much, too, with Stack's image reflected in a mirror as he both enters the hotel hallway and as he leaves Bacall's room. Bacall, playing a character who herself is in the business of authoring commodity objects (the Hadley advertisements), regards all of this with silent uncertainty, her patient but concerned walk through the hotel room keeping everything, including Stack, at arm's length.

In the subsequent scene in which Stack tries to convince Bacall to stay—she has fled to the airport to fly back to New York—the conversation condenses all of this ambivalence into a tidy bit of dialogue. Lucy confesses that, while the hotel room looked beautiful in the evening, it would have looked awfully ugly in the morning. And here proceeds a mostly unconvincing exchange in which Kyle convinces Lucy that a marriage to her might redeem him, and cure him of his drinking. Yet it is a sign of the ongoing doubt Lucy feels about this man, even after she marries him, that she will continue to keep the objects that define his social sphere at arm's length throughout the next part of the film, after she marries Kyle and is introduced to the Hadley patriarch. And surely this is one reason why Sirk wanted to cast Bacall—for her ability to continue to project an intelligent, cautious remove from the bounty her character's marriage into the Hadley family provides. There is no better example of Bacall's work in this film than her initial night in the hotel with Stack, after Lucy has agreed to stay. Sirk's camera dollies in toward the open glass door, through which we see Lucy and Kyle sleeping in their bedroom. Reflections of the waves, clouds, blue sky, and trees are glimpsed in the windows, and the scene is bathed in the kind of cool blue light that acts as something of a counterpoint to Stack's own heavy, orangey fleshiness. Bacall, waking, looks over at Stack. Kyle is fast asleep. Getting up, she circles around to Stack's side of the bed, adjusting his pillow, and in doing so finds a small pistol underneath. She picks it up, and cradles it in her hands. The music, sudden strings, suggests revelation, psychological torment, suspense. But Bacall's treatment of this object is more measured and cool, almost as if she knew she would find it there. The tips of her fingers lightly cradling the pistol, she turns around, walks over to a glossy white end table, and places it there, on the edge, and then looks out the window, the music acting not as an expression of her inner torment but as a counterpoint to the measured range of gestures she projects in the scene. Bacall herself guides our attention away from the music and toward the cool blue light spread across her, its coldness, in the context of this presumably warm night in Miami, a much more suitable complement to her emotions.

Bacall's presence and movement here, in other words, reminds us that Sirk's style does not so much "express," through music and *mise-en-scène*, emotions that her character is repressing, as is often assumed in the family melodrama, and in much writing on Sirk. Instead, her movement distinguishes various elements of Sirk's style, and defines each element in terms of its suitability to a cinematic expression of her character's own ambivalence about the man she has agreed to marry. The music suggests one response—perhaps the response of the viewer, aching to invest the scene with emotional energy—but Bacall's presence guides us back to the light, the cool blue which is a truer sign of her character's ambiguous position at this moment in the narrative. There is a degree of unknownness here, provoked by the question of why this smart, intelligent woman, very nearly running her own ad agency (she is just a secretary, she tells us, but we never see her boss), would ever want to agree to the terms Mitch is offering. In his study of the forties melodrama, Stanley Cavell has suggested that an "unknownness" in the central female leads, in contrast to the progression toward public knowledge and identity (conferred through marriage) in the thirties screwball comedies, is central to the genre's themes: "A certain choice of solitude (figured in a refusal of marriage) as the recognition that the terms of one's intelligibility are not welcome to others—at least not as the basis for romantic investment in any present other whom those terms nominate as eligible—is, as suggested, what the idea of unknownness comes to" (*Contesting Tears* 12). In his book, Cavell does not extend his thoughts to the fifties melodramas or to Sirk's films, yet it is notable that in *Written on the Wind* Bacall has both nominated herself for marriage (in agreeing to wed Stack) but at the same time holds onto a degree of unknownness, in refusing to "marry" herself to either the social world around her (she detaches herself from the gun, Kyle's way of handling social problems, buried beneath the pillow) or to Sirk's total use of expressive *mise-en-scène* (Bacall's position in the sequence attaching itself more closely to the cool blues of the light and distancing itself from the emotional outburst of the musical score). In this, she claims a perhaps even more complicated and tortured claim on "unknownness" than the female figures in the forties films Cavell studies, at once nominating herself for marriage (a marriage, it should be said, that is some distance away from the "suburbs and mortgage" she jokingly refers to in the 21 Club) but also distancing herself coolly from that nomination, as if this position of ambivalence were still necessary, at this stage, to finally make herself known.

The work Stack and Bacall perform together in *Written on the Wind* creates a very certain kind of a couple: a man, Kyle Hadley, who authors his life through the decadent arrangement of largesse in the social space around him, and a woman, Lucy Moore, who positions herself ambivalently in that same social world, aware and perhaps desirous of its material benefits but wary of its possible compromises. The couple they create here is thrown into even sharper relief when compared to their performance of love in a film made two years later, Jean Negulesco's underappreciated melodrama *The Gift of Love* (1958), the only other film in which Stack and Bacall appeared together. (One early sign in *The Gift of Love* that the film will be quite different from Sirk's is that while Kyle in *Written on the Wind* is a raging alcoholic, Stack's character in *The Gift of Love* has never touched a drink.) *The Gift of Love* tells the story of a physicist, played by Stack, who meets and falls in love with a receptionist, played by Bacall. Their courtship is brief: in the opening credits sequence, five years pass by, as they court, wed, and begin married life. Five years into this marriage, Bacall's character, Julie, will discover she has a heart condition; she has very little time left. Her role as wife, in the film, is to arrange and maintain a private life for her husband, Stack's William, who, so busy with being a physicist, is unable to spend much time at home. Key to her plan to maintain domestic harmony is to adopt a young child, Hitty (Evelyn Rudie). In contrast to Lucy Moore in *Written on the Wind*, everywhere in *The Gift of Love* Julie works to make herself unambiguously known—she would not fit in with Cavell's study of the unknown woman in the melodrama, for she clearly nominates herself as helpmeet to Stack's professional man without any trace of ambiguity. And Bacall's performance in *The Gift of Love* makes her character known through the way in which she positions herself, without ambivalence or torment, into social spaces implicitly figured as very much the patriarchal world in which Stack's character works and lives.

Yet there is a subtle and interesting way in which Bacall's performance in *The Gift of Love* nevertheless interjects into that patriarchal social world an autonomous, self-defined feminine presence. The film's narrative signals this, to some extent, in her character's adoption of a child who will survive her (the young girl, in one scene, dresses just like Bacall, as if to suggest that this adoptive daughter will become the posthumous replacement for the wife). But Bacall's performance, even before the narrative moves in this direction, suggests her character's ability to make herself autonomously known in the story's social world. On their first date, Bacall takes Stack to a small bar, encouraging him to enjoy a martini to help his sleep deprivation. The scene is an inverse of the first 21 Club sequence in *Written on the Wind*, in which Kyle orders the drinks and sets the stage: this bar is Bacall's hideaway, not his; she orders the drinks and sets the stage. (She is so conscious of her control over the *mise-en-scène* of the bar that when she accidentally pushes the wrong button on the small, wall-mounted jukebox behind their table, she makes an effort to point it out, as if to declare that the romantic music emanating from its tiny speakers wasn't the inflection of this social stage she was quite looking for.) Stack's character, despite sleep deprivation, is wily enough to recognize female performative agency at work, and he seeks to maintain his control by, first, pointing the lamp on the restaurant table toward her face, so he can get a look at her, and then encouraging her to excuse herself to the powder room, so he can get another look, now at her legs. But the scene is less rich as an example of Stack's character wielding the "male gaze" typical of a certain kind of Hollywood cinema, than it is of Julie's (and Bacall's) way of performatively pushing against male demands with self-assured, performative distinction. After Stack gestures with the lamp, Bacall slings it back toward him, remarking that its harsh brightness is no doubt highlighting her pores. But in the corresponding shot of Bacall *before* Stack moves the lamp forward, and then again after the light has been put back into its centered position, she looks just the same as when the light is pointed directly on her face, the diegetic source lamp wielded by Stack as a means to stake his claim on this space causing, in fact, no change at all in the glamorous, high-key lighting that unambiguously works to complement our beloved star. And, then, a few beats later, Bacall, at Stack's behest to "visit the washroom," does get up from the table, walking a few steps in front of it, facing away from Stack, then pirouetting to display herself to Stack and the camera before perching herself screen-right on a small green stool next to their booth (figure 7.5). She is ostensibly giving in to Stack's demands to display herself, and indeed, if another actress besides Bacall had been cast to play Julie, the total effect might have been one of objectification. But at no point during her movement does Bacall suggest anything less than an alive, thinking subjectivity inhabiting a way of moving, turning, and sitting not in order to acquiesce to the look of the man but rather because she is content to be looked at as an alive and assured presence, a woman who reasserts her command over the social space of this bar in a way that makes her confidence and inner thoughtfulness known to us (if not known, quite yet, to the increasingly intoxicated William). Throughout *The Gift of Love*, Bacall's character, while Stack's William is busy with his physics, will continually retreat to spaces (which the

Figure 7.5. Robert Stack and Lauren Bacall in *The Gift of Love* (Twentieth Century-Fox, 1958).

film codes as "feminine") that she inhabits and controls, including the domestic home itself, an abode largely separated from the laboratory work space in which Stack's character spends most of his time.

By contrast, Bacall's Lucy in *Written on the Wind* is not only less known than Julie, and not only a woman who refuses to fully nominate herself, and the meaning of her life, through marriage to a man; her presence as a figure in the social world of the Hadley clan finally never transcends an ironic detachment that the earnest and fulfilled Julie in *The Gift of Love* seems not to need. Lucy, though, needs this irony because, in contrast to Julie, Lucy is unable to inscribe a feminine space of autonomy or agency apart from the patriarchal Hadley world. But neither is she fully subsumed in the Hadley clan; she never settles comfortably into coupledom with Stack in the film, and the scenes with Hudson, too, are full of unfulfilled longing. Her most intimate companion in *Written on the Wind* is, indeed, not an object or another player (it is certainly not Stack, who, as we have seen in the hotel room scene earlier, is rendered as a physical husk of materiality rather than a loving companion), but rather the camera itself. At times, the camera will be the private witness to Bacall as she discloses expressions and gestures (apart from the view of any other character), rendering both the camera and us (even more than Hudson's Mitch) as Lucy's most intimate confidante in this foreign Hadley world; and at other moments the camera will, during moments of Lucy's greatest suffering at the hands of Kyle or his sister, frame Bacall in such a way so as to refrain from exploiting her distress as mere narrative or psychological information, preserving a certain degree of privacy for the character, a privacy that is her last outpost of autonomy in the Hadley world.

There are two key examples of this in the film. The first is during Marylee's infamous dance, midway through the film, a delirious montage that results in the death of the Hadley patriarch (Robert Keith). Critics have written much about Malone's extraordinary performance in the scene, but I want to focus on Bacall's figuration within this sequence, and the camera's relationship to it. The montage rhythmically interrelates three different spaces in the Hadley home: the Hadley office, in which the father interrogates one of Marylee's young suitors, with Mitch watching on; the staircase on which the father, after dismissing this kid, will die of a heart attack; and Kyle's bedroom, unseen in the montage itself but the room from which Lucy will emerge when she hears the senior Hadley collapse on the staircase. Bacall's moment in this sequence is brief, and it comes near the end, as Marylee's whirlwind nears its conclusion. It occurs over three shots (figures 7.6, 7.7, and 7.8). In the first, Bacall runs, from screen left to screen right, to the edge

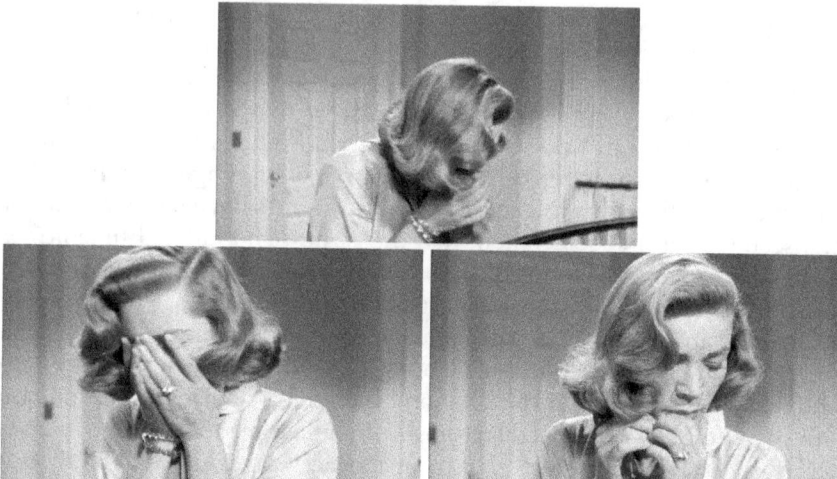

Figures 7.6, 7.7, and 7.8. Lauren Bacall, pouring her face and eyes sorrowfully into her hands, in *Written on the Wind* (1956).

of the stair railing, peering down below, in a medium-shot. Through a dolly movement, the shot inches into a close-up, as Bacall brings her hands to her face in horror at the collapse of Hadley. The shot cuts on Bacall's gesture with her hands before she can complete it, showing us two more shots—another of Malone, continuing her dervish, and then another of Hudson, helping the ailing Hadley patriarch at the bottom of the staircase—before returning to Bacall, who pours her face into her hands while turning away from the death down below, as the camera, through its continuing dolly, completes its reframing of her in a tight close-up. The camera's relationship to Bacall's performance is, in this sequence, quite different from its framing and presentation of Hudson, Malone, and Keith. Hadley's death, and Hudson's attempt to save him, are both framed in, first, a high-angle shot of Hadley gripping the top of the stair railing before tumbling to his death below in a canted shot taken from the bottom of the steps, and, then, another high-angle shot, of Hudson's feet as he runs to Hadley's side. The images of Marylee, by contrast, are set at, first, eye-level, before transitioning to a slight low-angle as her whirlwind reaches its climax, with a panning camera striving, throughout, to, as Ken Eisenstein has put it, "catch" Marylee as her dance in the pink negligee finds her moving closer and closer to the left edge of the frame (185). The canted, high-, and low-angle images of Hadley serve to visually figure a character fate unfolding in a moment of performance, while the panning camera, struggling to keep up with a fervently moving figure, declares its subservience to a quicksilver movement choreographed for Marylee's sole pleasure.

But the image of Bacall pouring her face and her eyes sorrowfully into her hands—a moment of performance that is itself spread out across three images interrupted by Hadley's death and Marylee's tumultuous tango—is framed with a dolly shot that tracks in toward her face, as if these hand gestures, and the face they briefly obscure, were our only possibility for intimate human connection in the scene. Further, it is significant that it is Bacall's face toward which we are moving, for she is a figure whom, in this film, as in *To Have and Have Not* and *The Big Sleep*, is rarely approached this way: she is most often either presented to us in long shot, so that we may see her confident stride across the frame or her assertive inhabitation of one sliver of it; or she is framed in a steady close-up, in which she may wield the famed "look," or perhaps deliver a saucy line of dialogue to Humphrey Bogart. But here the camera now presses toward Bacall as if she were about to unveil a singular and momentary revelation of personality, untethered to previous characters played or to star persona developed hitherto (and perhaps unconnected to anything we have known about Lucy up until this moment in the picture), its revelation prompted by this horrible death sparked by a dance in another room. But if something is revealed here, only we know it; at no other point in the film will Lucy discuss Hadley's death. That the final of these three shots of Bacall serves as the punctuation mark of the sequence only intensifies this feeling, suggesting that the force of the entire sequence now rests heavily, and privately, on her character's shoulders.

The second moment I want to describe, involving a close or intimate, and diegetically undisclosed, relationship between an element of Bacall's performance and Sirk's camera, happens later, when Mitch confronts Lucy about her pregnancy. Believing himself impotent, Kyle suspects Mitch is the father. After the climax of the argument, which intensifies in closely framed shots and reverse-shots, cut to a medium-shot, with Bacall positioned on the left side of the frame, facing away from the camera, and Stack, winding up to strike her, positioned in the center, and facing toward it. And that is where the camera stays throughout the duration of the shot, behind Bacall, framing the punch—certainly the most violent narrative moment between any of the couples we have encountered in this book—so that we hear (amplified on the film's soundtrack) but do not see the blow land on her face. If, in the earlier moment, the camera moved toward Bacall, pressing toward her face as she covered it with her hands, here it remains behind her, catching her fall (against the side of the bed and, then, face-first, on the floor) so as to prevent, throughout the shot, her face from being exposed to the frame, the physical or psychological violence of the moment unexploited by the lens. This is a different sort of "catch" than the one performed by the camera in the dance sequence with Marylee, in which a twirling figure's movements are successfully (if breathlessly) kept in view. Here, the point of the catch is to prevent Bacall's face from coming into view—it is only seen, briefly, from above, once Rock Hudson runs in to answer her distress, threatening to kill Stack's Kyle unless he leaves. But this moment of chivalry pales in comparison to the camera's own implicit refusal to intervene in the battle between a couple, viewing it from a slightly removed perspective, here achieved not through the visual intervention of a material object in the field of the frame but through a camera position that, in its intimate feeling for Bacall as a figure, refuses to render explicit or tawdry its central lead actress's performance of suffering. Even in this moment of violence, she is granted a space of privacy, her unknownness respectfully preserved—her pain is felt by the film, not exploited.

If Bacall's Lucy remains the unknown woman of melodrama throughout Sirk's film, then by contrast, Dorothy Malone's Marylee, an unmarried woman so completely in touch with her desires that she cannot but help make them known, clearly inscribes what she wants, through gesture, poise, color, and dance, in the film's *mise-en-scène*. We have, of course, met Malone earlier in these pages, as the bookshop clerk in *The Big Sleep*. In his direction of Malone in that film, as Peter William Evans points out, Howard Hawks preferred a "cooler style" in contrast to the "bravura kinetics" on display in her performance in *Written on the Wind* (51). And unlike Malone's cool customer in the Hawks film, who seems quite at home with treating her encounter with Marlowe as a one-time fling, Marylee in *Written on the Wind* desires, obsessively, *total* commitment. Like Lucy, she is also interested in marriage, but in contrast to both Cavell's forties women and Lucy, she does not seem to quite need marriage to make herself known or socially present. And unlike Bacall in this film, who carves out an autonomous space from the emotional stirrings of the music and color through her disclosures of privacy to the camera, Dorothy Malone will move through and across frames as if everything Sirk is doing (with music, with color, with light, with cutting, with blocking) is just for her, a hungry claim on *mise-en-scène* that conveys the full force of her character's overflowing desire. (And, unlike her brother ordering up drinks in the 21 Club, Marylee does not need servants to command social space: she can do it with her body alone.) In contrast to Bacall's tendency to develop intimate rapports with the camera in this film (while also distancing herself from the emotional vibrations of music), Malone's performance gets close to cutting and color, two devices exploited through her performance to make explicit Marylee's efforts to unambiguously inscribe her identity into the film's *mise-en-scène* and to develop a connection with the viewer that has less to do with the private disclosure to the camera than it does with the more public display of body and emotion through the forward movement generated by these three techniques. As Malone's whirlwind dance in the pink negligee has been extensively analyzed in previous literature, and as I have already described it at some length through my interest in describing the distinction of Bacall's presence within that sequence, I wish to focus on three other scenes with Malone that illustrate her performative relationship with elements of Sirk's style, as her character (unsuccessfully) courts Rock Hudson, the man of her dreams, a dream she perhaps shares with a large number of the audience. The power of these moments emerges not only through Malone's relationship to other aspects of Sirk's direction, but also through the way in which her character is depicted as courting a purely imaginative figure.

The first of these scenes occurs by a river. It couples her with Hudson in a partially imaginary space. The scene begins with a dissolve superimposed, briefly, over the final shot of the previous scene, in which Mitch confesses to his father his love for Lucy Moore (figure. 7.9). The effect of the dissolve, for a moment, is to position Marylee, fading in gradually through the dissolve, on the left side of the frame, opposite Hudson, fading out gradually through the dissolve on the right. "Is she in love with you?" Mitch's father asks, wondering if his affections for Lucy Moore are shared. "Strictly one-sided," Hudson answers, and as he stoically gazes offscreen, the shot dissolves into the image of Malone walking to the river. As the camera tracks with her, the superimposition ends and Hudson dissolves into the present image, his disappearance rhymed with the appearance of a solid tree trunk, as if in visual corollary to both positive and negative conceptions of Hudson as an actor (as either a "solid" presence in the frame or, less charitably, a performer with the range of a tree trunk; for more on the divided reception of Hudson as actor, see Mercer, especially 69–71). For Marylee, in the sequence, too, the tree trunk is a surrogate for Mitch; as she walks by it, she reaches out to it, with an outstretched left hand, grasping one of its edges and letting her hand linger, with a slight caress, on another edge of bark before sitting down on the grass to lean against it. Where moments with Bacall have confirmed Lucy's slight detachment from her social world and from certain of Sirk's own stylistic gestures, Malone here positions Marylee as desiring a connection with the plenitude of the natural world, signaled through her gaze at the body of water before her (its vegetation reflected in the water itself reflective of the dream of Mitch she is presently having). Malone, too, modulates her gestures and movements in complete emotional synchronization with Sirk's style. After she sits down next to the tree trunk, Sirk cuts to a closer medium-shot of Malone, prompting the actress to lean forward eagerly toward this water which will in a moment trigger the dream of a childhood memory, a childhood shared, of course, with Mitch. For a moment, Malone is secure in her reverie—knees cradled up against her chest, her arms hugging her knees, she is at once entirely self-contained and completely at ease with the natural world surrounding her. But then, a gesture that seems to come entirely from within: she picks up a rock and skips it on the surface of the water. This cues another cut, a closer medium-shot positioned in front of Malone, as she looks, with unease now, at the rippling water offscreen. A voiceover, of Mitch, Kyle, and Marylee as children, playing at this river, drifts in on the soundtrack; the emotions on Malone's face are synched directly to the words the voices speak (a frown at the sound of Kyle's voice, a proud smile and nod at the end of young Mitch's). Nostalgic music punctuates the sequence, but Malone's desire for this imagined past is very presently felt: as these memories bubble up inside her character, Malone gasps with desire, breathing heavily and leaning forward slightly with every breath, every time pulling back only to gasp and lean forward ever so slightly again. The moment is then marked by two unforgettable gestures. In the first, Malone raises her fingers to her pink-painted lips, as she recalls, on the voiceover, a moment as a child when she used mulberry juice as makeup. In the second, after perhaps feeling something of the disappointment at the distance between her childish play with mulberry juice and her adult use of lipstick, she turns back to the tree, now clutching at its bark with her outstretched right hand, gazing forlornly at heart-bounded initials etched into the side of the tree: MH + MW. Outside this heart, near the middle of the bottom edge of the frame, are another pair of initials etched on the tree: KH, uncoupled with anyone else, and outside the boundary of the heart binding MH and MW together (figure 7.10). Malone contemplates this for a moment. Then she turns away from the camera, and toward the tree, and cries.

If we were to imagine that the couples discussed in this book had engraved their initials on an imaginary cinephilic tree—to take the names of the actors themselves in the initials: CL and JB; ML and WP; KH and CG; GT and DA; LB and HB; DK and JK—we might also simultaneously remind ourselves that each of these couples, although firmly etched in our memories as if on this massive hunk of tree made to stand,

Figures 7.9 and 7.10. Dorothy Malone, courting a dream in *Written on the Wind* (Universal, 1956).

for Malone and Marylee, as Rock Hudson, we might also remember that each of these memorable couples do their share of imagining and projecting fantasy onto the other, just as Marylee does. For JB, there is the fantasy of turning CL into a magisterial star, one that he might possess and desire; for ML, the desire that WP do something other than live off her money, that is, that he occasionally deign to work as the private eye she idealizes him to be in her mind's eye; for KH, a hopeful gaze at the archeologist CG, desiring in him more than mere rationality; in DA, gazing upon a painting of GT, and seeing in her a way out of his station; for both LB and HB, the designation of monikers ("Slim" and "Steve") that creatively characterize a potential lover; for DK and JK, the fantasy that their courtship might surmount social pressures and impossibilities. Yet there is something altogether more tragic here, I think, in Malone's projection of fantasy onto Hudson in *Written on the Wind*. There is, first, the fact that he is not even present in this scene, and will never be present in the scene she most imagines and desires; she is projecting her desire onto a natural landscape that, as the rock she throws earlier in the scene suggests, can only respond with indifferent ripples. And there is, second, the fact that her fantasy projections are based on a childhood that probably did not quite ever exist the way she imagines it in voiceover—did she ever dress her lips with mulberry juice, or is this only a fantasy of what she would have liked her childhood to be, so that her ways of dressing for Hudson in the present day might reverberate with a shared history that goes deeper than perhaps it ever did in reality? There is in Malone's performance in the film a responsiveness to every element of environment that counterpoints Bacall's ironic detachment and reserve, but it is a responsiveness that occurs in the midst of one enormous absence: Hudson, the figure toward which her every movement seems directed, even when he is not there.

Critics often focus on Marylee, and Malone's performance, as an example of "overstated playing" (Evans 51), modulated to the expressive hysterics of melodramatic design. But Malone's performance, delightfully histrionic at times, is not bereft of subtlety, and Marylee, as a character, not incapable of control. In a later scene, as if in an attempt to adapt these fantasies born by the river to a reality, Malone will bring Hudson to this river's edge, to share a picnic with him; Sirk initially frames them, on the left side of the shot, opposite another couple, on the right, rowing a boat down the river, perhaps symbolic of the drifting away of any possible coupledom between them, or a sign that Marylee's courtship of Mitch is now entering something resembling a social, rather than purely imaginative, space. Yet what is most striking about this picnic scene is Marylee's control over its diegetic staging: she arranges the picnic blanket and the meal; she jokingly disposes of some ants disturbing their presence; and she removes a bottle of champagne, hidden during some earlier offscreen moment, from behind a fallen tree trunk resting behind them, as if to suggest her staging of this scene, in the fine tradition of *découpage*, has indeed been quite pre-planned. Most striking of all is that the large tree trunk figured in Malone's earlier solo scene by this river, the same tree trunk that stood in place for Hudson and bore their initials carved on its surface, is now kept almost entirely out of frame, as if Marylee herself had made every effort to arrange this *mise-en-scène* so as to keep an unpleasant and unfulfilling history of fantasy, signaled by the initials, out of view. Certainly, where Bacall's character, earlier in the film, marked her distance from certain elements of *mise-en-scène* surrounding her, Malone, by contrast, attempts to take full control of them, arranging this picnic in ways that might help her realize a future companionship with Mitch.

Marylee's effort in this scene and others is to take the Hudson character out of his usual position in the film as observer and make him a participant: she does not want him to merely watch her be, she wants him to be with her. John Mercer has discussed a gradual shift in Hudson's star persona, writing that while the actor began his career in roles that exemplified self-assured, and romantically accessible, masculinity, "in both of these later films [*All That Heaven Allows* (1955) and *Written on the Wind*] he is more akin to the everyman or narrator/observer . . . positioned in one way or another as an outsider" (73). In *Written on the Wind*, in particular, Mercer notes that "Hudson's acting style is productively played off against the more histrionic dramatic registers" of Malone, rendering Hudson's Mitch "a witness to the emotional decay that wealth and privilege brings" and "an archetype, a model of idealized masculinity, one that is not only unattainable by Kyle Hadley but by the vast majority of the film's audience" (78). However, there are moments in *Written on the Wind* in which Malone gets strikingly close to drawing Hudson out of his observer status. Prior to the picnic scene, Marylee and Mitch find themselves at a Hadley soiree commemorating Kyle and Lucy's one-year anniversary. A tracking crane shot draws us inside the mansion, as the chatter of fluttery debutantes and chiseled fraternity boys discussing football games gives way to the more fluid presence of Malone, looking for Hudson in the center of the frame. Against all this typical and boring masculinity and femininity swirling around her, Marylee wants something else—not a socialized form of courtship (signaled by the normative discussion of football we hear on the soundtrack—"I never know who's got the ball!" one of the debutantes dimly exclaims) but a flirtation that might be hers. She finds Mitch, eventually, in his old bedroom, virtually unchanged (with its sports banners and design) from his childhood. He is plucking a ukulele, both he and instrument bathed in blue moonlight. Marylee walks into the room, a drink in each hand, offering him one. She begins to walk in a circle around him, remembering "all those wonderful afternoons we used to spend here"—on those afternoons when it was too cold to go down by the river. "Those wonderful lost afternoons," she remarks, and as she circles in front of Hudson we notice a cigarette burning at one end resting on the endtable next to him, reminding us that this scene will not be about a shared quality of time between two lovers but rather of time's ephemeral drifting away. Marylee's dialogue situates the scene as the inverse of their shared moments down by the river, and her most memorable gesture in the scene, too, works to establish the moment as a counterpoint to our earlier introduction to that river. Where, in the first of the river scenes, a sturdy tree-trunk substituted for Hudson in the frame, Hudson is, in this bedroom scene, figured as liquid: Malone, her drink in hand, sits down next to Hudson, who reclines on a couch, and leans in to him, bringing her glass to her lips and then to his, as if she were positioning herself to drink him up. It's a moment that reminds us of Marylee's ongoing attempts to dissolve Hudson's solidness into something more malleable and fluid, something more sensuous, so as to better remove him from his status as observer. This idea is also suggested by the dialogue, in which Marylee reminds Mitch of their childhood skinny-dipping together. All of this flirtation almost works: moments later, when the two of them return to the party outside, Mitch and Marylee dance. Mitch seems close to relinquishing his observer status. But it is only for a moment: in contrast to Marylee's movements in the dance, in which Malone's free-flowing movements are timed to the rhythms in the music, Hudson's dancing is restrained and bound, his pleasure in the moment never resulting in an abdication of his solid, fundamentally observational presence. By the end of the scene, Mitch has found another, less demonstrative dance partner, with whom he observes the pleasure Marylee takes in her social exhibitionism. Mitch, for a moment, was becoming malleable; this moment drifts away. Where the picnic scene marks an earnest attempt by Marylee to court the man of her dreams, and where the party scene indicates a certain degree of progress in removing Mitch from his observational liminality, Malone's subsequent scenes in the film return her to a soloist position, as she employs gesture and movement not in order to woo another but rather to indulge ecstatically, and for its own sake, in the acrid pleasures of her obsessive, frustrated desire.

Where others have wooed, Marylee weeps. And, of course, since it is Rock Hudson being courted in these scenes, we are reminded that just as Mitch is a difficult man to woo, Hudson, despite or perhaps because of his outrageous beauty, is a difficult actor to win over in analysis. In *Written on the Wind* he tends to be a rather sturdy, stoic figure whose recessive presence often strikes an ambiguous note, no matter how much our love for him compels us to get close to his performance and its possible meanings. Hudson, after all, doesn't do a lot of his own flirting in this movie; his connection with Bacall arrives mostly through their shared sense of ironic detachment in relation to the Hadleys, rather than any internally burning desire we are privy to. Hudson's presence also signifies a certain crisis of performance, wherein certain affects or intensities impossible to depict in the censored bounds of Classical Hollywood cinema begin to break apart the very foundation of flirty heterosexual *découpage* this book has studied. Elena del Rio, for example, discusses Malone's stylized dance sequence later in the film as "a force unto itself, lacking cause/origin as well as effect/goal" (54), as if Marylee's failure to woo Mitch in earlier sequences were not a failure at all (as is perhaps suggested by the final shot of the film) but rather a display of her own boundless desire. Further complicating the film's depiction of heterosexual courtship, of course, are the shifting cultural meanings attached to Hudson as a star across his career and after his death, rendering any empirical reading of his gestures, movements, and expressions especially unstable (see, for further discussion, Klinger 127).

The performances in *Written on the Wind*, although we may love them, cannot finally find those gestures of love it has been the privilege of characters discussed earlier in this book to discover; they finally cannot flirt with time, nor imagine new space, even as they suggest the need for different qualities of time and different spatial contexts for love. Only in the modern cinema to come would an effort be made to pick up the pieces.

Coda

Modern Love

There is no shortage of enchanting performers in Contemporary Hollywood cinema, but the surrounding context in which the viewer's heart is made to beat through gesture, movement, and expression has significantly altered since the 1950s. Classical Hollywood is largely an actor-driven cinema, with genres providing different frameworks for performance and auteurs inflecting gesture with style in various ways, and with relatively longer shot durations giving us room to contemplate the qualities of time different actors grant to us. By contrast, in Contemporary Hollywood, the intensification of certain filmmaking strategies often forcefully intervenes in our appreciation of film acting. David Bordwell's influential concept of "intensified continuity" has usefully described how Contemporary Hollywood's style involves an increase in editing tempo, a greater number of cuts, a more limited use of lens lengths, closer framings in dialogue scenes, and a more freely moving camera ("Intensified Continuity" 16–21). A cinema built on quick cuts, close framings, and virtuosic camerawork presents the film performer as one fragment among many, a figure not always or necessarily shaping the rhythms of that world. The actor, in this situation, is used by the filmmaker to paint a vision of the world, a figure whose gesture, movement, and expression are inscribed as a part of that vision—but, in contrast to the performance-driven films encountered earlier in this book, no longer a figure who structures style through gesture, movement, and expression. If the viewer finds herself touched by the intensity of Contemporary Hollywood style, the actor is, arguably, merely one current within a larger filmic intensity, rather than the point of intensity's origin.

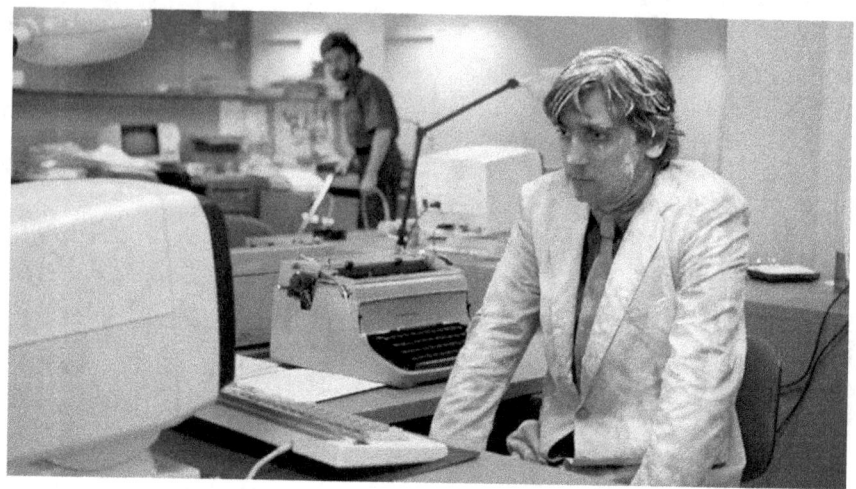

Figure C.1. Griffin Dunne in *After Hours* (Geffen Company, 1985).

Take, for example, Martin Scorsese's *After Hours* (1985), a film that can be regarded as a postmodern variation on at least one of this book's three chosen genres, the screwball comedy (with its city streets and intensely fractured human relationships, the film also bears slight traces of noir and melodrama). *After Hours* is a breathless film, but its kinetic rhythms are, throughout, in counterpoint to the movements of its hapless protagonist. The opening tracking shot cuts a diagonal movement across a New York City office, the camera embodying an excitement and verve for life that, hilariously, is *not* echoed by our first view of Griffin Dunne's work-weary Paul Hackett. When the viewer meets Dunne in these opening scenes, he is training Bronson Pinchot in the use of a computer program integrally connected to whatever business this business is in the business of conducting; yet he could not look more bored, more detached, less kinetic than the camera which has come to greet him. This may be the biggest difference between *After Hours* and the cinema discussed earlier in this book: it is the director, the auteur, who gets our heart beating first. It will then be the actor's job to find his place within this propulsive motion.

This is because *After Hours*, although full of delightful performances, is not, in the sense that the classical films discussed in the earlier part of this book are, an actor-driven film: where it could be reasonably claimed that many classical films situate the actor as the driving force behind the propulsion of classical style, this film is driven by

Martin Scorsese, with the auteur occasionally giving the performer the wheel. And certainly Griffin Dunne, although a terrific performer, is, in terms of star quality, no Cary Grant—and Rosanna Arquette and Linda Fiorentino and Teri Garr and Catherine O'Hara (playing a quartet of women Dunne encounters during one sleepless night on the streets of New York City), while quite interesting and funny and mysterious and assertive, do not command the singular pride of place in *After Hours* as Hepburn, Lombard, or Loy would in traditional screwball comedy. This fact is reflective of the entire point of the film: Dunne cannot consummate any sort of beginning to a relationship with any of these women, who continually slip away from our view almost as quickly as they are introduced. Rosanna Arquette dies of a suicidal overdose (a morbid spin on screwball comedy's metaphorical interest in mental illness); Linda Fiorentino, like a femme fatale walking into screwball from noir, falls asleep during one of Hackett's boring stories; Teri Garr's awkward courtship of Dunne is interrupted, grotesquely, by the death of a mouse; and Catherine O'Hara, convinced that Dunne is a thief, stalks him across the city streets, pasting "WANTED" posters bearing Dunne's hapless visage along the way. The very speed of the film's rhythms insures that the man will not be able to defer his time with these women, will not find time to flirt or properly judge the quality of time he has spent with them. So the fact that Dunne's poor Hackett cannot develop a relationship—or even just have sex—with any of these women not only suggests something important about the social context in which the film was made (at the dawn of wider awareness of the AIDS crisis, in which impulsive copulation is stopped short by paranoia and fear of one's social others), it also implies that the creation of a couple will either no longer be the driving force of much Hollywood cinema, or will be cloaked in a veil of irony that must be pierced for the heart to beat earnestly.

So while *After Hours* is very funny, and while it inherits the breakneck speed of the finest screwball comedies, it does not suggest, as *Twentieth Century* and *The Thin Man* and *Bringing Up Baby* do, that the couples it contains might change the space through their love. Throughout the film, any attempt Griffin Dunne makes to connect with a romantic partner is immediately complicated by some hilariously or tragically absurd external intervention (a horrifying book of burns and scars; a waiter doing a pirouette; a suicide). And after each of these events, New York City remains just as it was before, impassive to the events of the humans crawling about within it. Further, the film presents these characters to us without histories: this is not a comedy of remarriage, or even marriage, but rather a film about women and men passing in the night, trying to carve something relatively permanent out of a world that is changing around them but which does not change because of them.

The first moment Griffin Dunne and Rosanna Arquette meet one another in the film suggests Scorsese's ironic twist on the traditional first encounter between the man and the woman in screwball comedy. After a long and typically unsatisfying day of work, Dunne finds himself sitting in a café. He is reading Henry Miller's *Tropic of Cancer*. A plaintive performance of Bach's "Air Overture Number 3 in D" plays on the soundtrack. Rosanna Arquette spots him.

There is something in the *découpage* of this first scene of ironic courtship in *After Hours* unmotivated by character movement or gesture, a camera movement that Scorsese will at times include in his films (there is a similar camera movement in *Taxi Driver* [1977], when we see Scorsese track laterally and away from the Robert De Niro character at a moment of profound embarrassment). This sequence in *After Hours* begins with a two-shot of Dunne reading, at a table, from over Arquette's shoulder, as she spies him before he looks up at her (figure C.2). (How long has she been looking? And has all this time been spent looking at him, or perhaps also at something behind him?) After this moment, Scorsese will track in toward Arquette as she begins the conversation (she likes Henry Miller, she tells him, because he spits in the

Figure C.2. Scorsese's camera encounters potential lovers in *After Hours* (Geffen Company, 1985).

face of art—a line of dialogue that functions in acerbic counterpoint to the lovely Bach music that floats in the background). The camera does not bring us closer to Arquette, however, in any existential or personal sense—she is not playing a character who we will in any meaningful sense "get to know"—but rather to a lurid red light, streaming in from the window offscreen, that plays on the right side of her face. A quick cut to Dunne, now in close-up, as he reacts. Then back to Arquette. Now back to Dunne: remarkably, although Scorsese had a moment earlier cut closely to him, he now begins from the position of a medium-shot, before dollying, in a quarter-circle, around him, bringing us again to where we were, a close shot of Dunne as he begins his patter about Miller with Arquette. That we should have to back out again after having already been brought close to a character is perhaps a reminder that no sort of intimate connection has yet been forged: a cut back to Arquette shows that she is only half-listening to Dunne, her eyes darting back and forth from him to something she spies behind him. Scorsese cuts to another two-shot, again from behind Arquette's shoulder. She gets up. The camera now follows, the first character-motivated camera movement in the sequence. She sits down, settling into an intimate two-shot that will trigger a series of shot-reverse shot angles that only intensify the irony behind the sequence. It is, after all, not toward Dunne she's moving; she is fascinated by the waiter at the counter, who—arms raised to his chest in a semicircle, as if he were courting a ghost—has attracted her attention. The two laugh at him—he is like any other odd person you might run into in New York City—and the sequence settles into a conversation that ends with Arquette giving Dunne not her number, but rather the number of her roommate, a sculptress who might sell him a Plaster-of-Paris, bagel-and-cream-cheese paperweight. (The sequence is like a Deleuzian conception of courtship: Arquette, rather than wooing this man through words, is saying "any-words-whatever," a kind of truly irrational screwiness that is the inversion of the secretly rational screwball heroine's interest in winning over the man with carefully orchestrated flighty behavior.) The conversation does not go where Dunne had, in all likelihood, hoped it would go, and before too long, Arquette leaves—the foreplay had hardly even begun.

Rather than change the space of this little, unassuming café, this moment of too-brief flirtation ends with Dunne haplessly trying to inscribe the phone number she has given him on his copy of the Miller, before darting out of the café, which remains, at the end, quite as he left it. Our hero's pen fails to work; and so he is unable to write down this number in a close-up of Miller's text, in which the phrase *boldness of approach* is viewable, that boldness of approach it is difficult for us to imagine poor Paul Hackett ever quite having in any encounter with any woman, including the ones he meets in the present film.

The characters cannot change the space, cannot envision an alternative idea of love, because the film itself presents the proscenium upon which they perform their desire as a thoroughly and already vexed one, continually under threat from different ways of living and loving that poor Paul Hackett, for one, having wandered into a SoHo he does not understand, knows nothing of. The film's sense of space as vexed is also suggested by its saliently mixed genre status. Is the film a screwball comedy? It is certainly funny, and surreal—and in its way, it moves as quickly as *Bringing Up Baby* or *His Girl Friday*. Is it noir? These city streets are dark, and rain-swept—and Catherine O'Hara, who stalks the hero in the final third of the picture, is some kind of comical femme fatale, to be sure. Lesley Stern, in a provocative reading of the film, has suggested that *After Hours* is a horror film, positing that it "arouses in us a sense of traumatic resonance, a sense of being at the mercy of undefined forces" (91), forces that manifest themselves in various and increasingly absurd guises (Scorsese's hovering camera, which remains fixed on while relatively autonomous from the characters; the waiter dancing with ghosts; Arquette's bagel-shaped paperweight). *After Hours* offers its genre markers less as prosceniums for performance than as temporary points of identification, signposts that give the viewer breathing room before being swept up again by the sheer forward movement of Scorsese's picture.

Of course, despite this shift in the filmic style which structures the context of screen performance—a shift that *After Hours* does a good job of exemplifying—movie couples continue to abound in Contemporary Hollywood cinema, even as movies have either problematized or rendered ironic the heterosexual couple at the center of many narratives (see Wexman 183–85). Additionally, as Martha P. Nochimson points out, couples in recent films, due to changes in the economics of the film industry and the challenge to film by television and other media, no longer enjoy the serial repetition of couples in Classical Hollywood; the repeated appearances of the same actors cast as a pair of lovers, today, is more likely to occur on television series rather than in cinema (Nochimson uses as two examples Bruce Willis and Cybill Shepherd, and David Duchovny and Gillian Anderson, across several seasons of *Moonlighting* [1985–1989] and *The X-Files* [1993–2002, and 2016], respectively; see 237–63). When the same pair of performers do appear across a number of films together, their performances are frequently marked by a sense of irony and melancholy—the failure of love in the face of personal neurosis and social encumbrances—an idea exemplified by the recurring pairing of Woody Allen and Diane Keaton across several of Allen's films (Nochimson 263–74).

Some scholars have argued that this destabilization of the couple in contemporary films has progressive undercurrents. Reidar Due has intriguingly suggested that contemporary art cinemas problematize the centrality of the couple by placing them in a wider dialogue with the evolving and complex social contexts in which they live. Due questions the extent to which characters in recent films have the agency to shape or change the world in which they live, remarking that "love's relation to place [in recent cinema] characterizes it as a phenomenon without boundaries: for the place in which the lovers live is itself both material and social, historical and economic, a limit and a source of identity" (123). Adrian Martin has echoed this sentiment when he writes of a contemporary, post-1968 cinema that smashes open the intimacy of space enjoyed by the classical couple—think Katharine Hepburn and Jimmy Stewart enjoying champagne poolside, or Myrna Loy and William Powell retreating to a private space, beyond the glimpse of the audience—a smashing-open that means to pry open the "secluded chamber and force the young characters back out into the world ... The free figures must reenter history, and join a new, collective narrative" (210). Of course, the story of love I have told in these pages has suggested that, to an important extent, this intimate chamber drama of classical cinema was always open to at least a third eye—the eye of the loving viewer who, in her apprehension of gesture, movement, and expression that exceeded the line of sight of at least one member of the loving pair, opens the intimate space of the classical love story to a larger social world that might interpret it in a larger frame of desire. Indeed, sometimes characters actively desire this third, and indeed many more, eye(s)—John Barrymore and Carole Lombard, who theatrically solicit our loving response; or Lauren Bacall and Humphrey Bogart, whose performative rhythms in *To Have and Have Not* are inscribed in the larger social context grooving along with them. But just as frequently this story of love encounters an intimacy that reduces the range of its public and social expression: Gene Tierney and David Andrews remain unknowable in their love in *Laura*, playing as they always do for a future time; and Lauren Bacall and Rock Hudson in *Written on the Wind* develop complex and at times contrapuntal relationships to Sirk's style (and in Hudson, we find a recessive actor who occupies observational positions in the social world of the narrative, his characters avoiding that risk of legibly inscribing personal desire through a social performance). Such moments in the story I have told gesture toward the complex situation of performance found in both Contemporary Hollywood as well as much of art cinema, performance that continues to inscribe feeling through gesture and expression but which is no longer so assured of changing the space of its filmic world.

All of these questions regarding the place of the actor, and the screen couple, in recent cinema deserve further consideration. What I hope to have offered in these final pages is the beginning of an answer to a question: Given these changes in film style and given the destabilization, new stylization, and hybridization of the genres in which actors appear, how does our love for the actor shift, change, evolve? *After Hours*, in counterpoint to screwball comedy and in follow-up to the melancholic visions of noir and melodrama, offers an ambiguous and at times even tortured presentation of love's possibilities, framing the performance of courtship and flirtation with a sharper and often more pessimistic sense of irony. Where Cary Grant in *Bringing Up Baby* eventually adapts to Katharine Hepburn's fast-paced rhythms, poor Paul Hackett in *After Hours* can never quite adjust to the speed of modern love, and is merely along for a ride that offers plenty of fleeting contact with fascinating women but promises no hope of future romantic fulfillment.

This example is not meant to suggest that love, in Contemporary Hollywood, is consistently performed as ironic, or melancholic, or as a failure. Plenty of contemporary films, indeed most and perhaps too many of them—too numerous to name here—end happily, and project confidence in the ongoing ability of the couple to overcome (if not progressively change) social form. Some films (very few within Hollywood, however) are even beginning to move beyond heterosexuality as a prerequisite for coupledom. But how many of these couples breathlessly change the space of the film we are watching? In giving space and time for their performers to create characters who woo, flirt, and measure the quality of time they might enjoy with a lover, films as varied as *Twentieth Century*, *The Thin Man*, *Bringing Up Baby*, and *To Have and Have Not*, whatever their limitations, remain vital examples of the kinds of unanticipated and repeatedly dazzling sparks two human beings projected on film might create with one another. These films still work on us and for us; despite the fact that decades have passed since their production, they remain invigorating experiences. And even in those films in which love fails, or projects itself into an uncertain future time—*Laura*, *Tea and Sympathy*, *Written on the Wind*—the ongoing effort to create space and time in which to woo another, within a social form that does not always accommodate it, is moving. If, in the classical films I have studied, movement and gesture work within a space that is to some degree designed as a proscenium for performance, in contemporary films style often assumes the shape of an external or social force that bears down on the characters, or it conveys the emotional timbre of a subjectivity unable to connect with another in the frame.

These final pages form a suggestive punctuation mark to this book, and the possible beginnings for another study on the performance of love in contemporary cinema, a fall into or for modern love.

Works Cited

Affron, Charles. *Cinema and Sentiment*. Chicago: University of Chicago Press, 1982.
———. *Star Acting: Gish, Garbo, Davis*. New York: Dutton, 1977.
Agee, James. *Agee on Film: Criticism and Comment on the Movies*. New York: Modern Library, 2000.
Andrew, Dudley. *What Cinema Is!: Bazin's Quest and Its Charge*. Malden, MA: Wiley-Blackwell, 2010.
Aragon, Louis. "On Décor." Trans. Paul Hammond. *French Film Theory and Criticism: A History/Anthology, 1907–1929*. Ed. Richard Abel. Princeton, NJ: Princeton University Press, 1988: 165–68.
Archer, William. *Masks or Faces?: A Study in the Psychology of Acting*. London: Longmans, Green, 1888.
Bacall, Lauren. *By Myself*. New York: Knopf, 1978.
Balázs, Béla. "The Close-Up," in *Critical Visions in Film Theory: Classical and Contemporary Readings*, eds. Timothy Corrigan, Patricia White, and Meta Mazaj. Boston and New York: Bedford/St. Martin's, 2011.
Barnard, Timothy. *Découpage*. Montreal: Caboose, 2014.
Baron, Cynthia. "Film Noir: Gesture Under Pressure." In *Genre and Performance: Film and Television*, ed. Christine Cornea. Manchester, UK: Manchester University Press, 2010: 18–37.
Baron, Cynthia, and Sharon Marie Carnicke. *Reframing Screen Performance*. Ann Arbor: University of Michigan, 2008.
Barthes, Roland. *A Lover's Discourse: Fragments*. New York: Hill and Wang, 1978.
———. *Camera Lucida: Reflections on Photography*. New York: Hill and Wang, 1981.
———. *Mythologies*. New York: Hill and Wang, 1972.
Basinger, Jeanine. *I Do and I Don't: A History of Marriage in the Movies*. New York: Knopf, 2012.
Baudelaire, Charles. *The Painter of Modern Life, and Other Essays*. Trans. Jonathan Mayne. London: Phaidon Press, 1964.
Behlmer, Rudy. *Behind the Scenes: The Making of . . .* Hollywood, CA: Samuel French, 1989.

Bollas, Christopher. *Being a Character: Psychoanalysis and Self Experience.* New York: Routledge, 1992.

Bordwell, David. "Intensified Continuity: Visual Style in Contemporary American Film." *Film Quarterly* 55, no. 3 (Spring 2002), 16–28.

———. *Narration in the Fiction Film.* Madison, WI: University of Wisconsin-Madison, 1985.

Bordwell, David, Janet Staiger, and Kristin Thompson. *The Classical Hollywood Cinema: Film Style & Mode of Production to 1960.* New York: Columbia University Press, 1985.

Britton, Andrew. *Katharine Hepburn: Star as Feminist.* New York: Continuum, 1995.

Brooks, Louise. *Lulu in Hollywood.* Minneapolis: University of Minnesota Press, 2000.

Buckland, Warren. "Bodies in Filmic Space: The Mise en Scène of 'Courtship Readiness' in *The Big Sleep*." In *Senses of Cinema* 66 (March 2013).

Camper, Fred. "The Films of Douglas Sirk." In *Screen* 12, no. 2 (Summer 1971): 44–62.

Cavell, Stanley. *Cities of Words: Pedagogical Letters on a Register of the Moral Life.* Cambridge, MA: Belknap Press of Harvard University Press, 2004.

———. *Contesting Tears: The Hollywood Melodrama of the Unknown Woman.* Chicago: University of Chicago Press, 1996.

———. *Pursuits of Happiness: The Hollywood Comedy of Remarriage.* Cambridge, MA: Harvard University Press, 1981.

Chambers, Whitman. Revised treatment of *To Have and Have Not.* 3 January 1944. Jules Furthman Papers. Margaret Herrick Library.

Chandler, James. *An Archaeology of Sympathy: The Sentimental Mode in Literature and Cinema.* Chicago: The University of Chicago Press, 2013.

Chion, Michel. *The Voice in Cinema.* Trans. Claudia Gorbman. New York: Columbia University Press, 1999.

Clayton, Alex. *The Body in Hollywood Slapstick.* Jefferson, NC: McFarland & Co., 2007.

Creekmur, Corey K. "Cinephilia and Film Noir." *A Companion to Film Noir.* Eds. Andrew Spicer and Helen Hanson. Malden, MA: Wiley-Blackwell, 2013: 67–76.

deCordova, Richard. "Genre and Performance: An Overview." In *Star Texts: Image and Performance in Film and Television.* Ed. Jeremy G. Butler. Detroit: Wayne State University Press. 115–24.

del Rio, Elena. *Deleuze and the Cinemas of Performance: Powers of Affection.* Edinburgh: Edinburgh University Press, 2008.

DiBattista, Maria. *Fast-Talking Dames.* New Haven, CT: Yale University Press, 2001.

Dimendberg, Edward. *Film Noir and the Spaces of Modernity.* Cambridge, MA: Harvard University Press, 2004.

Doane, Mary Ann. *The Emergence of Cinematic Time.* Cambridge, MA: Harvard University Press, 2003.

Due, Reidar. *Love in Motion: Erotic Relationships in Film*. New York: Columbia University Press, 2013.
Dyer, Richard. *Heavenly Bodies: Film Stars and Society*. London: Routledge, 2005.
———. *Stars*. London: British Film Institute, 1998.
Eisenstein, Ken. "They Are Like Black Lakes Troubled by Fantastic Moons." In *Framework: The Journal of Cinema and Media* 50, no. ½ (Spring & Fall 2009): 183–89.
Elsaesser, Thomas. "Observations on the Family Melodrama." In *Home is Where the Heart Is: Studies in Melodrama and the Woman's Film*. Ed. Christine Gledhill. London: British Film Institute, 1990.
———. "Vincente Minnelli." In *Vincente Minnelli: The Art of Entertainment*. Ed. Joe McElhaney. Detroit: Wayne State University Press, 2009, 79–96.
Evans, Peter William. *Written on the Wind*. London: British Film Institute, 2013.
Eyman, Scott. *Ernst Lubitsch: Laughter in Paradise*. New York: Simon & Schuster, 1993.
Farber, Manny. *Farber on Film: The Complete Film Writings of Manny Farber*. New York: Library of America, 2009.
———. *Negative Space*. New York: Da Capo, 1998.
Fassbinder, Rainer Werner. "Fassbinder on Sirk." *Film Comment* 11, no. 6 (November–December 1975): 22–23.
Frank, Nino. "A New Kind of Police Drama: The Criminal Adventure." *Film Noir Reader 2*. Eds. Alain Silver and James Ursini. New York: Limelight Editions, 1999: 15–20.
Fujiwara, Chris. *The World and its Double: The Life and Work of Otto Preminger*. New York: Faber and Faber, 2008.
Gehring, Wes. *Carole Lombard: The Hoosier Tornado*. Indianapolis: Indiana University Press, 2003.
Gerstner, David A. "The Production and Display of the Closet." In *Vincente Minnelli: The Art of Entertainment*, ed. Joe McElhaney. Detroit: Wayne State University Press, 2009, 275–94.
Gibbs, John. *Mise-en-Scène: Film Style and Interpretation*. London: Wallflower Press, 2002.
Gledhill, Christine. "Introduction." In *Stardom: Industry of Desire*, ed. Christine Gledhill. London: Routledge, 1991: xii–xx.
Godard, Jean-Luc. *Godard on Godard*. Trans. Tom Milne. London: Da Capo, 1986.
Grant, Cary. Letter to Katharine Hepburn. May 29, 1984. Katharine Hepburn Collection. Margaret Herrick Library.
Grosz, Dave. "The First Legion: Vision and Perception in Sirk." In *Screen* 12, no. 2 (Summer 1971): 99–117.
Hake, Sabine. *Passions and Deceptions: The Early Films of Ernst Lubitsch*. Princeton, NJ: Princeton University Press, 1992.
Hall, Gladys. Correspondence with Selznick International Pictures about changes to an article on Carole Lombard, as demanded by Lombard, August 19, 1938. Gladys Hall Collection, Margaret Herrick Library.
Hammett, Dashiell. *The Thin Man*. New York: Vintage Books, 1992.

Hansen, Jim. "Mod Men." In *Mad Men, Mad World: Sex, Politics, Style and the 1960s*. Eds. Lauren M. E. Goodlad, Lilya Kaganovsky, and Robert A. Rushing. Durham, NC: Duke University Press, 2013, 145–60.

Harvey, James. *Movie Love in the Fifties*. New York: Knopf, 2001.

———. *Romantic Comedy in Hollywood from Lubitsch to Sturges*. New York: Knopf, 1987.

Hecht, Ben. *A Child of the Century*. New York: Simon and Schuster, 1954.

Hickman, Darryl. DVD commentary. *Leave Her to Heaven*. 20th Century Fox Studio Classics, 2005.

Hirsch, Foster. *The Dark Side of the Screen: Film Noir (Revised Edition)*. Cambridge, MA: Da Capo Press, 2008.

Jollimore, Troy A. *Love's Vision*. Princeton, NJ: Princeton University Press, 2011.

Keathley, Christian. *Cinephilia and History, or the Wind in the Trees*. Bloomington: Indiana University Press, 2006.

Kendall, Elizabeth. *The Runaway Bride: Hollywood Romantic Comedy of the 1930s*. New York: Knopf, 1990.

Klevan, Andrew. *Disclosure of the Everyday: Undramatic Achievement in Narrative Film*. Trowbridge, Wilts., UK: Flicks Books, 2000.

———. "Expressing the In-Between." In *Lola Journal* 1 (2011). Accessed online at http://lolajournal.com/1/in_between.html.

———. *Film Performance: From Achievement to Appreciation*. London: Wallflower Press, 2005.

———. "Living Meaning: The Fluency of Film Performance." In *Theorizing Film Performance*, ed. Aaron Taylor. New York: Routledge, 2012. 33–46.

Klinger, Barbara. *Melodrama and Meaning: History, Culture, and the Films of Douglas Sirk*. Bloomington: Indiana University Press, 1994.

Krieger, Murray. *Ekphrasis: The Illusion of the Natural Sign*. Baltimore: John Hopkins University Press, 1992.

Kuleshov, Lev. *Kuleshov on Film: Writings*. Berkeley: University of California Press, 1974.

Leider, Emily W. *Myrna Loy: The Only Good Girl in Hollywood*. Berkeley: University of California Press, 2011.

Lennon, Tom. Letter to Katharine Hepburn. August 7, 1935. Katharine Hepburn Collection, Margaret Herrick Library.

Loy, Myrna. *Being and Becoming*. With James Kotsilibas-Davis. New York: Knopf, 1987.

Martin, Adrian. *Mise-en-Scène and Film Style: From Classical Hollywood to New Media Art*. New York: Palgrave, 2014.

Mast, Gerald. *Howard Hawks, Storyteller*. New York: Oxford University Press, 1982.

McCarthy, Todd. *Howard Hawks: The Grey Fox of Hollywood*. New York: Grove Press, 1997.

McCourt, James. "Douglas Sirk: Melo Maestro." In *Film Comment* 11, no. 6 (November–December 1975): 18–21.

McElhaney, Joe. *The Death of Classical Cinema: Hitchcock, Lang, Minnelli*. Albany, NY: State University of New York Press, 2006.

———. "Howard Hawks: American Gesture." *Journal of Film & Video* 58, no. 1/2 (Spring/Summer 2006). 31–45.

———. "Lauren Bacall: The Walk." In *The Cine-Files* (Spring 2014). Accessible online at http://www.thecine-files.com/wp-content/uploads/2014/06/McElhaney.pdf.

———. "Medium-Shot Gestures: Vincente Minnelli and *Some Came Running*." In *Vincente Minnelli: The Art of Entertainment*, ed. Joe McElhaney. Detroit: Wayne State University Press, 2009, 322–35.

Mercer, John. *Rock Hudson*. London: British Film Institute, 2015.

Mercer, John, and Martin Shingler. *Melodrama: Genre, Style, Sensibility*. London: Wallflower, 2004.

Mitry, Jean. *The Aesthetics and Psychology of the Cinema*. Bloomington: Indiana University Press, 1997.

Morin, Edgar. *The Stars*. Minneapolis: University of Minnesota Press, 2005.

Morris, Mary. "Lauren Bacall: Girl with 'The Look.'" In *P.M. New York*, December 3, 1944.

Naremore, James. *Acting in the Cinema*. Berkeley: University of California Press, 1988.

———. *The Films of Vincente Minnelli*. New York: Cambridge University Press, 1993.

———. *More than Night: Film Noir in its Contexts*. Berkeley: University of California Press, 1998.

Nochimson, Martha P. *Screen Couple Chemistry: The Power of 2*. Austin: University of Texas Press, 2002.

Paul, William. *Ernst Lubitsch's American Comedy*. New York: Columbia University Press, 1983.

Paz, Octavio. *The Double Flame: Love and Eroticism*. New York: Harcourt Brace, 1995.

Peacock, Steven. *Colour*. Manchester, UK: Manchester University Press, 2010.

Peberdy, Donna. "Acting and Performance in Film Noir." *A Companion to Film Noir*. Eds. Andrew Spicer and Helen Hanson. Malden, MA: Wiley-Blackwell, 2013: 318–34.

Perkins, V. F. "Hawks's Comedies." *Howard Hawks: American Artist*. Eds. Jim Hillier and Peter Wollen. London: British Film Institute, 1996.

Phillips, Adam. *On Flirtation: Psychoanalytic Essays on the Uncommitted Life*. Cambridge, MA: Harvard University Press, 1994.

Pomerance, Murray. *The Eyes Have It: Cinema and the Reality Effect*. New Brunswick, NJ: Rutgers University Press, 2013.

Pryor, Thomas M. Review of *Laura*. *New York Times*, October 12, 1944.

Ray, Robert B. *The ABCs of Hollywood*. New York: Oxford University Press, 2008.

Rigaut, Jacques. "Mae Murray." In *The Shadow and Its Shadow: Surrealist Writings on the Cinema*. Ed. Paul Hammond. San Francisco: City Light Books, 205. Originally printed in *Littérature* (Paris) 1 (March 1922): 18.

Rollyson, Carl E. *Hollywood Enigma: Dana Andrews*. Jackson: University Press of Mississippi, 2012.

Rothman, Ellen K. *Hands and Hearts: A History of Courtship in America.* New York: Basic Books, 1984.
Rothman, William. *Must We Kill the Thing We Love?: Emersonian Perfectionism and the Films of Alfred Hitchcock.* New York: Columbia University Press, 2014.
———. "Silence and Stasis." In *The Language and Style of Film Criticism.* Eds. Alex Clayton and Andrew Klevan. London and New York: Routledge, 2011: 107–20.
Russon, John. *Bearing Witness to Epiphany: Persons, Things, and the Nature of Erotic Life.* Albany, NY: State University of New York Press, 2009.
Salzberg, Ana. *Beyond the Looking Glass: Narcissism and Female Stardom in Studio-Era Hollywood.* New York: Berghahn, 2014.
Sarris, Andrew. "Ernst Lubitsch: American Period." In *Cinema: A Critical Dictionary (Volume Two)*, ed. Richard Roud. New York: The Viking Press.
Schatz, Thomas. *Hollywood Genres: Formulas, Filmmaking, and the Studio System.* New York: McGraw-Hill, 1981.
Schivelbusch, Wolfgang. *The Railway Journey: The Industrialization of Time and Space in the 19th Century.* Berkeley: University of California Press, 1986.
Silver, Alain, and James Ursini. *Film Noir Reader 2.* New York: Limelight, 1999.
Sobchack, Vivian. *The Address of the Eye: A Phenomenology of Film Experience.* Princeton, NJ: Princeton University Press, 1992.
Sperber, A. M., and Eric Lax. *Bogart.* New York: William Morrow and Co., 1997.
Stern, Lesley. *The Scorsese Connection.* Bloomington: Indiana University Press, 1995.
Stern, Lesley, and George Kouvaros, eds. *Falling for You: Essays on Cinema and Performance.* Sydney: Power Publications, 1999.
Stewart, David Ogden, and Sidney Buchman. *Holiday* screenplay; revised final version, February 22, 1938. George Cukor Collection, Margaret Herrick Library.
Swindell, Larry. *Screwball: The Life of Carole Lombard.* New York: Morrow, 1975.
Thomson, David. *Movie Man.* New York: Stein and Day, 1967.
Thompson, John O. "Screen Acting and the Commutation Test." In *Stardom: Industry of Desire*, ed. Christine Gledhill. London and New York: Routledge, 1991: 183–97.
Thompson, Kristin. *Breaking the Glass Armor: Neoformalist Film Analysis.* Princeton, NJ: Princeton University Press, 1988.
Tierney, Gene, with Mickey Herskowitz. *Self-Portrait.* New York: Wyden Books, 1979.
Toles, George. "Writing About Performance: The Film Critic as Actor." In *The Language and Style of Film Criticism*, eds. Alex Clayton and Andrew Klevan. London: Routledge, 2011, 87–106.
Tynan, Kenneth. *Curtains: Selections from the Drama Criticism and Related Writings of Kenneth Tynan.* London: Longmans, 1961.
Wexman, Virginia Wright. *Creating the Couple: Love, Marriage, and Hollywood Performance.* Princeton, NJ: Princeton University Press, 1993.
Willemen, Paul. *Looks and Frictions: Essays in Cultural Studies and Film Theory.* Bloomington: Indiana University Press, 1994.

Winnicott, D. W. *Playing and Reality*. New York: Basic Books, 1971.
Winokur, Mark. "Improbably Ethnic Hero: William Powell and the Transformation of Ethnic Hollywood." In *Cinema Journal* 27, no. 1 (Autumn 1987): 5–22.
Wood, Robin. *Howard Hawks*. Detroit: Wayne State University Press, 2006.
Worland, Rick. "Humphrey Bogart and Lauren Bacall: Tough Guy and Cool Dame." In *What Dreams Were Made Of: Movie Stars of the 1940s*, ed. Sean Griffin. New Brunswick, NJ: Rutgers University Press, 2011: 70–95.

Index

Adam's Rib (George Cukor, 1949) 79
Affron Charles, 19, 26–27, 28–29
After Hours (Martin Scorsese, 1985), 240–46
After the Thin Man (W. S. Van Dyke, 1936), 63, 80
Aherne, Brian, 88
All That Heaven Allows (Douglas Sirk, 1955), 236
Allen, Woody, 245
Anderson, Gillian, 244
Anderson, Judith, 124
Andrews, Dana, 119–46, 196, 245
Aragon, Louis, 124
Arquette, Rosanna, 241–44
Arthur, Jean, 42
Asta the dog, 62–63, 80
Ayres, Lew, 93

Bacall, Lauren, 8, 29, 42, 119, 147–82, 185–86, 192–97, 206, 209–33, 235–38
Balázs, Béla, 25–26, 28
Barbarian, The (Sam Wood, 1933), 67–68
Barlow, Joy, 165, 167
Barnard, Timothy, 9–10
Baron, Cynthia, 43, 75, 76
Barrymore, John, 8, 33–55, 58, 59, 72, 104, 115, 119, 120, 156, 245
Barrymore, Lionel, 178–79, 181

Big City Blues (Mervyn LeRoy, 1932), 148
Big Sleep, The (Howard Hawks, 1946), 8, 29, 45, 147, 152, 165–72, 192, 231–32
Bill of Divorcement, A (George Cukor, 1932), 87
Bogart, Humphrey, 8, 29, 45, 119, 141, 147–82, 192, 194, 206, 231, 245
Bordwell, David, 239
Boyer, Charles, 147, 185, 187, 188–89
Breathless (Jean-Luc Godard, 1960), 151
Breen, Joseph, 74
Bringing Up Baby (Howard Hawks, 1938), 7, 13, 29, 36, 81, 83, 85, 96–104, 105, 107–9, 115, 152, 155, 241, 244, 246
Britton, Andrew, 90, 96
Brooks, Louise, 49, 149
Buckland, Warren, 167

Camper, Fred, 215
Carnicke, Sharon Marie, 43, 75, 76
Casablanca (Michael Curtiz, 1942), 148–50, 157, 178
Cavell, Stanley, 8, 15, 40, 49, 57, 59, 113, 166, 226–27, 232
Chambers, Whitman, 158–59

Index

Chandler, Raymond, 165
Chion, Michel, 61
Clayton, Alex, 97
Clift, Montgomery, 27–28
Cobweb, The (Vincente Minnelli, 1955), 147, 185–94, 198
 drapes in, 186, 190, 193–94
Colbert, Claudette, 6
Confidential Agent (Herman Shumlin, 1945), 147
Connolly, Walter, 48, 76, 80
Consolation Marriage (Paul Sloane, 1931), xv–xvii, 67
Cooper, Gary, 20–21, 187
Creekmur, Corey K., 122–23
Cukor, George, 58, 86–87, 90, 91, 104, 108, 112, 113
Curtiz, Michael, 148, 150, 157

Dark Passage (Delmer Daves, 1947), 147, 173–78, 181–82
Darrin, Sonia, 186–86
Daves, Delmer, 172–73
Davis, Bette, 149
Day, Doris, 192
De Niro, Robert, 242
deCordova, Richard, 9
découpage, 7, 9–12, 18, 59, 202, 209, 212, 222, 236, 238, 242
del Rio, Elena, 238
Design for Living (Ernst Lubitsch, 1933), 20–22
DiBattista, Maria, 59, 76, 97
Dimendberg, Edward, 121
Dixon, Jean, 90
Duchovny, David, 244
Due, Reidar, 245
Dunne, Griffin, 240–43
Dunne, Irene, xvii
Dvorak, Ann, 148–49

ekphrasis, 20
Elsaesser, Thomas, 195–96, 213, 223
Evans, Peter William, 209, 232

Farber, Manny, 42, 172

Fiorentino, Linda, 241
Forbes, Ralph, 53
Francis, Kay, 14, 16–17, 19–20, 65–66, 69
Fujiwara, Chris, 124, 126

Gable, Clark, 6, 42, 59
Garbo, Greta, 24–25, 27, 90
Garr, Teri, 241
Gerstner, David A., 196–98
Gift of Love, The (Jean Negulesco, 1958), 226–29
Gish, Lillian, 25–26, 27, 185, 187–89
Godard, Jean-Luc, 9–12, 18, 23, 59, 151, 209, 211, 215
Goulding, Edmund, 25
Grahame, Gloria, 141, 185
Grant, Cary, 7–8, 53, 58, 83–115, 119–20, 123, 152, 156, 194, 241, 246
Great Profile, The (Walter Lang, 1940), 49
Grosz, Dave, 215
Gwenn, Edmund, 86

Hake, Sabine, 15
Hall, Gladys, 41
Harlow, Jean, 75, 76, 80
Harvey, James, 15, 48, 61, 65, 213–14
Hatchet Man, The (William A. Wellman, 1932), 178
Hawks, Howard, 33, 39, 42, 45, 54, 55, 91, 97–98, 104, 108, 115, 150, 155–57, 164, 172–73, 179, 181, 232
Hawks, Nancy, 150
Hepburn, Katharine, 7–8, 11, 36, 53, 58, 79, 81, 83–115, 119–20, 123, 152, 156, 192–93, 241, 245–46
Hickman, Darryl, 128–29, 203–4
High Sierra (Raoul Walsh, 1941), 150
Hirsch, Foster, 121
His Girl Friday (Howard Hawks, 1940), 42, 244
Hitchcock, Alfred, 5
Holiday (George Cukor, 1938), 53, 83–84, 90–97, 99, 115

Hopkins, Miriam, 12–14, 16, 20–21, 187
Horton, Edward Everett, 90
Howard, John, 104
Howard, Leslie, 149–51
Hudson, Rock, 147, 192, 197, 209, 212, 216–22, 224, 229–30, 232–33, 235–37, 245
Hussey, Ruth, 104, 106
Huston, John, 148, 150, 172–73, 178, 181

In a Lonely Place (Nicholas Ray, 1950), 141
Irving, George, 97
It Happened One Night (Frank Capra, 1934), 49

Jewel Robbery (William Dieterle, 1932), 65–66, 69

Karns, Roscoe, 46
Keathley, Christian, 7, 22
Keaton, Diane, 245
Keeper of the Flame (George Cukor, 1943), 79
Kendall, Elizabeth, 59
Kerr, Deborah, 192, 196–207
Kerr, John, 8, 185, 192, 196–207
Key Largo (John Huston, 1948), 29, 147, 172–73, 178–82, 193
Klevan, Andrew, 19–20, 22, 23, 75, 85, 106
Knudsen, Peggy, 166
Kouvaros, George, 19
Kuleshov, Lev, 24

Laura (Otto Preminger, 1944), 8, 119–46, 175, 194, 245–46
Leave Her to Heaven (John M. Stahl, 1945), 128–29
Leigh, Janet, 5
Libeled Lady (Jack Conway, 1936), 40, 57, 74–80
Little Caesar (Mervyn LeRoy, 1931), 178

Lombard, Carole, 7–8, 33–55, 58–59, 72, 104, 115, 119–20, 241, 245
Loy, Myrna, xv–xviii, 6–9, 11, 28, 30, 53, 57–81, 104, 114, 115, 119–20, 192, 241, 245
Lubitsch, Ernst, 12–15, 17, 19–23, 193

Malone, Dorothy, 45, 165–67, 169–72, 197, 212, 216–17, 229–30, 232–38
Maltese Falcon, The (John Huston, 1941), 125, 148, 150–51
Manhattan Melodrama (W. S. Van Dyke, 1934), 59–60, 65
March, Fredric, 20–23, 40, 187
Marshall, Herbert, 12–17, 19–20, 26–27, 130–31
Martin, Adrian, 7, 10, 186
Martin, Dean, 196
Mask of Fu Manchu, The (Charles Brabin, 1932), 66–68
Mast, Gerald, 167
McCourt, James, 216
McElhaney, Joe, 39, 42, 155, 157, 169, 191–93, 195–96
Mercer, John, 212, 233, 236
Miller, Henry, 242–43
Minnelli, Vincente, 8, 29, 185–207
mise-en-scène, 9–10, 12, 15, 24–25, 29, 39, 120–21, 185–87, 191, 195, 209, 211, 213, 222–27, 233, 236
Mitchum, Robert, 119
Montgomery, Robert, 173
Moore, Dennie, 86
Morin, Edgar, 48
Morris, Mary, 155
Murder, My Sweet (Edward Dmytryk, 1944), 125
Murray, Mae, 24–25
My Man Godfrey (Gregory La Cava, 1936), 7, 36, 38–40, 55

Naremore, James, 49, 60, 84, 90, 92, 94, 98, 112, 124, 186, 196
Negulesco, Jean, 227

Nielsen, Asta, 25–26
No Man of Her Own (Wesley Ruggles, 1932), 42
Nochimson, Martha P., 2, 7, 64, 69, 244–45
Nolan, Doris, 90
Nothing Sacred (William A. Wellman, 1937), 36, 40, 55
Novarro, Ramon, 67–68

O'Brien, Pat, xv–xvi
O'Hara, Catherine, 241, 244
O'Sullivan, Maureen, 62
One Way Passage (Tay Garnett, 1932), 65
Out of the Past (Jacques Tourneur, 1947), 119

Paley, Natalie, 88
Parrish, Gigi, 45
Pat and Mike (George Cukor, 1952), 79
Patrick, Gail, 37
Paul, William, 15, 16
Paz, Octavio, 64
Peacock, Steven, 216–17
Penthouse (W. S. Van Dyke, 1933), 59
Peberdy, Donna, 120
Petrified Forest, The (Archie Mayo, 1936), 149–50
Philadelphia Story, The (George Cukor, 1940), 45, 58, 75, 84, 104–14, 206
Phillips, Adam, 38, 102
Pinchot, Bronson, 240
Place in the Sun, A (George Stevens, 1951), 27–28, 29
Playmates (David Butler, 1941), 49
Pomerance, Murray, 3–5, 7
Powell, William, 6–8, 30, 36–38, 40, 53, 57–81, 104, 115, 119, 120, 151, 156, 192, 245
Pre-Code cinema, 22, 65–67, 69
Preminger, Otto, 119, 125–27, 133, 135–36, 138–39, 141, 144–45, 196

Price, Vincent, 124–25, 134–35
Prizefighter and the Lady, The (W. S. Van Dyke, 1933), 59
Psycho (Alfred Hitchcock, 1960), 5

Raksin, David, 134, 136–37
Ray, Nicholas, 141
Ray, Robert B., 105
Razor's Edge, The (Edmund Goulding, 1946), 130–32
Rigaut, Jacques, 24–26, 28
Robinson, Edward G., 29, 178
Rollyson, Carl E., 126
Romeo and Juliet (play), xv–xvi
Rothman, Ellen K., 122
Rothman, William, 36, 40, 132
Rudie, Evelyn, 227
Russon, John, 63–64

Salzberg, Ana, 3–4, 11
Scarlet Pimpernel, The (Harold Young, 1934), 151
Schatz, Thomas, 96
Schivelbusch, Wolfgang, 22, 43
Scorsese, Martin, 240–43, 244
Shanghai Gesture (Josef von Sternberg, 1941), 128
Shepherd, Cybill, 244
Shingler, Martin, 212
Silver, Alain, 125
Sirk, Douglas, 8, 29, 192, 194, 197, 209–38, 245
Sobchack, Vivian, 173
Stack, Robert, 147, 197, 209–17, 220–29, 231–32
Stahl, John M., 128
Stern, Lesley, 19, 244
Stewart, James, 45, 104, 105–6, 109, 110–13, 245
Sylvia Scarlett (George Cukor, 1935), 86–90, 96, 115

Taylor, Elizabeth, 27–28
Tea and Sympathy (Vincente Minnelli, 1956), 8, 185, 192, 193, 196–207, 246

Technicolor, 211, 214, 216
Tempest, The (Sam Taylor, 1928), 41
Thin Man, The (Dashiell Hammett novel), 57
Thin Man, The (W. S. Van Dyke, 1934), 7, 30, 40, 57–74, 75–76, 78–80, 140, 212, 241, 246
Thirteen Women (George Archainbaud, 1932), 67–68
Thomson, David, 91
Thompson, Kristin, 126
Three on a Match (Mervyn LeRoy, 1932), 148
Tierney, Gene, 8, 119–46, 175, 196, 245
To Be or Not to Be (Ernst Lubitsch, 1942), 55
To Have and Have Not (Howard Hawks, 1944), 8, 147, 153–65, 169, 172, 176, 179, 181, 245–46
Tobacco Road (John Ford, 1942), 128
Toles, George, 27–28, 29
Tourneur, Jacques, 130
Tracy, Spencer, 76, 79, 192
Trouble in Paradise (Ernst Lubitsch, 1932), 12–14, 16–18, 19–20, 193
True Confession (Wesley Ruggles, 1937), 55

Twentieth Century (Howard Hawks, 1934), 29, 33–55, 104, 241
Tynan, Kenneth, 24–26, 28

Ursini, James, 125

Van Dyke, W. S., 59, 70
Vickers, Martha, 165–66, 169

Way of a Gaucho (Jacques Tourneur, 1952), 130, 132
Webb, Clifton, 124, 126, 128, 133–35, 137
Wexman, Virginia Wright, 2–3, 7, 149–50, 244
Where the Sidewalk Ends (Otto Preminger, 1950), 135
Widmark, Richard, 147, 185, 187
Willemen, Paul, 213
Willis, Bruce, 244
Winnicott, D. W., 84–86
Winokur, Mark, 65
Woman of the Year, The (George Stevens, 1942), 79, 114
Wood, Robin, 115, 152
Worland, Rick, 150
Written on the Wind (Douglas Sirk, 1956), 8, 147, 193, 209–38, 245–46

www.ingramcontent.com/pod-product-compliance
Lightning Source LLC
Chambersburg PA
CBHW070756230426
43665CB00017B/2383